IMAGES
of America

TIOGA AND COLLINSVILLE

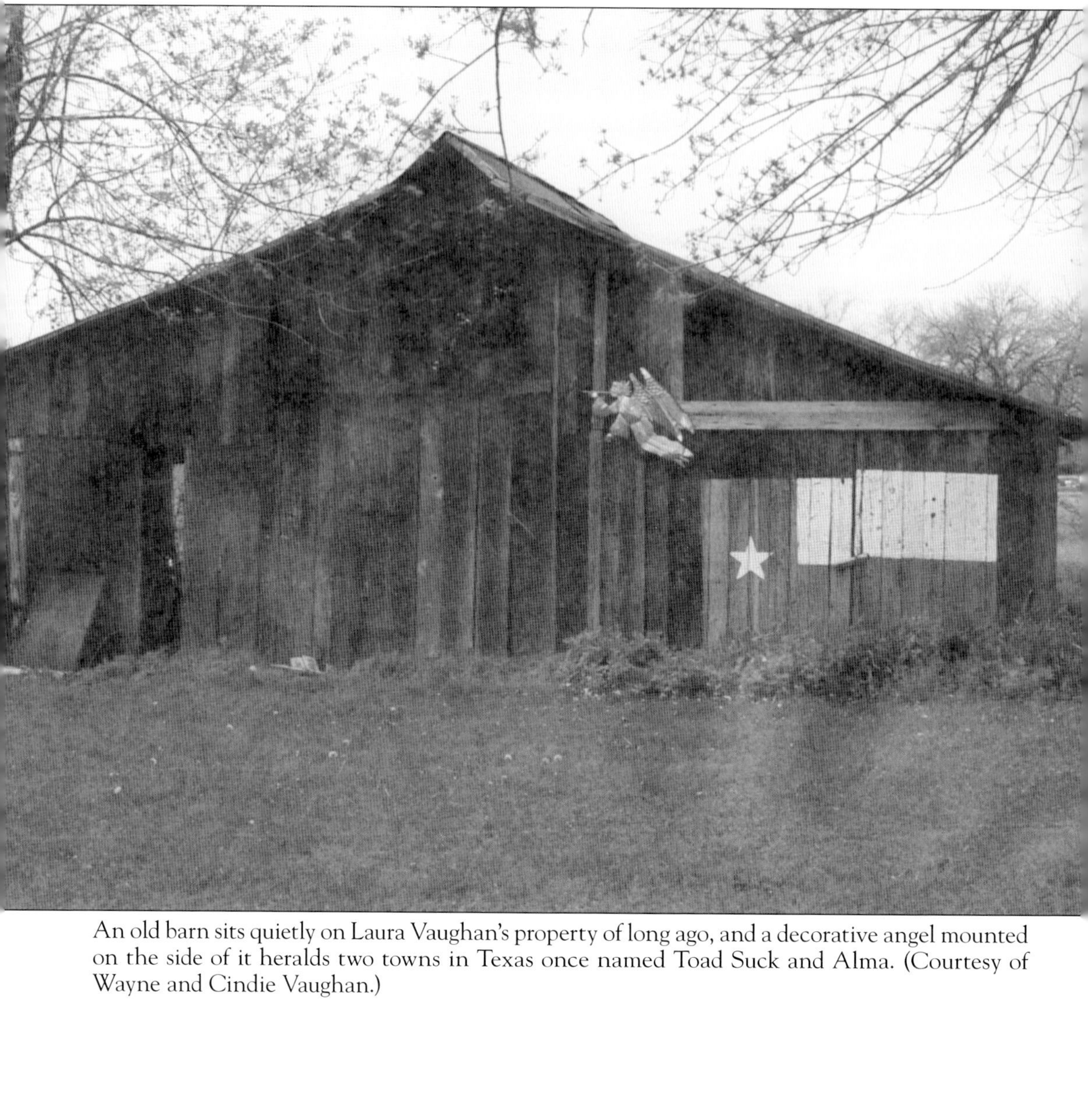

An old barn sits quietly on Laura Vaughan's property of long ago, and a decorative angel mounted on the side of it heralds two towns in Texas once named Toad Suck and Alma. (Courtesy of Wayne and Cindie Vaughan.)

ON THE COVER: Pictured are Tioga's Texas Rangers of Company T, Tioga, Texas, in the early 1900s. The two men in front wearing dark coats are Capt. J.L. Webb First (left) and Col. Matt Bradley. The men are facing west toward the railroad in front of Lee Brown's store, where the rangers would meet upstairs. The post office was on the left of the two-story building; it was the first public office. The gable of the structure belonged to the Texas Hotel. Unfortunately, all of these buildings burned in 1909. (Courtesy of James Hilliard.)

IMAGES
of America

TIOGA AND COLLINSVILLE

Don and J.R. Davenport

ARCADIA
PUBLISHING

ISBN 978-1-4671-3127-8

Published by Arcadia Publishing
Charleston, South Carolina

Printed in the United States of America

Library of Congress Control Number: 2013952330

For all general information, please contact Arcadia Publishing:
Telephone 843-853-2070
Fax 843-853-0044
E-mail sales@arcadiapublishing.com
For customer service and orders:
Toll-Free 1-888-313-2665

Visit us on the Internet at www.arcadiapublishing.com

This book is dedicated to the townspeople of Tioga and Collinsville, their ancestors, and their descendants.

Contents

ACKNOWLEDGMENTS

A sincere thank you goes to all who contributed pictures, stories, encouragement, and confirmation for Images of America: *Tioga and Collinsville*. I enjoyed my visits with you and our walk through time. For those I have left out, please accept my sincerest apologies. My hope is this book will help preserve a part of a rich legacy so those who follow after can easily read of their heritage. Thank you, Laura Bruns, my editor, and Arcadia Publishing for allowing me to retrace time's footprints left on two Texas towns I grew up in.

INTRODUCTION

Texas has 254 counties, and Grayson County is home to Tioga and Collinsville. Each of these sister cities has its own municipal government, school district, and post office. They are different in many ways, yet they share one thing: bloodlines. Many current and past residents in each town have kinfolk in the other town. Why did these two towns in Texas, only seven miles apart, decide it was better to be independent of each other? Though there is not a definitive answer, it seems that folks of Tioga were headstrong to remain as is, and though Tioga has struggled in recent years it is on a comeback. Gene Autry, singing star and of silver screen fame, was born outside city limits of this country town, and Randy Travis, of country music fame, now calls Tioga home, as do several outstanding physicians.

Collinsville, located six miles north on Highway 377, also has its own municipal government, school district, and post office. It has been more successful in maintaining and adding population growth. Since its inception, the school district has maintained all grades required to graduate. Both towns support active schools and churches.

If the towns had joined forces, they could have been more prosperous and could have grown. Today, Tioga has a population of about 803, and Collinsville has about 1,600, and together that would be a nice-sized small town; however, there has never been any interest in combining the two.

The histories of both are interesting. For instance, Collinsville was originally called Toad Suck. Supposedly, it was the name of a saloon near the community. The saloon and the town got their names from the following belief: "You sit and drink until you swell up like a toad. Then, you go outside to go home, and if it is raining the mud will suck the shoes right off your feet." The name was later changed to Collinsville after two missionaries who settled in the area. Lodi Collins continued to live in the community after her husband passed on, and she was instrumental in forming the first free school in Texas, Collinsville Academy, where Greek, metaphysics, and "mental physics" (methods and practice for development of body, mind, and spirit) were taught.

Tioga actually was comprised of two towns, Alma and San Diego. To unify the towns, citizens put the name Alma on one side of a board and San Diego on the other. They then threw it up in the air, and Alma fell face up and was declared the winner. Unfortunately, when the railroad person in charge of officially naming towns took the name to Austin, he was informed the state already had a town named Alma. Not wishing to endure the sobering task of once again asking what residents wanted to name their town, he took it upon himself to name it Tioga. He was from Tioga, Pennsylvania, and thought that was good a name as any. Tioga also was a term Native Americans in the North used to describe the meeting of two rivers or "at the forks."

The true stories behind the names of the two towns most likely rests somewhere between fact and fiction. In more recent years, it was debated that Tioga be changed to Autry Springs after its native son Gene Autry, but the majority of residents resisted, and thus Tioga remains.

Through the years, Tioga has supported six banks operating at different times, a movie house, four grocery stores, mineral bath hotels, a beauty shop, a barbershop, and a train depot. It also has had a 12-grade school, a jail, a car dealership, and five churches.

Union Pacific trains still roll day and night through Tioga. Texas Pacific was the original owner of the ribbon of silvery tracks that serve these sister cities; now, it is the Union Pacific. Many years ago, when the sound of the train whistle echoed through the stillness of the night, it must have brought comfort to the two struggling communities as they realized it brought visitors to try the mineral baths of the area and perhaps the funds to help build a better community. The railroad also carried young men of the area off to war in 1941. It brought some back home on furloughs and sadly some in flag-draped coffins. No longer in existence, both depots were striking, as old photographs attest. Somehow, both cities were cheated out of their beautiful depots that should have been kept and cherished, but time—as well as structures, people, and the two towns—moves on.

Tioga was home to Texas senator Olan R. Van Zandt, who was blind but still knew every inch of Tioga like the back of his hand. Rev. Henry Ball, who baptized Speaker of the House Sam Rayburn, also called Tioga home. Later, Reverend Ball laid Rayburn to rest in nearby Bonham; four presidents were in attendance that day. Tioga was home to Gene Autry and now Randy Travis—it does not lack a rich legacy.

The same can be said of Collinsville. Although it has outgrown Tioga and has maintained an elementary school, middle school, and high school of academic quality for many years, it is still a small town. Also like Tioga, it is going through a growth spurt. The surrounding horse and cattle ranches support Collinsville in its quest to keep the friendly small-town atmosphere intact while striving for a prosperous future.

Collinsville has 12 grades of education and prides itself as being a town of academic excellence. For years, the 11-man Pirates football team of Collinsville High School, as well as the basketball, baseball, and volleyball teams, has placed trophies in glass cases that line the school's hallways. School spirit can be felt at any event or function. Each year, the graduating class sends many students off to college, the armed forces, and the business world. They are well equipped to meet the challenging goals the world has set. In their hearts, graduates hold onto the motto, "Once a pirate, always a pirate," and they vow to make their hometown proud. There is nothing quite like being raised in a small town where each student is known by name and is remembered by residents in prayer.

In 2012, Tioga Independent School District (ISD) added a freshman class to its academic endeavors. Plans are to add a grade a year until all 12 are once again active and available. Tioga has not had a full 12-grade school system since 1961. It has always had a school, but classes were cut back to eighth grade, and high school students were forced to go to Collinsville and then to Gunter ISD about 11 miles away. In 2012, the Tioga Bulldogs played six-man football for the first time in 62 years. The pride of the town could be seen and felt as the football tumbled through the autumn night air, and games of past generations were remembered. The football was retrieved after Tioga scored its first touchdown, and it was put in a display case and marked for history.

Images of America: *Tioga and Collinsville* provides residents with memories of the past and hope for a bright future, and each town vows to maintain its individuality as challenges are faced and time moves on.

One

TIOGA
THE EARLY YEARS

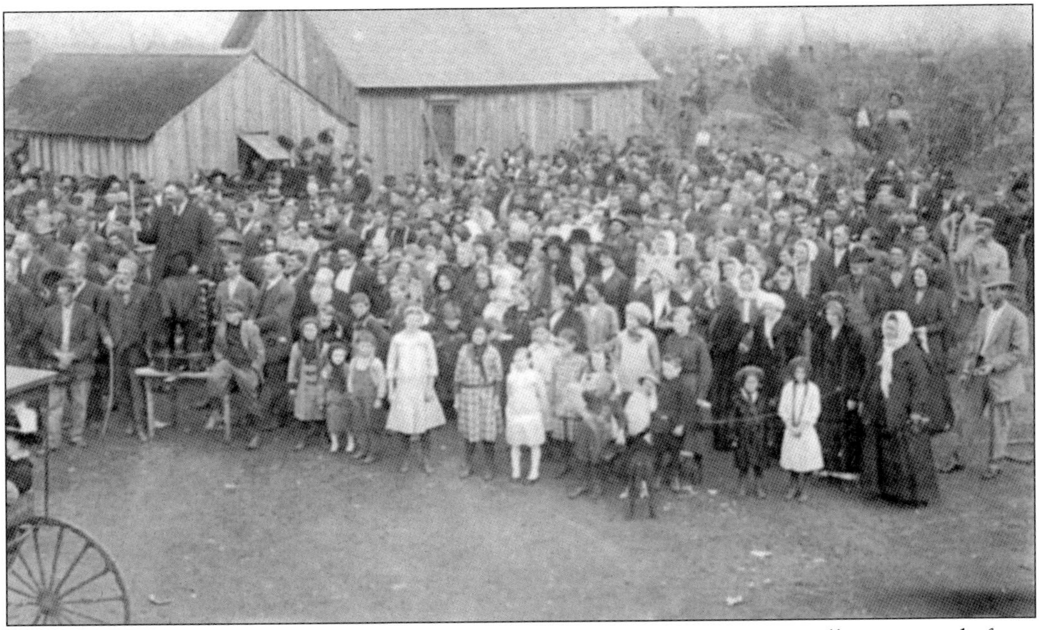

At the time a late-1800s photograph captured these residents, Tioga was actually comprised of two towns: Alma and San Diego. Wishing to settle on one name, they painted Alma on one side of a board and San Diego on the other. They threw the board in the air, and the name that fell face up would be the town's name. Alma was chosen, but when word of the name reached Austin, it was already taken. Not wishing to confront citizens once more to name their town, the railroad man who brought the message to the capital took it upon himself to name the town Tioga after a term used by Native Americans in the North. (James Hilliard.)

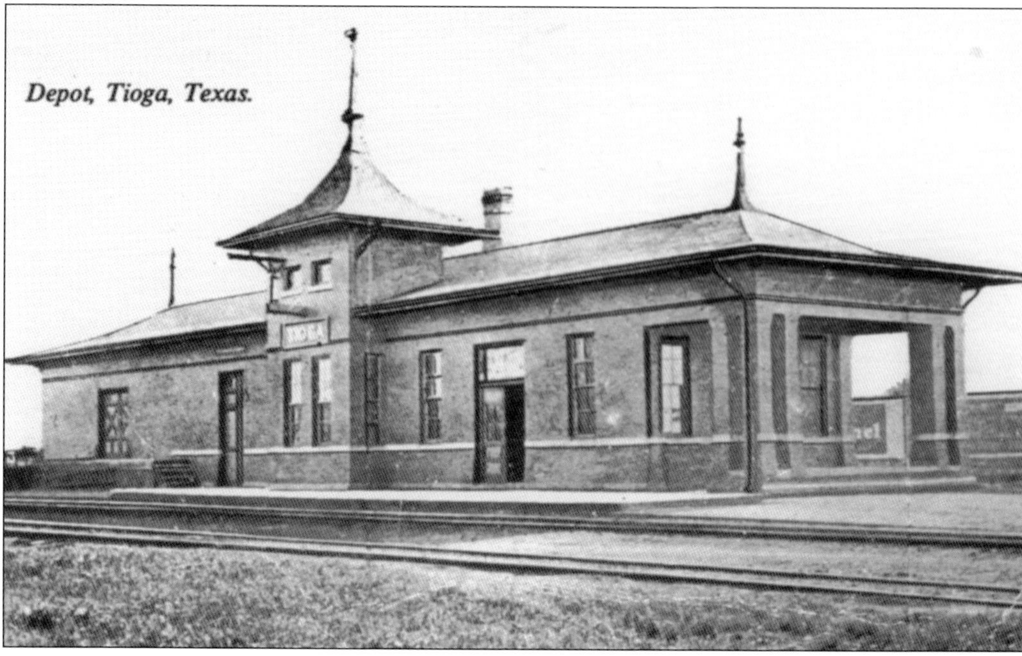

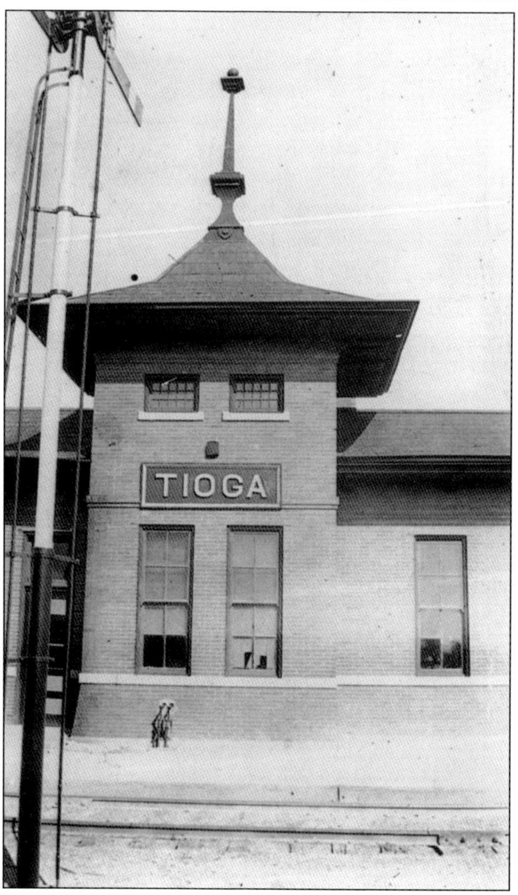

Tioga's train depot was architecturally beautiful. The railroad came to town about 1897, and the depot was built soon after. People came from all over the country to try the mineral waters in the area for their ailments, and the mineral bathhouses were busy. Later, one of Tioga's native sons, Gene Autry, would meet the trains and serenade visitors coming to town. One lady said, "That Autry kid is never going to amount to anything. All he does is play that guitar and sing." Autry's history tells a different story, though, as he went on to become a singing and silver screen star, proving the observer incorrect. This photograph was taken in the early 1900s. (James Hilliard.)

Here is another view of Tioga's train depot. No one knows why the town did not try to save it for future generations. The only trace of the depot that remains today is the concrete foundation (James Hilliard.)

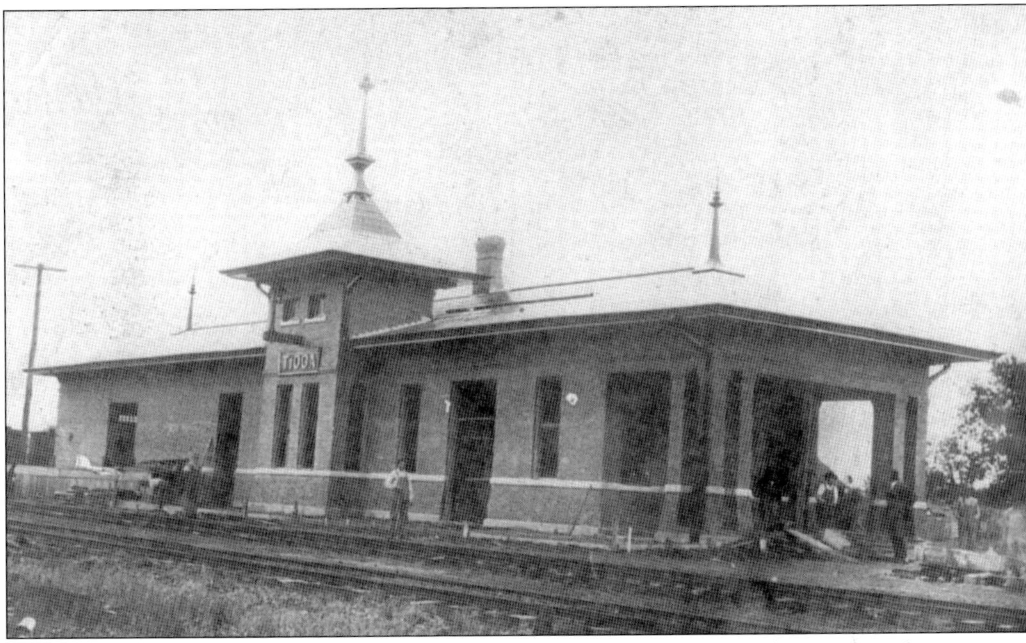

Pictured are people coming and going around the depot. It was a busy part of town, as it was where US soldiers were picked up and dropped off for duty. It was also unfortunately the destination of flag-draped coffins being brought home so that area sons could be laid to rest in nearby cemeteries. The depot was a piece of history that faded away in the 1950s when it was torn down. (James Hilliard.)

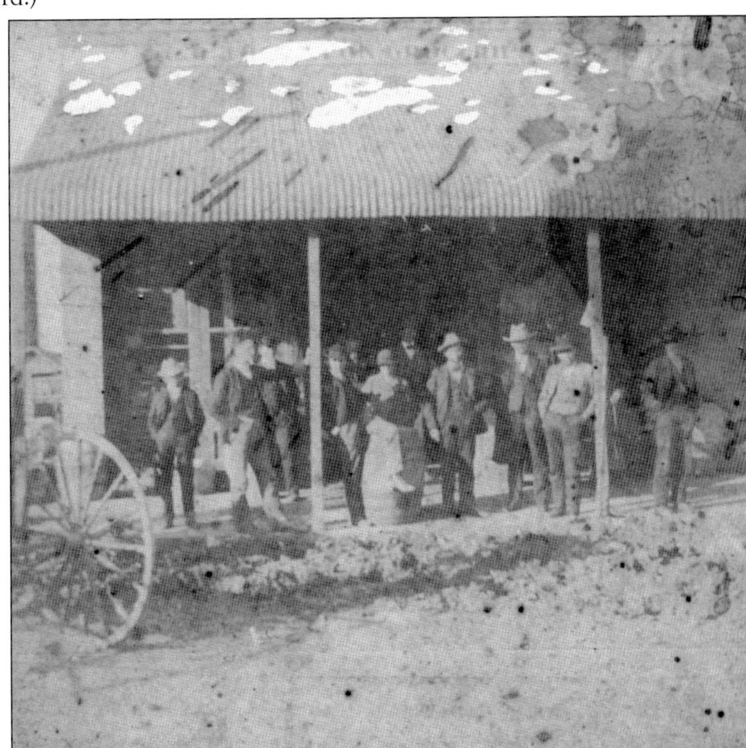

A group of men poses outside a storefront on Main Street in the early 1900s. Tioga was bustling with activity at the time. (James Hilliard.)

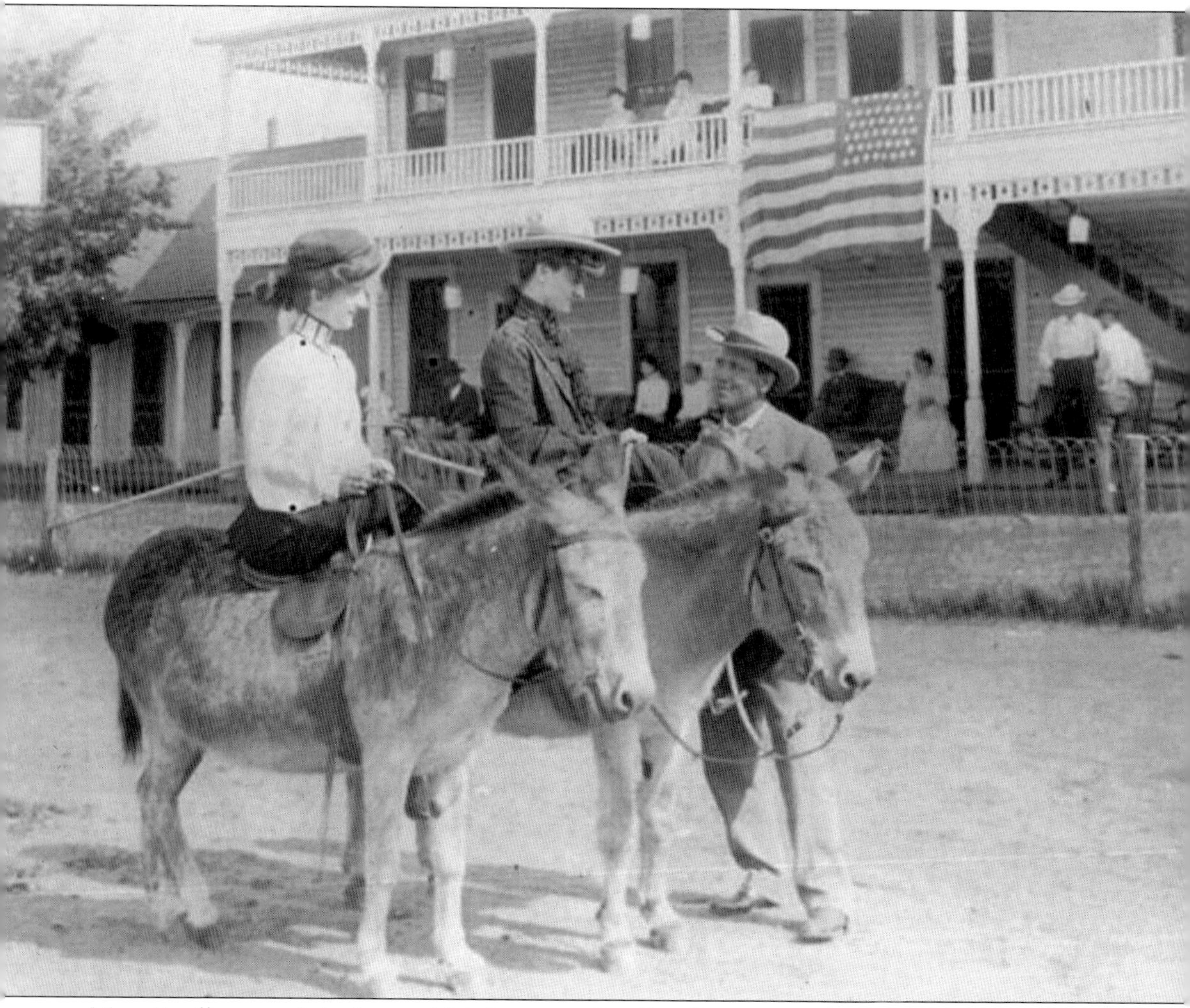

Matt Bradley stands in front of his business, Bradley Cottage, with two unidentified nieces riding donkeys. Bradley Cottage was a successful hotel and bathhouse during the mineral water boom, and the business it brought in was a blessing to Tioga. In later years, it served as a nursing home for the elderly. Note the flag flying behind Mr. Bradley and its 45 stars, indicating that this photograph was taken around the turn of the century. Bradley and his wife, Mattie, were active citizens in the promotion and growth of Tioga. Bradley Cottage was located on what is now Donation Street. (James Hilliard.)

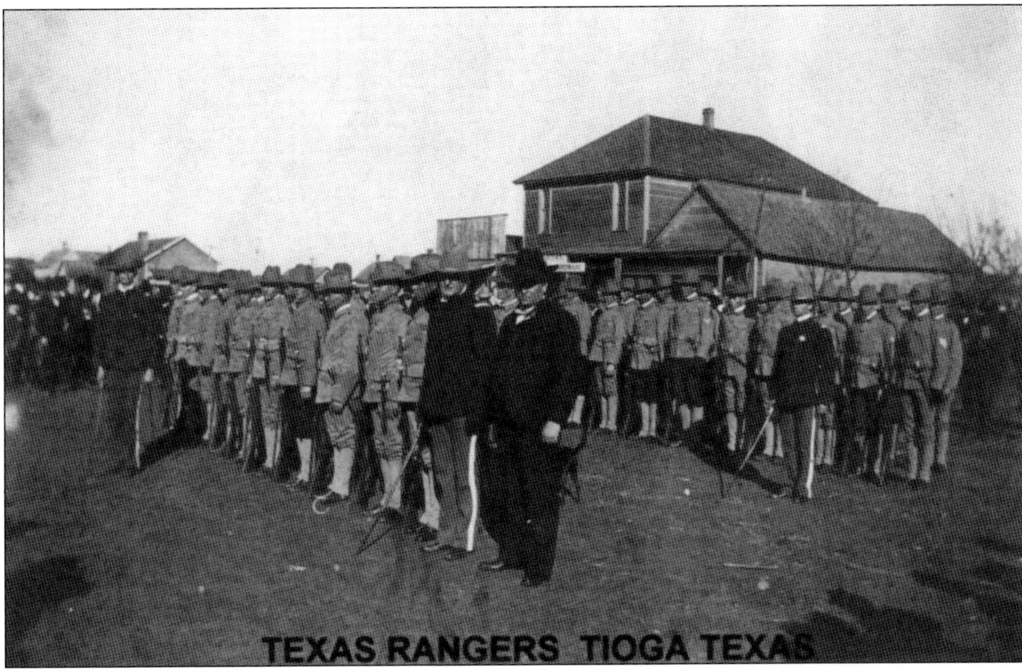

Pictured are Tioga's Texas Rangers, also known as the Home Guard. The two men in the foreground wearing dark coats are Capt. J.L. Webb First (left) and Col. Matt Bradley. The rest of the men in uniform are unidentified. (James Hilliard.)

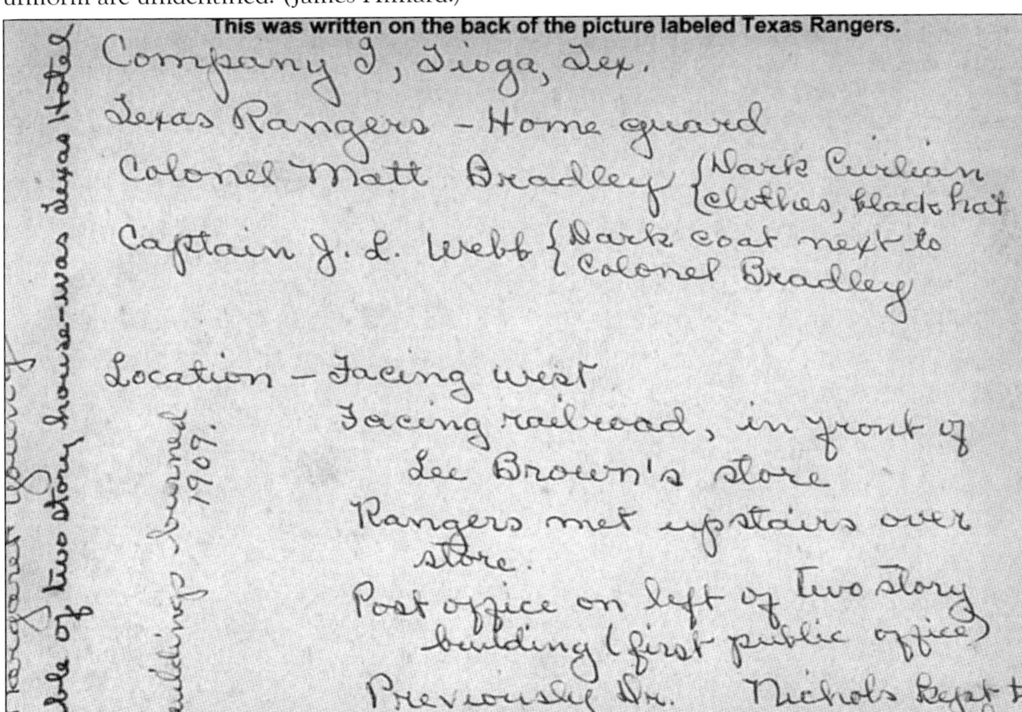

This was written on the back of the picture labeled Texas Rangers.

Company I, Tioga, Tex.
Texas Rangers – Home guard
Colonel Matt Bradley {Dark Civilian clothes, black hat
Captain J. L. Webb {Dark coat next to Colonel Bradley

Location – Facing west
Facing railroad, in front of Lee Brown's store
Rangers met upstairs over store.
Post office on left of two story building (first public office)
Previously Dr. Nichols kept th

gable of two story house–was Texas Hotel
Buildings burned 1907.

This hand-written note was attached to the photograph above of the Texas Rangers. It lists some of the buildings behind the men. (James Hilliard.)

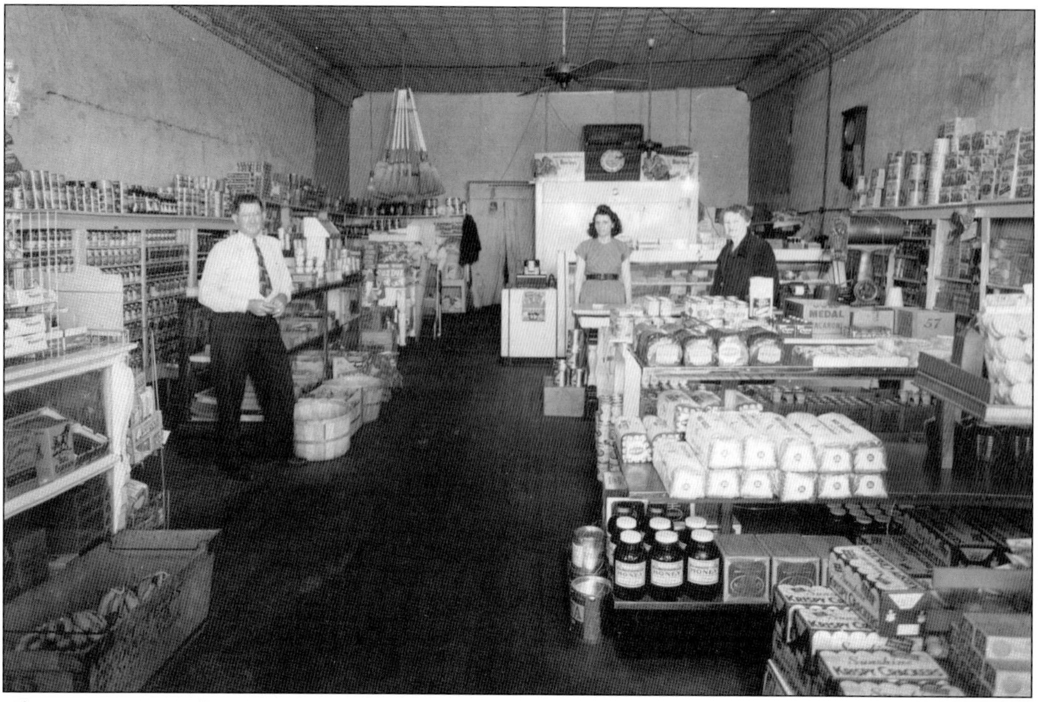

This is Henry Ball's grocery store in the 1940s. Henry is the man on the left. Ball was also known as Elder Ball or Reverend Ball. He preached at the Primitive Baptist Church in town. (James Hilliard.)

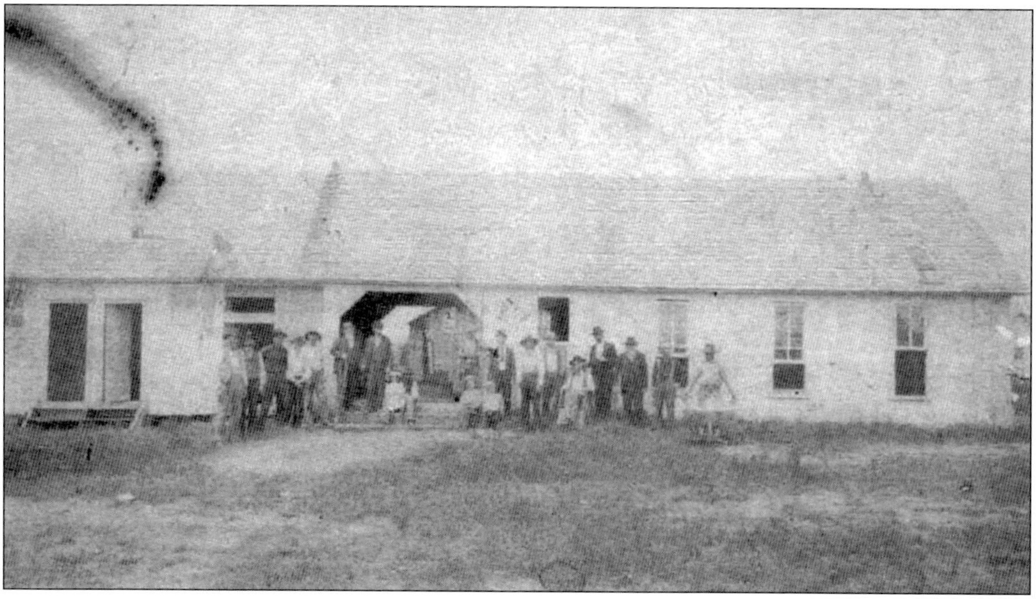

Pictured in the early 1920s is the old cotton gin in Tioga. (James Hilliard.)

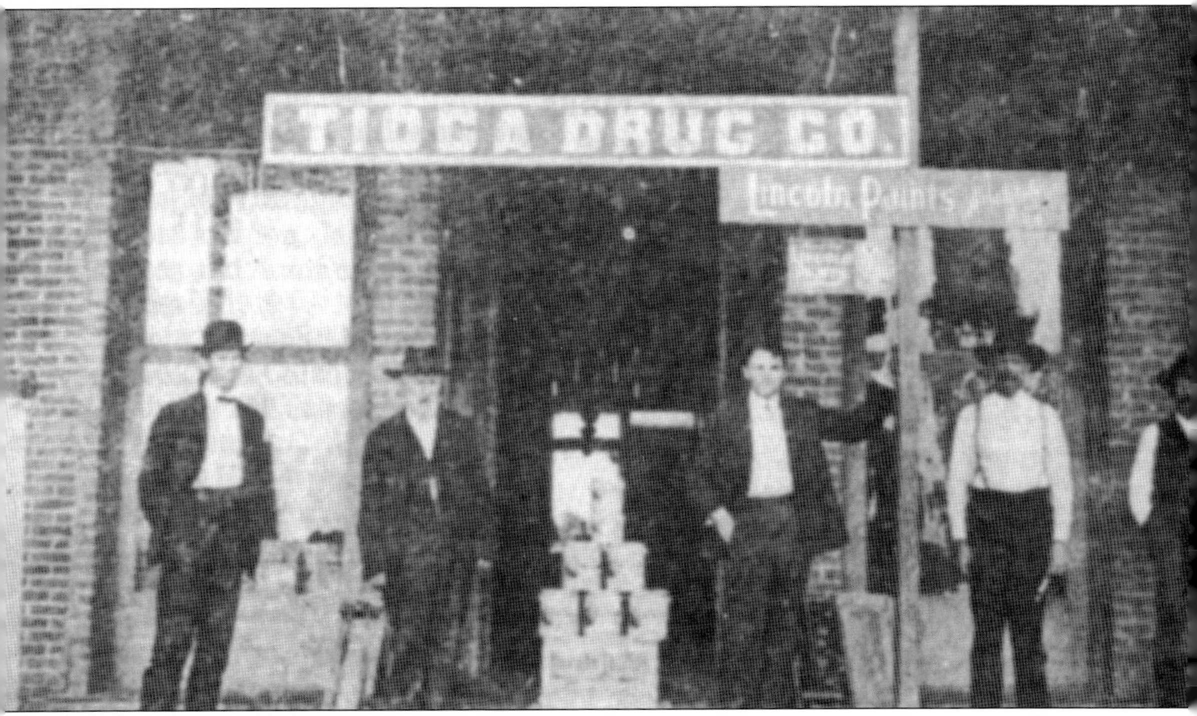

This was one of the first drugstores in Tioga at the turn of the century with a group of men standing out front for the camera. (James Hilliard.)

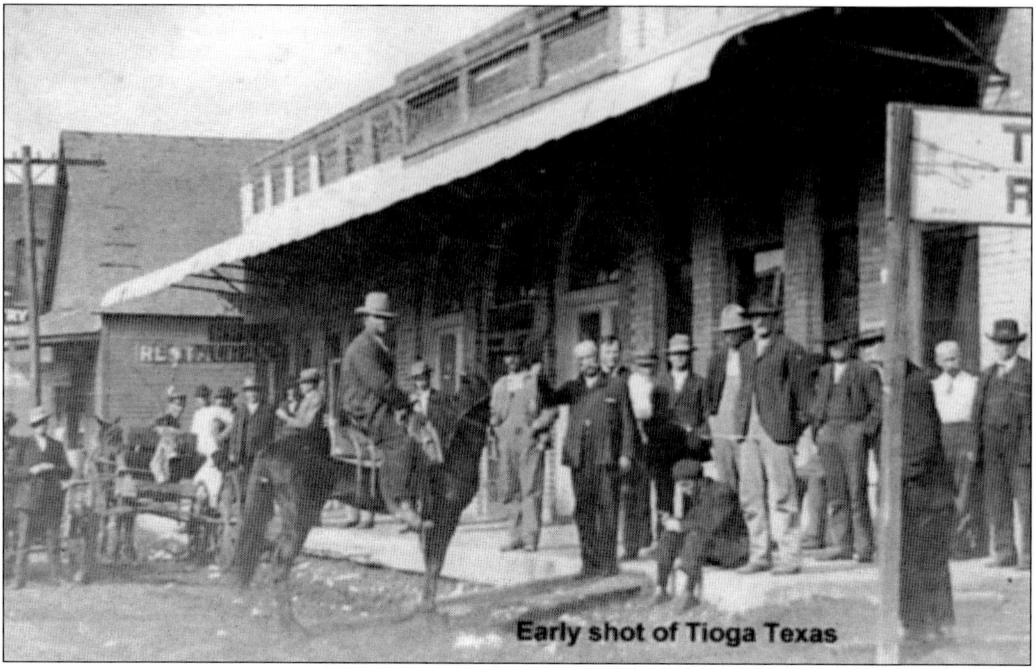

A bustling crowd is seen here on Main Street in the late 1800s. (James Hilliard.)

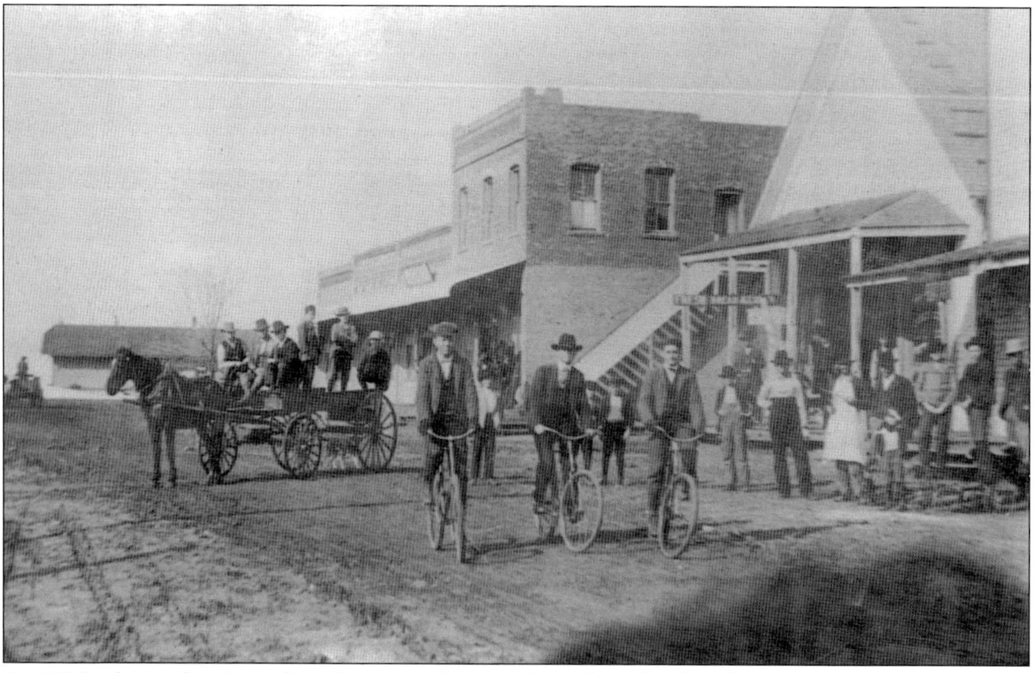

By 1910, about the time this photograph was taken, bicycles had become a popular mode of transportation and had replaced horses to some extent. These bicyclists are seen on Main Street. (James Hilliard.)

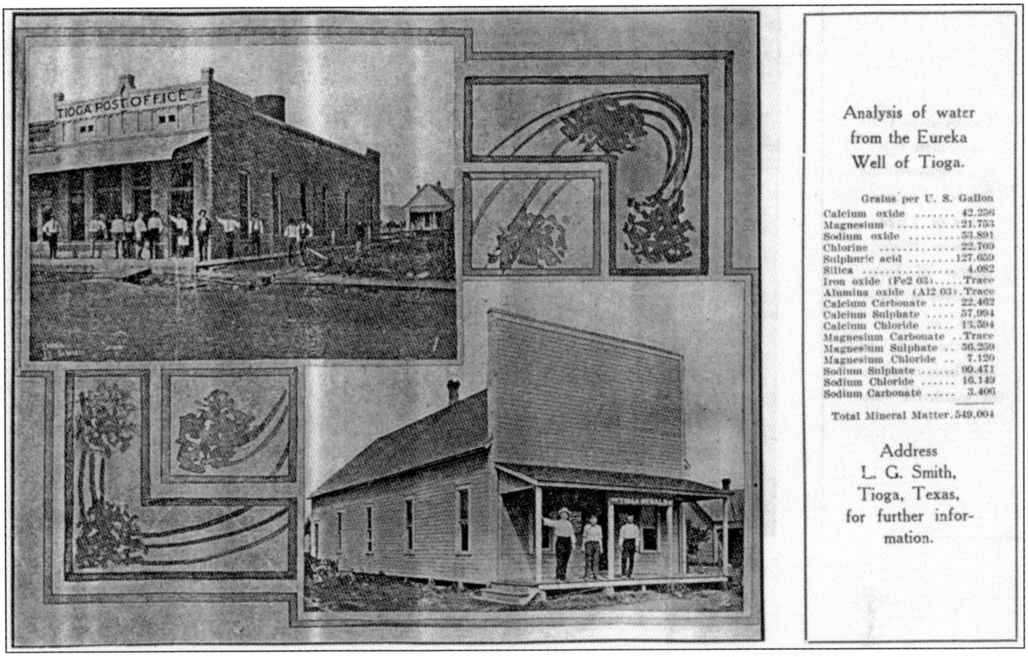

Here, the post office and early mineral water plant are pictured in the early 1900s. At one time, Dr. Nichols kept the mail in his office in a cigar box, so when a new, official post office was established, residents appreciated it. (James Hilliard.)

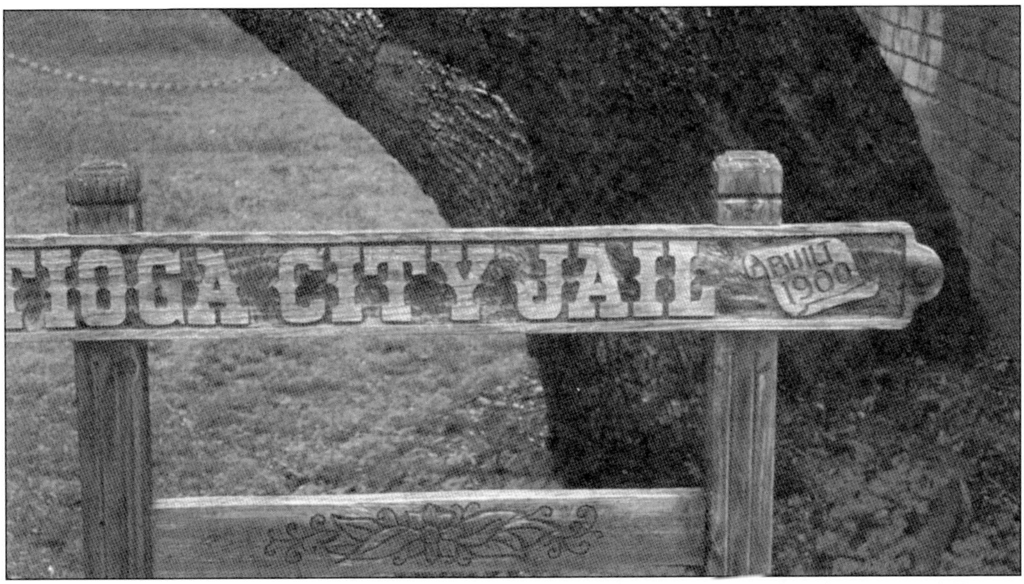

This sign out front of the city jail states that it was built in 1900 by the City of Tioga. (Authors' collection.)

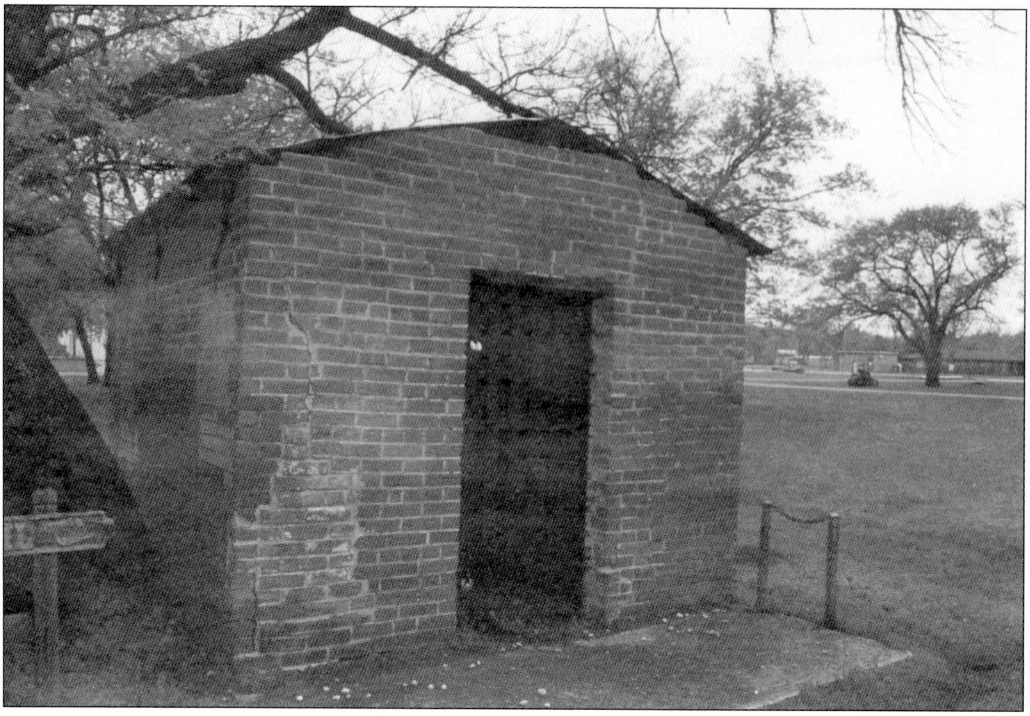

The bricks of Tioga's jail are cracked and crumbling now, yet one gets the feeling the old jail could still do its job. (Authors' collection.)

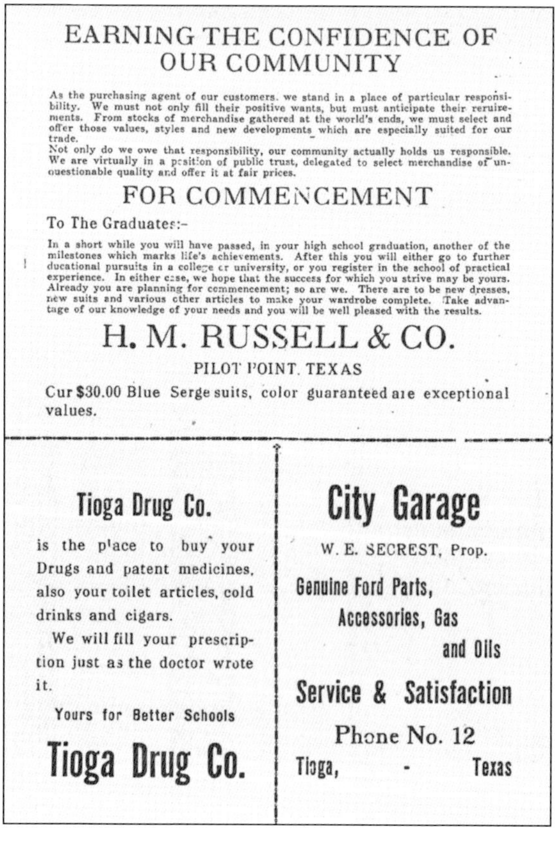

This ad ran in the *Tioga Herald* in the 1930s. The newspaper has long been silent, but at one time the town was affluent, ready for business, and able to support a newspaper. (James Hilliard.)

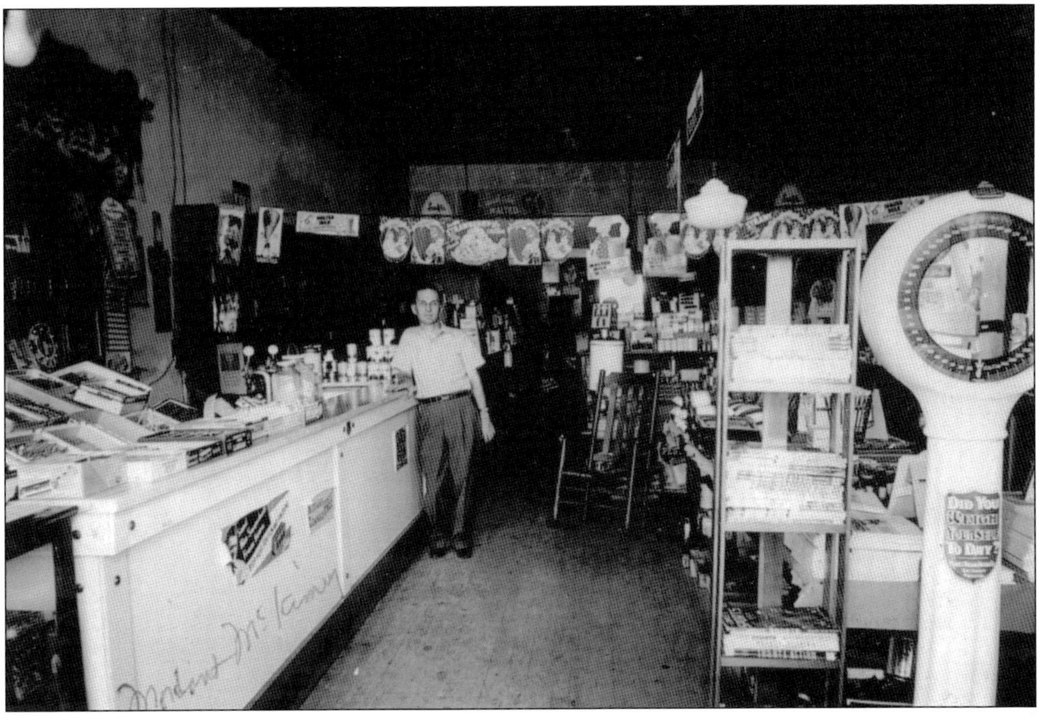

This drugstore, owned by Mordant McKinney in 1930, served the community with professional courtesy. Tioga no longer has a drugstore, but it hopes to include every modern-day need a town could want in the near future. As the school continues to grow, hopefully the town will along with it. (James Hilliard.)

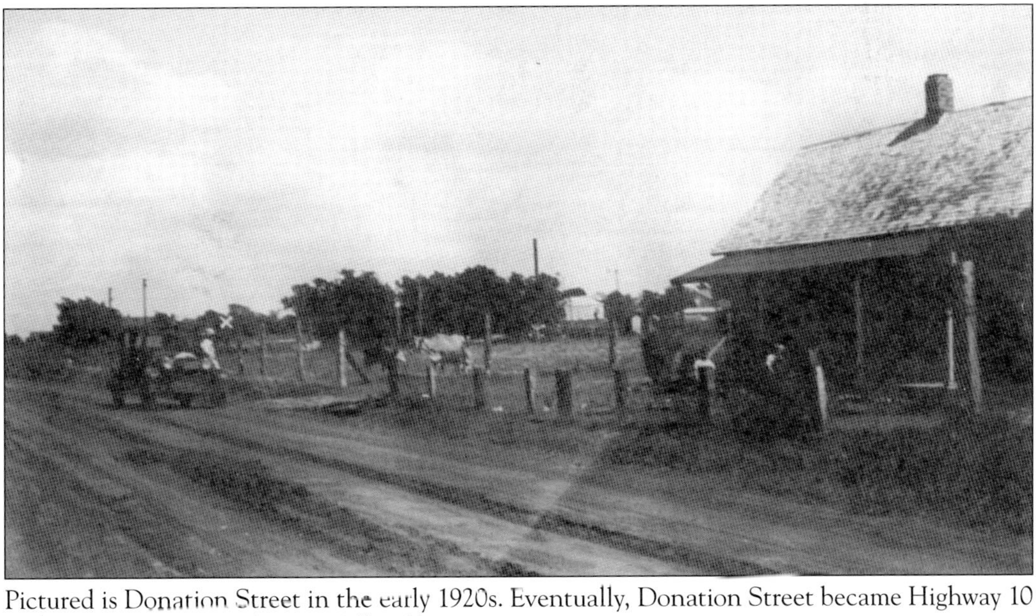

Pictured is Donation Street in the early 1920s. Eventually, Donation Street became Highway 10 and later Highway 99. (James Hilliard.)

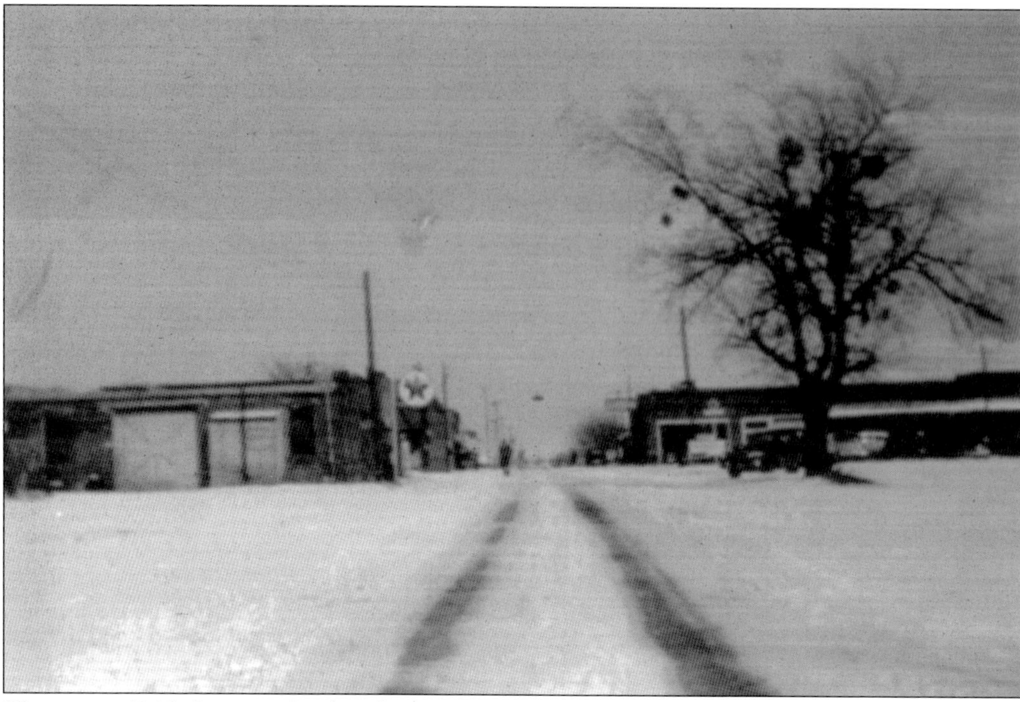

This is a c. 1946 photograph of Highway 10 going north on a winter's day. Woodall Chevrolet is on the right, and Walter Secrest's Texaco garage is on the left. (Authors' collection.)

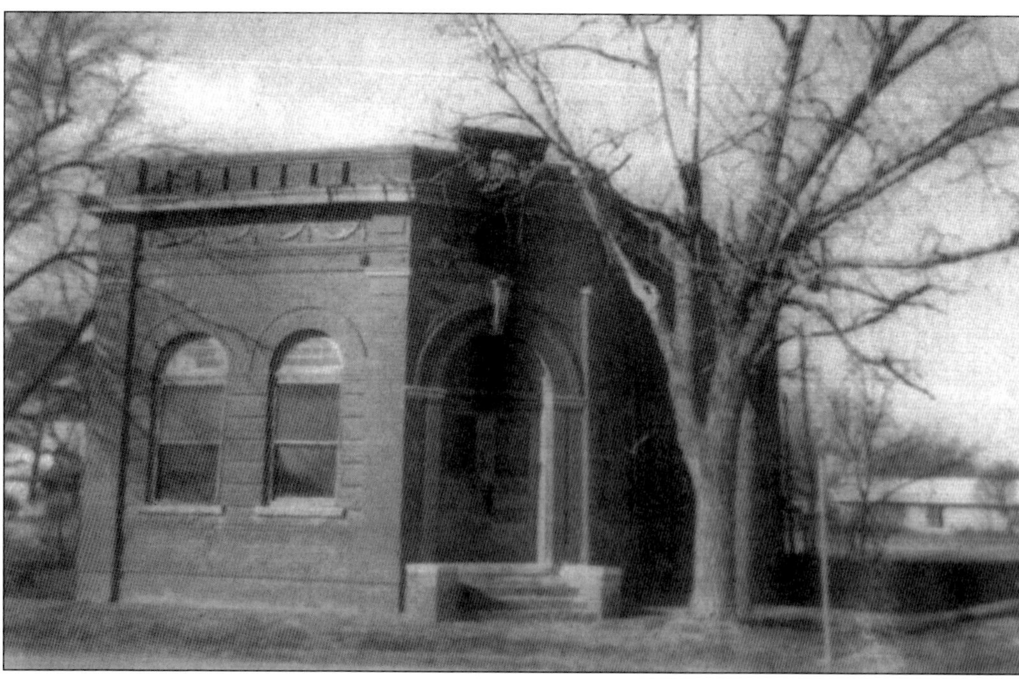

One of the first banks in Tioga later became the home of Mrs. Young and her mother, Mrs. Wadell. This image was taken in the 1940s. (James Hilliard.)

Pictured around 1915 is the original Tioga water tower, which was made of wood. (James Hilliard.)

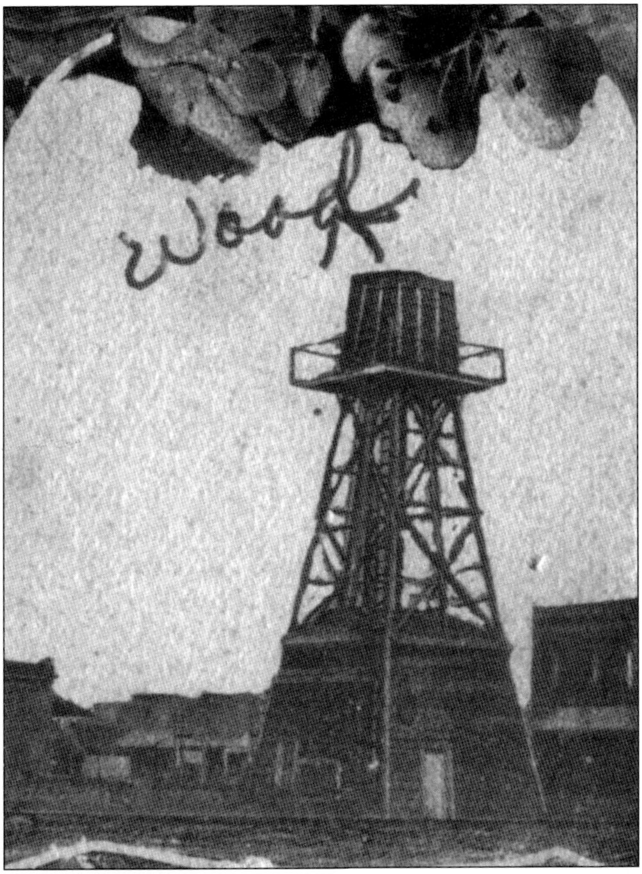

This c. 1900 photograph depicts a rural mail carrier on Main Street. Folks in town had not had a post office long before the rural communities were graced with a rural mail carrier. (James Hilliard.)

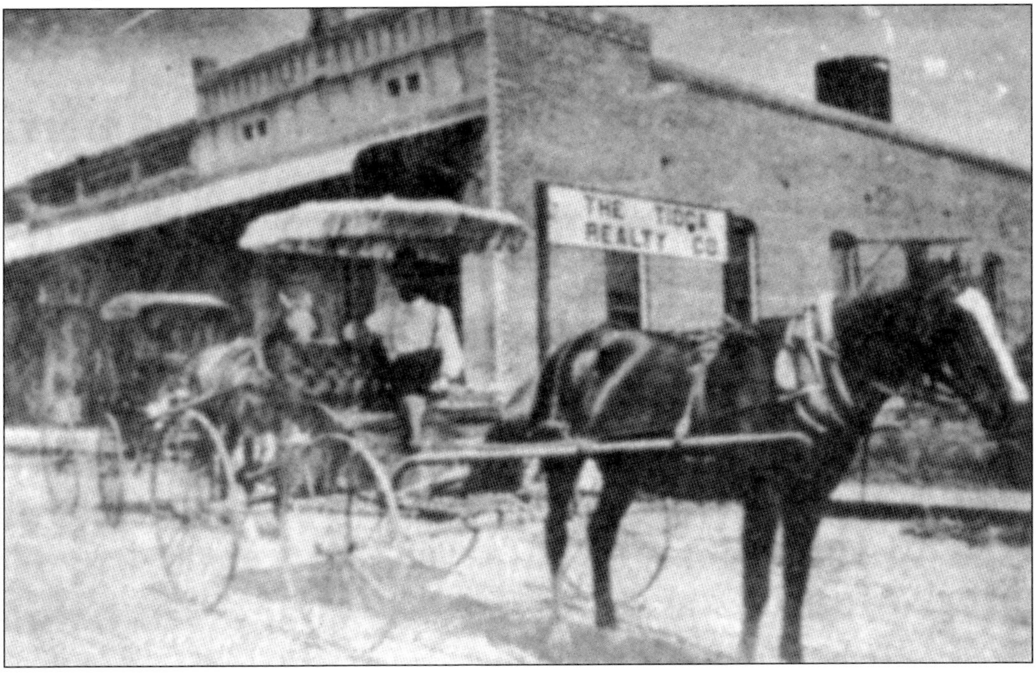

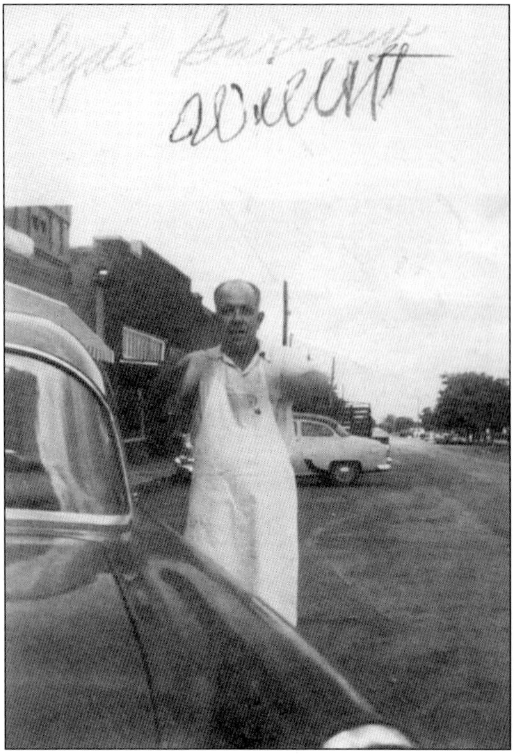

Clyde Willett was a butcher at Ball's grocery store from the 1940s to the 1960s. The Willetts were outstanding citizens of Tioga. (Wayne and Cindie Vaughan.)

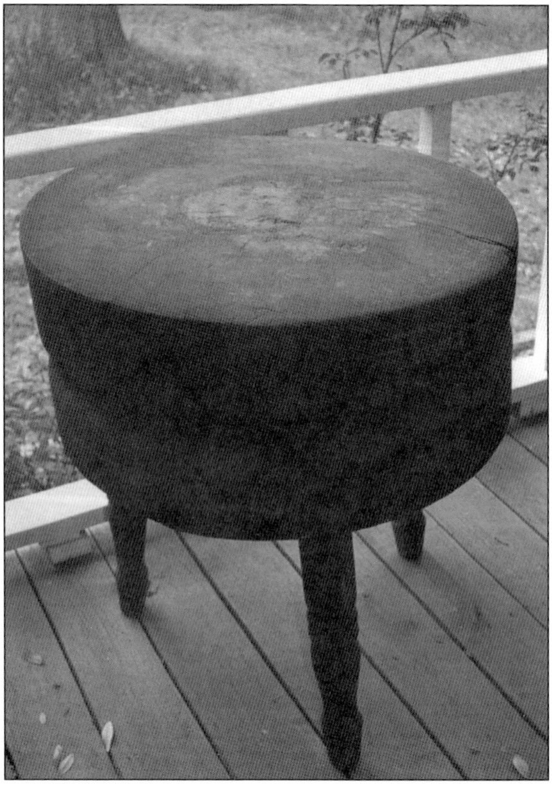

Clyde Willett used this butcher block in the grocery store for many years, and his grandson Wayne Vaughan now treasures it. (Wayne and Cindie Vaughan.)

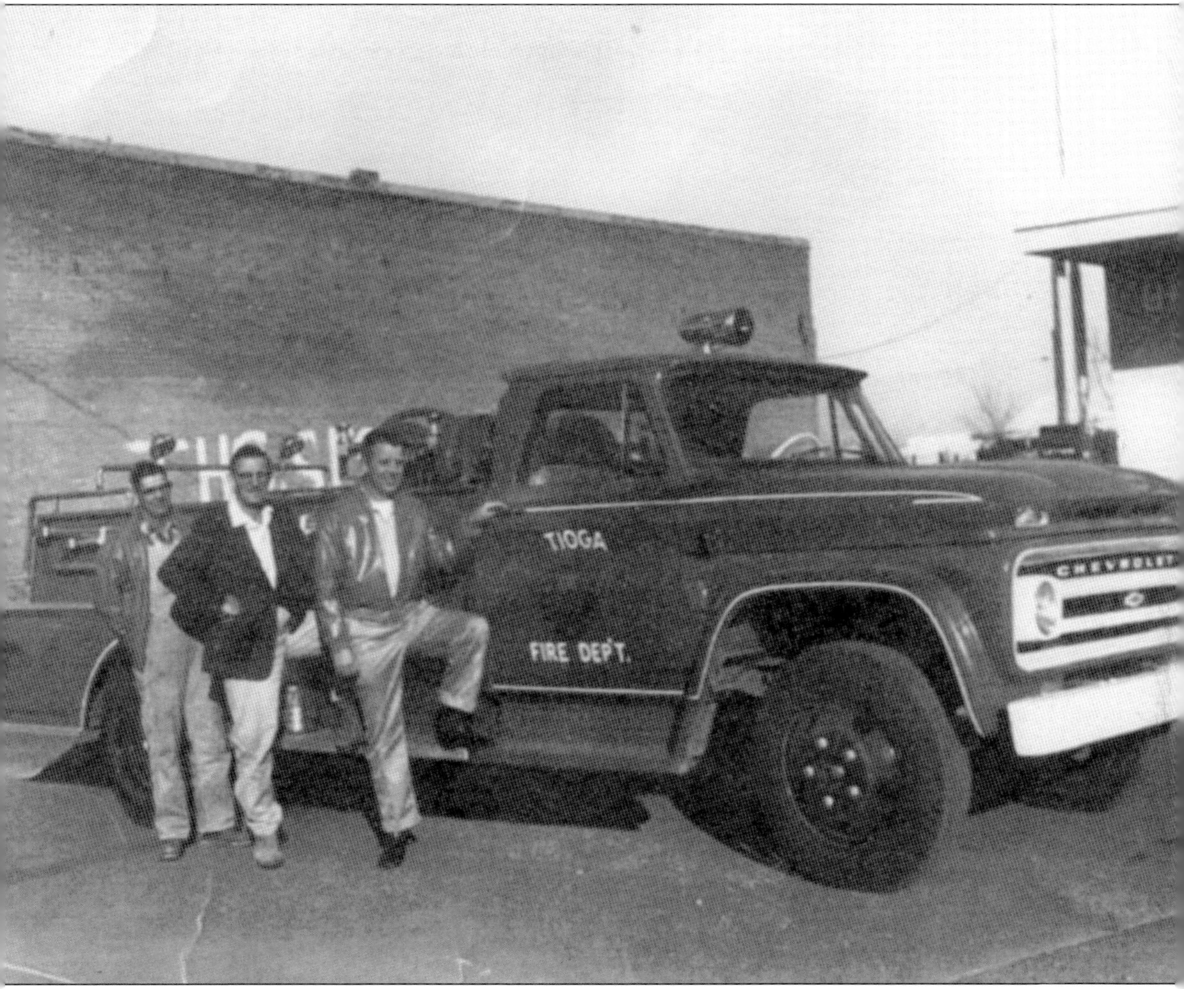

Some members of Tioga's volunteer fire department are pictured here. From left to right are C.W. "Bud" Davenport, Mayor William Kruger, and fire chief Billy Gene Mayo. (James Hilliard.)

HISTORY OF LEOPOLD AND MARY HERZIK BODORVSKY
By: Leona Bodovsky Leorwald &
Arvella Bodovsky McKnight

My Grandfather, Leopold Bordovsky was born in Moravia, Czech., Oct. 4, 1863. According to some of his children, he moved to Freistadt at an early age. This was before the Austrian-Prussian war and Freistadt was still located in Czech. After the war, the boundary of Austria and Czech. was changed and this city is now in Austria. The Czechs were being drafted by Austria into this war which he did not want to fight in, so he ran away at the age of 17 or 18. He made it to the Mediterranean or Atlantic which we do not know, and stowed away on a ship coming to America. He was discovered hiding in the boiler room and had to shovel coal to pay for his passage. He landed in New York and worked his way to Texas doing any odd jobs he could find. He settled in Fayette County, Tx. about 1882. His name was spelled "Bordovsky" but for some reason in later years the "R" was dropped and was spelled "Bodovsky".

My Grandmother, Mary Herzik was born in Moravia, Czech. July 30, 1863, twin sister of Molly. Her parents were Frantisek and Anna Herzik who are buried in Praha, Fayette County, Tx. Grandma and her twin were only 3 years old when they came to America by way of the Atlantic Ocean. Molly died on the way across and was buried in the Atlantic. My great-grandfather Herzik farmed some land in Fayette County. He advertised in the paper for a hired hand and Grandfather Bodovsky answered the ad and got the job. This is how he met my Grandmother. They were married Nov. 11, 1886 at St. Cyrill Church, Dubina Tx., Fayette County. Dubina is not a town, only a church and cemetery near LaGrange, Tx. They bought 20 acres of farm land in Fayette Co., a 6" walking plow, 1 mule, a double--shovel and a Georgia stock. They came to Grayson County in 1894 in a box-car with their five children at that time, along with the Frank Fries family. They bought about 170 acres of farm land at $15.00 per acre five miles east of Tioga. They lived in one room on the Latonskys farm near the old Schindler place in Pilot Point while their house was being built. Their new home consisted of four rooms downstairs and three rooms upstairs. Grandpa died on Aug. 11, 1911 and is buried at St. Thomas Cemetery in Pilot Point. Grandma died Oct. 21, 1950 and is also buried at St. Thomas.

Grandpa and Grandma had eleven children. They are listed on following page.

Family letters explain how the Bodovskys immigrated to Tioga, and cousins Arvella (née Bodovsky) McKnight and Leona (née Bodovsky) Leorwald compiled this brief write-up of how the Bodovsky clan arrived in Tioga, Texas. (Arvella McKnight.)

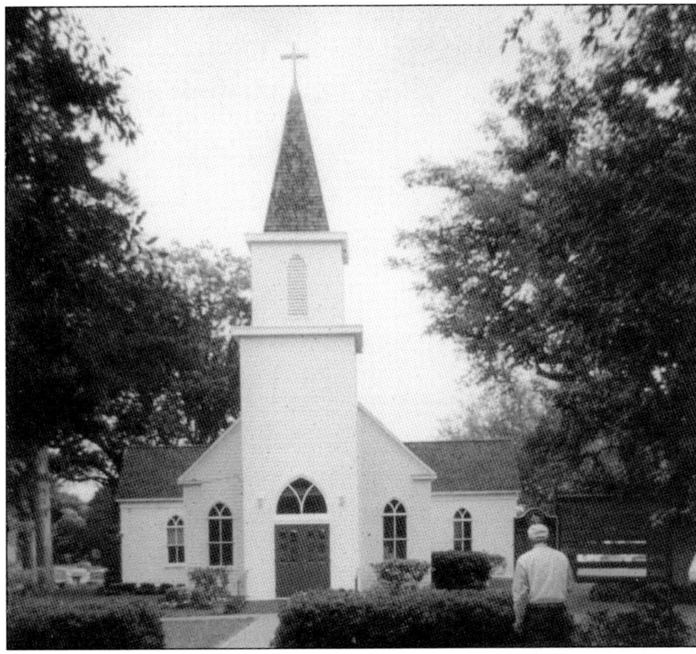

St. Cyril Catholic Church is located in Dubina, Texas. Leopold Bodovsky and Mary Herzik were married in this church in 1886. Dubina is no longer a town, as several fires and storms finally destroyed it; only the church and the cemetery remain. Czech immigrants founded the town, church, and cemetery around 1856. Leopold and Mary are the parents of Eugene Bodovsky. Eugene married Ruby Ragsdale, and Arvella (née Bodovsky) McKnight is one of their daughters. (Arvella McKnight.)

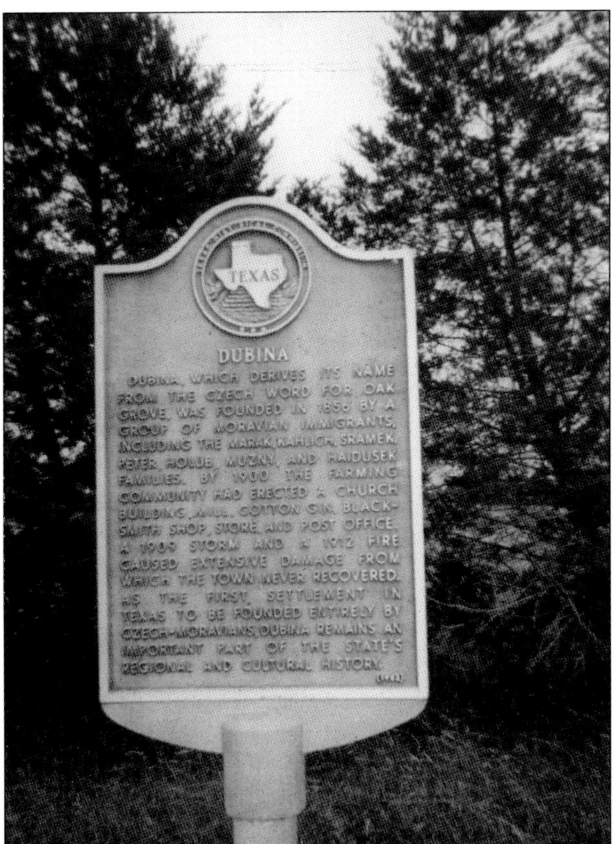

The plaque in front of St. Cyril Catholic Church in Dubina explains its formation and the Czech immigrants who lived there. Dubina is located near LaGrange, Texas. (Arvella McKnight.)

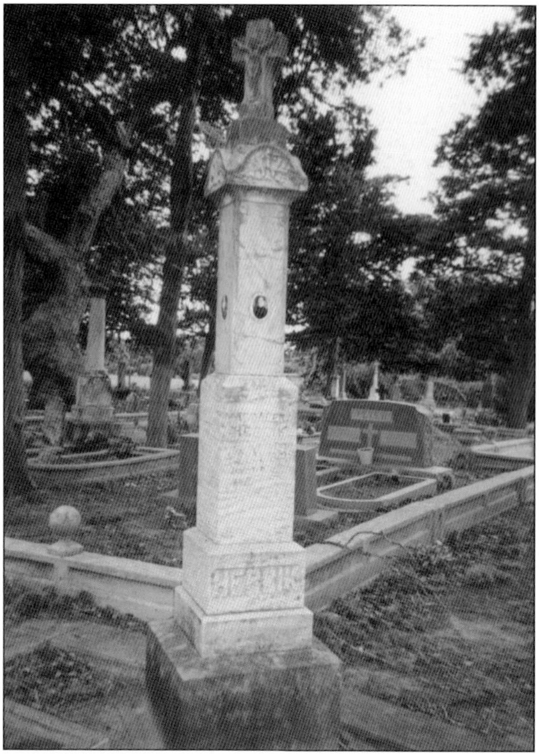

Located in the cemetery at St. Cyril Catholic Church in Dubina, Texas, is the headstone of Anna Herzik, mother of Mary (Herzik) Bodovsky. Anna is the great-grandmother of Arvella (Bodovsky) McKnight and her siblings. (Arvella McKnight.)

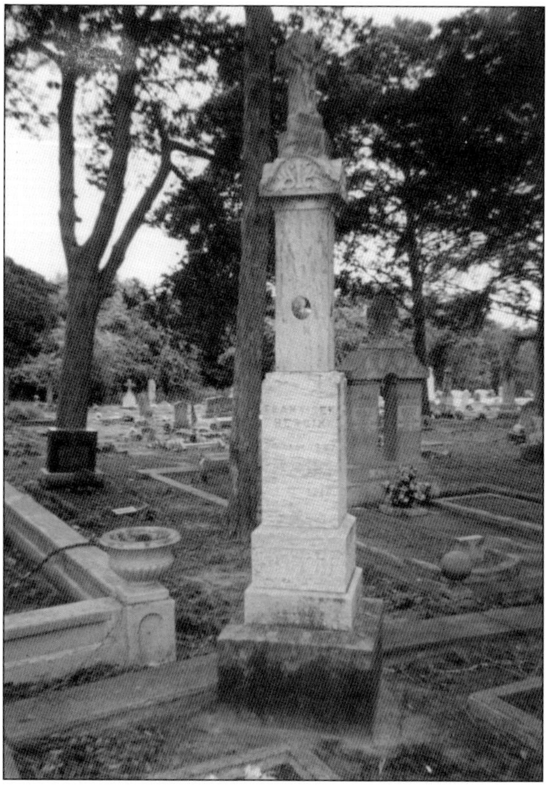

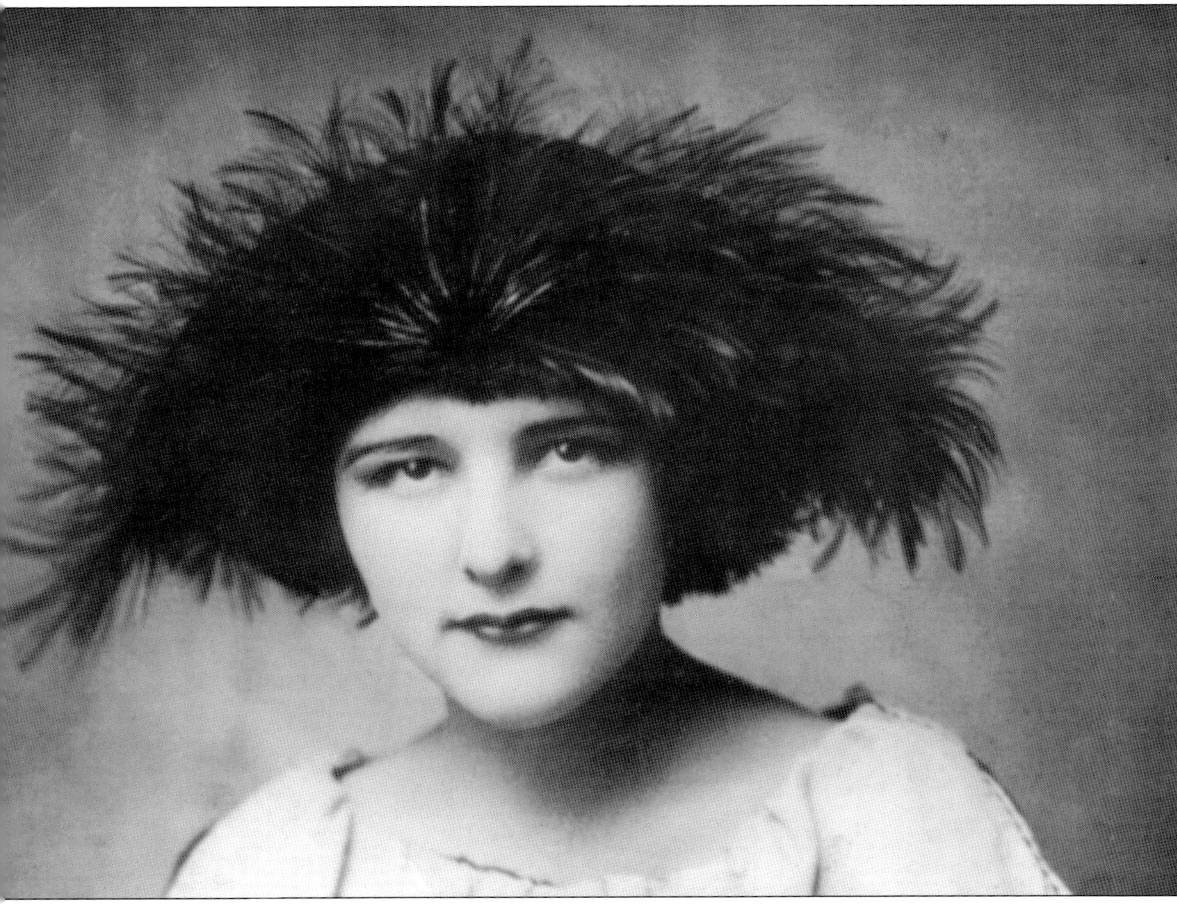

Ruby (Ragsdale) Bodovsky is pictured about 1920. Leopold and Mary (Herzik) Bodovsky were her husband's parents. Ruby was the mother of Arvella (Bodovsky) McKnight. (Arvella McKnight.)

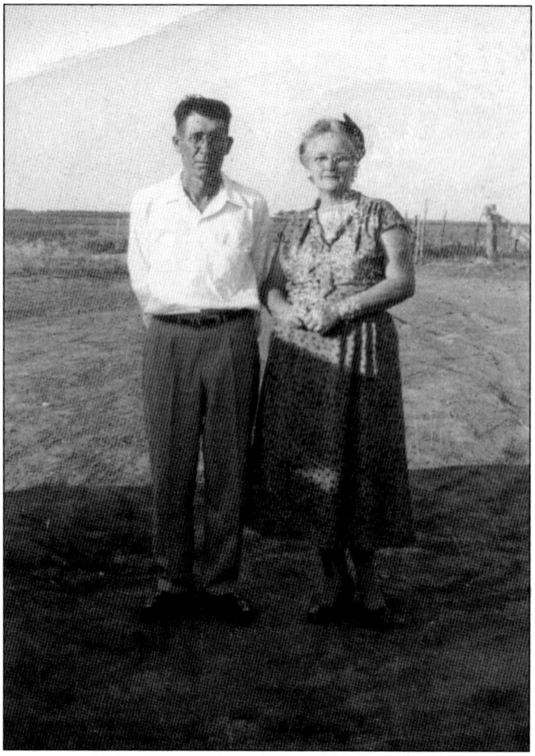

Eugene and Ruby Bodovsky are pictured around 1955. Eugene was killed shortly after this photograph when a train in Gunter, Texas, hit him. (Arvella McKnight.)

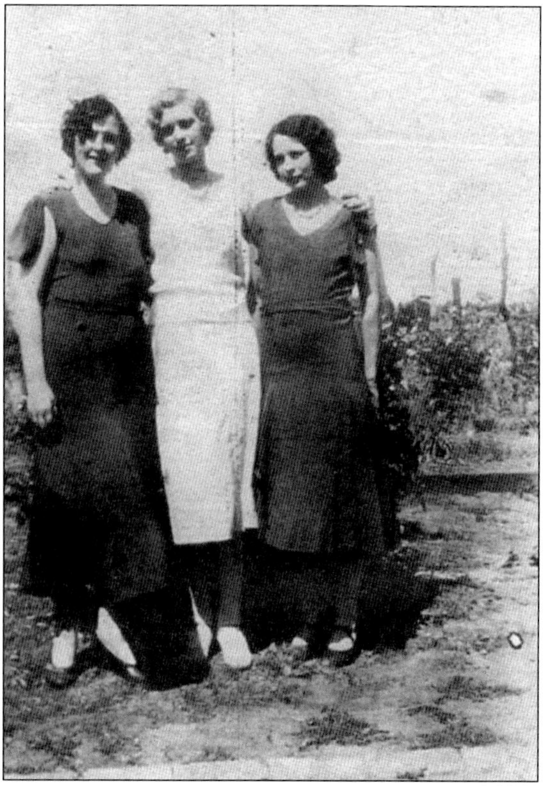

Pictured are, from left to right, sisters-in-law Ruby (née Ragsdale) Bodovsky, wife of Eugene; Elnora (née Scharff) Bodovsky, wife of Gilbert; and Dovie (née Williams) Bodovsky, wife of Raymond. This image was taken in the mid-1920s. Ruby's daughter Arvella McKnight still resides in the rural community outside Tioga, located close to Mount Carmel Church. (Arvella McKnight.)

Seen in the mid-1940s are Dan McKnight Jr. and Arvella Bodovsky. They are on the bridge crossing the creek on Scoggins Road. (Arvella McKnight.)

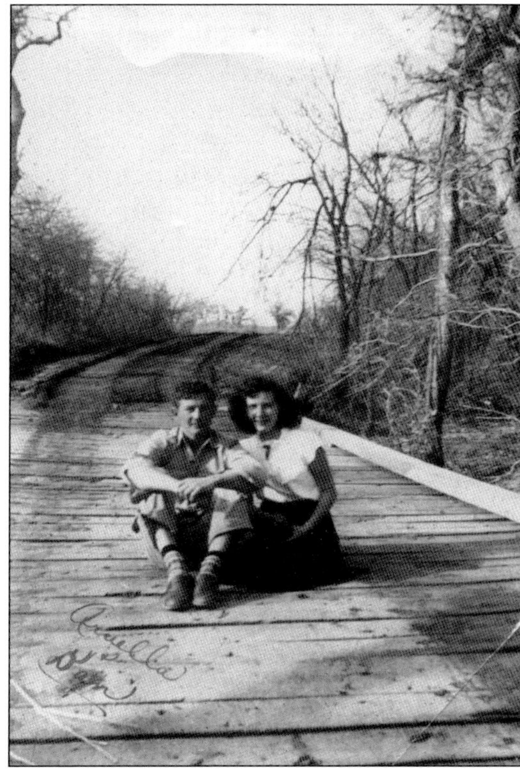

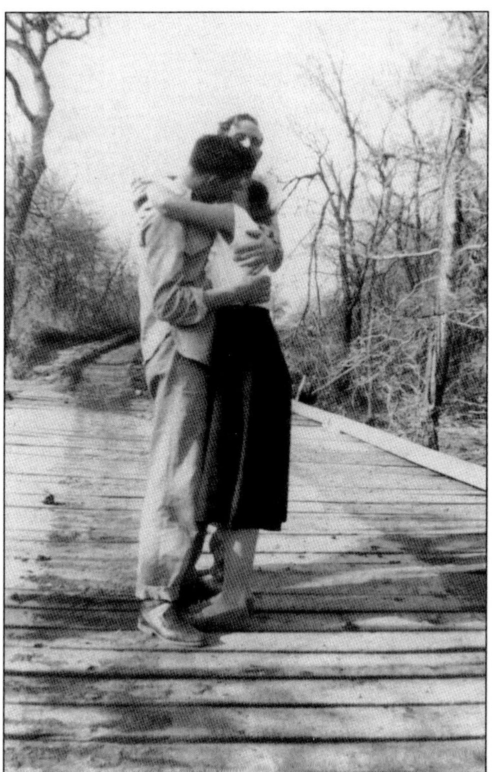

Here are Dan McKnight Jr. and Arvella Bodovsky again, this time with Jack Mullins in the background. Love surely must have been in the air, as Arvella and Dan Jr. went on to marry in 1949. They continued to live and raise their family in and around Tioga. (Arvella McKnight.)

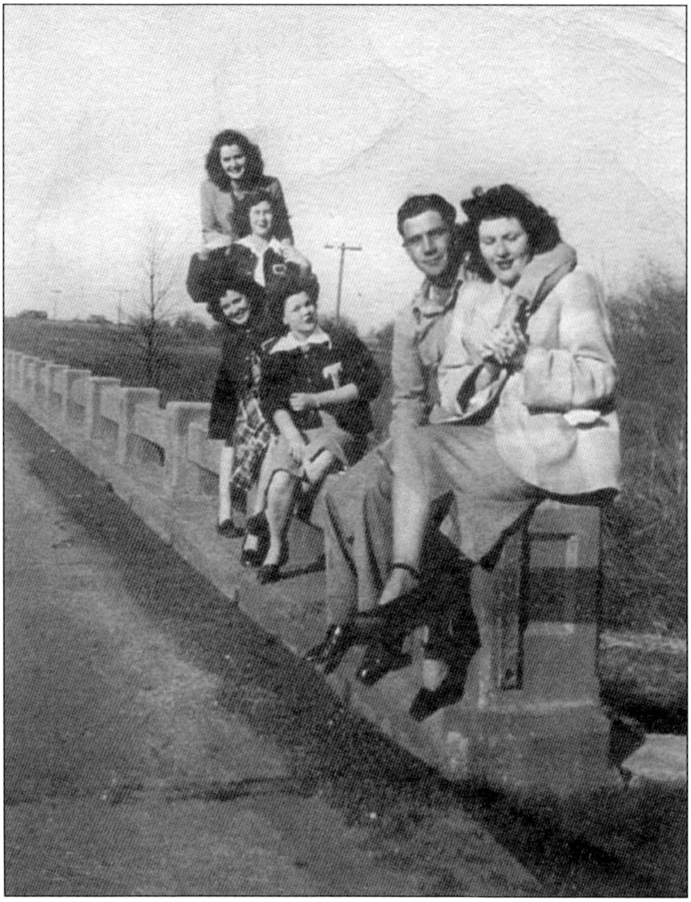

Pictured around 1950 are, from front to back, Dolores "Tommy" Bodovsky (another daughter of Eugene and Ruby Bodovsky), Bob Midkiff, Frankie Fullmore, Imogene Norris, and two unidentified girls. (Arvella McKnight.)

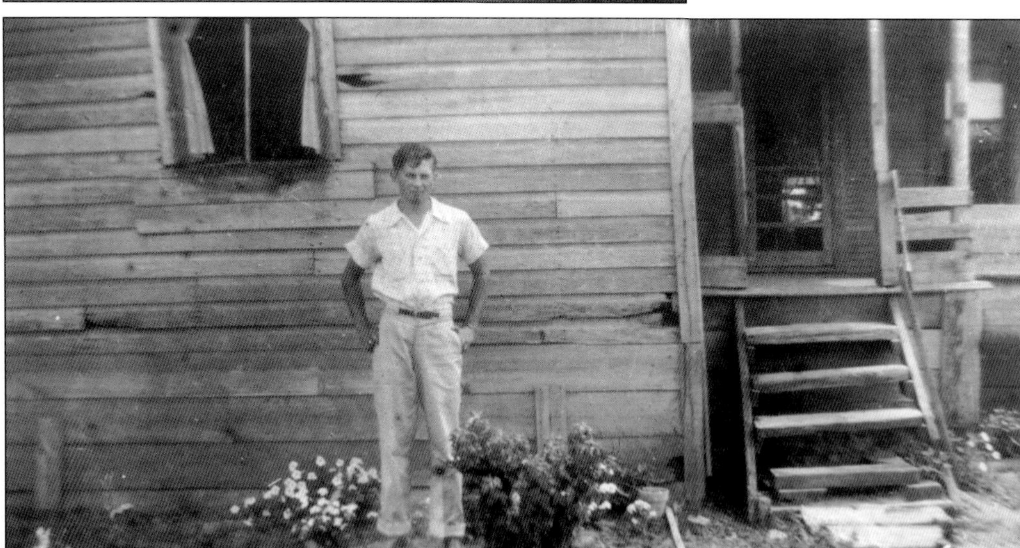

Dan McKnight Jr. is standing in front of an old house in Tioga around 1945. The McKnights are a long-standing family in the Tioga community. (Arvella McKnight.)

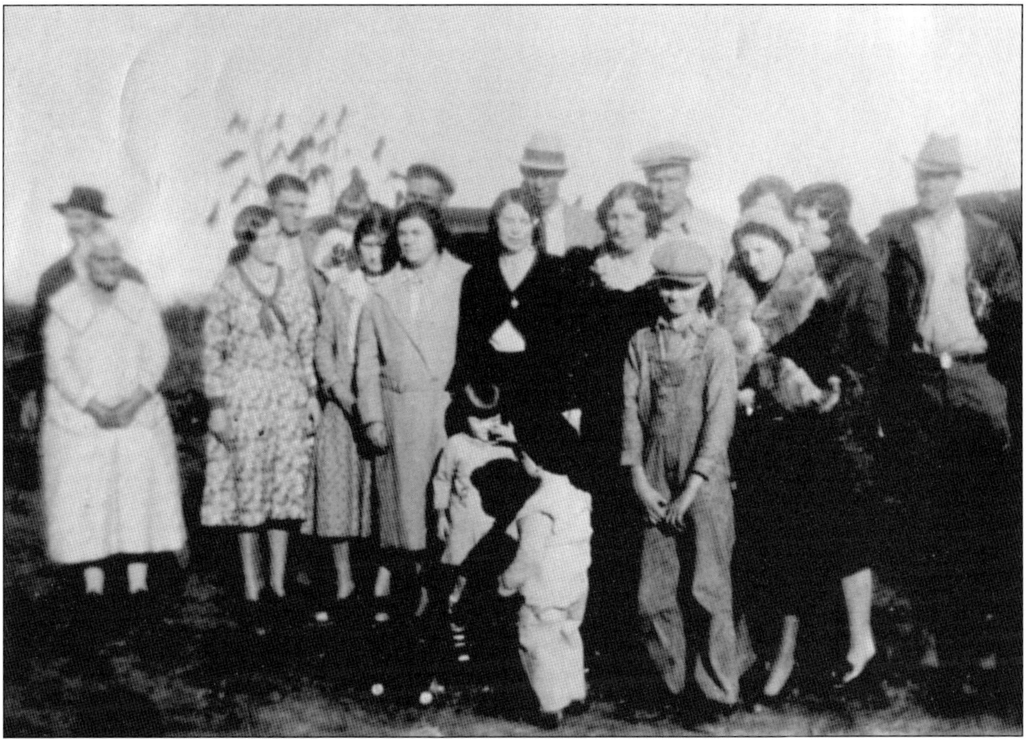

Here is the Morton family of Tioga in the 1930s. In no particular order, they are Grandpa and Grandmother Morton, Lena, Delmor, Lester, Rhoda, Peggy, Jack, Dressie, Irene, Floyd, Rudena, F. Tucker, and Maye Morton. (Arvella McKnight.)

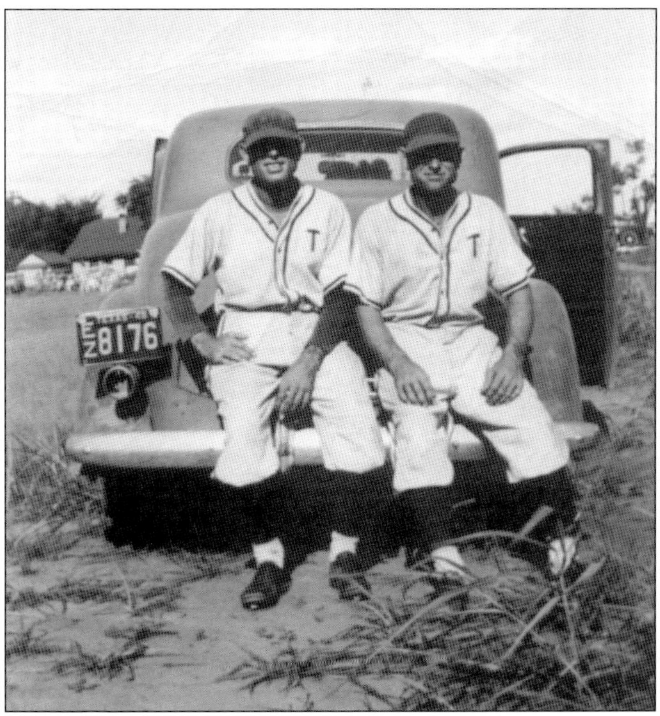

Pictured here in 1945 are, from left to right, Austin and Dude Carrigan. These brothers played for the Tioga baseball team. Not all the players on the team were from Tioga. Dude was a resident in Tioga for many years, but Austin moved away. (James Hilliard.)

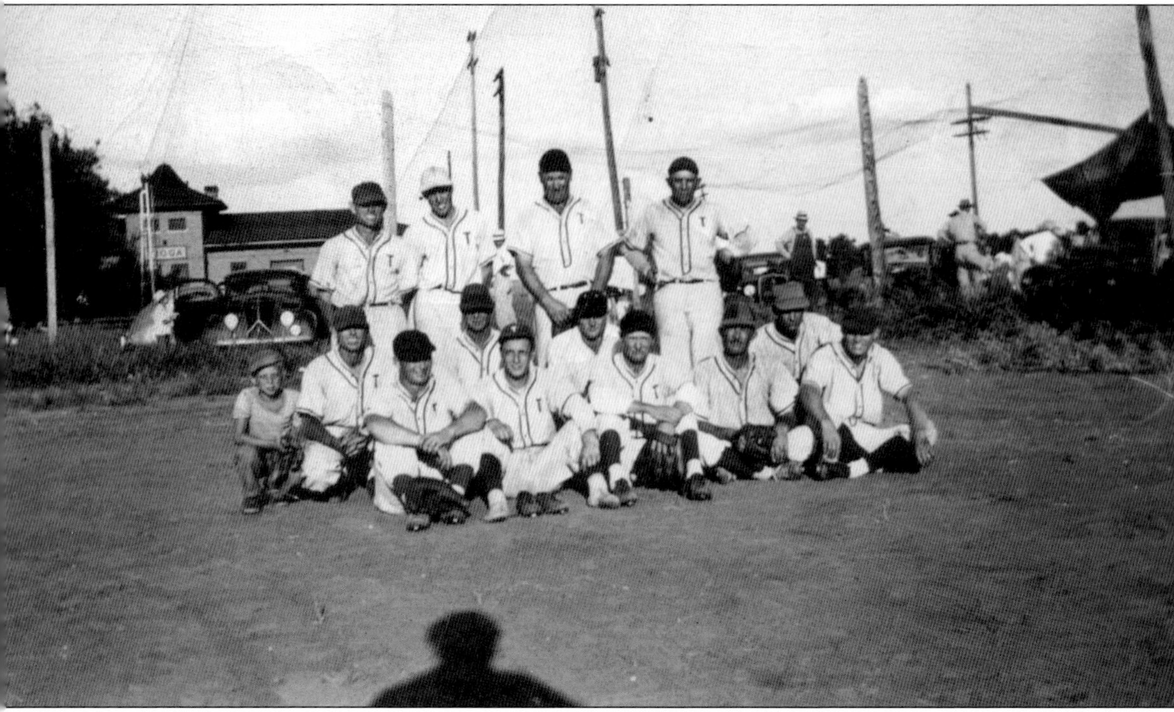

Here is the 1945–1946 Tioga baseball team, which was very competitive. (Authors' collection.)

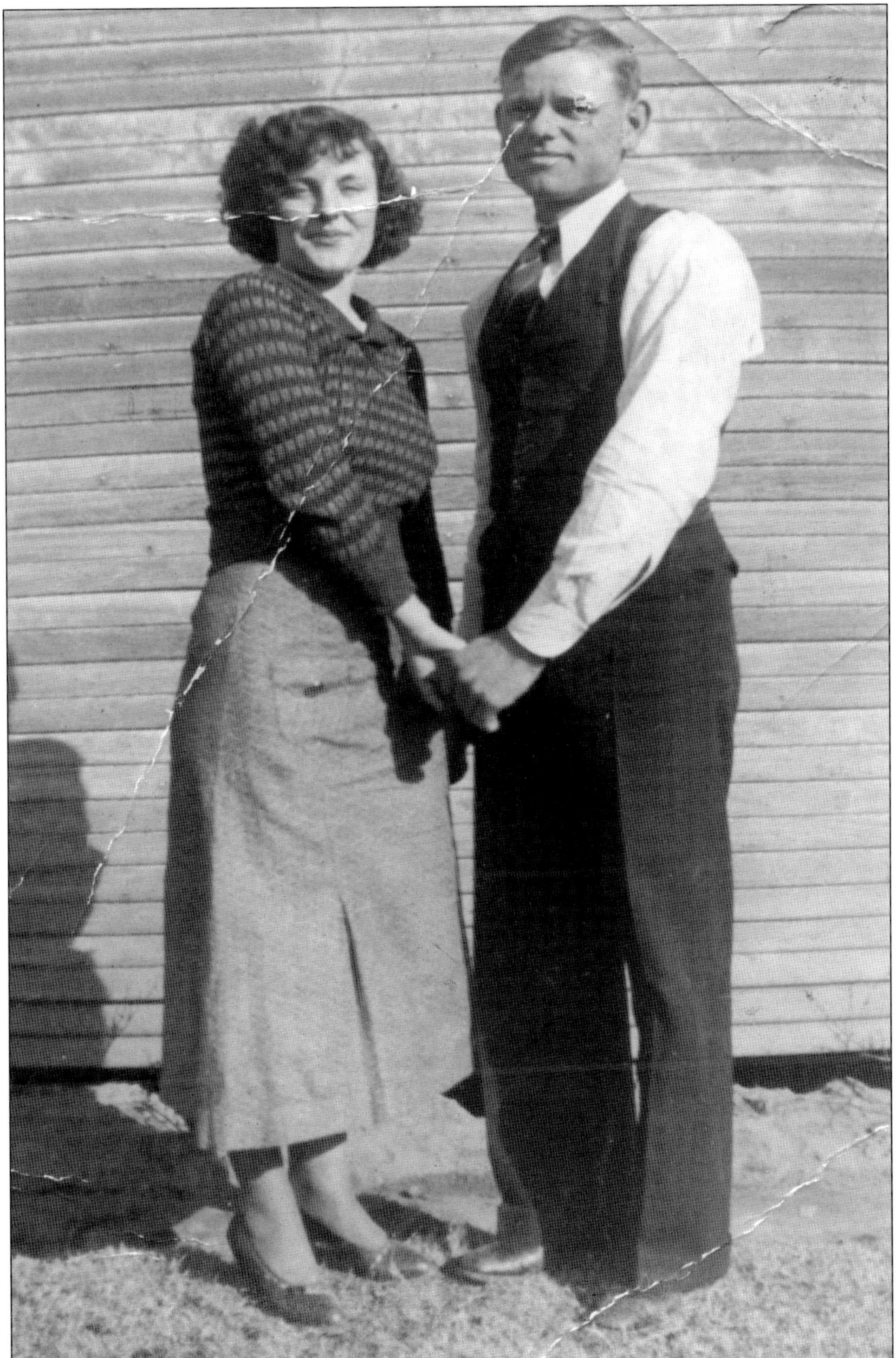

Pictured are Dude and Irene Carrigan. Dude played on the Tioga baseball team around 1945. (Arvella McKnight.)

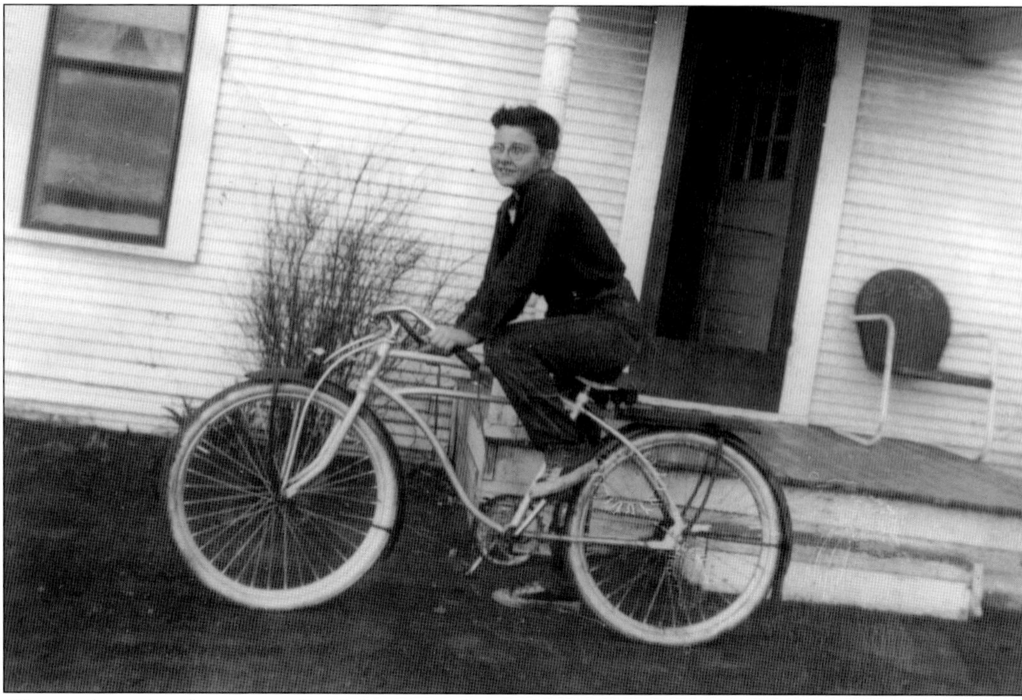

This is Jerry Bodovsky on his bike around 1945. Jerry was Arvella McKnight's brother. The Bodovskys were longtime residents of Tioga. (Arvella McKnight.)

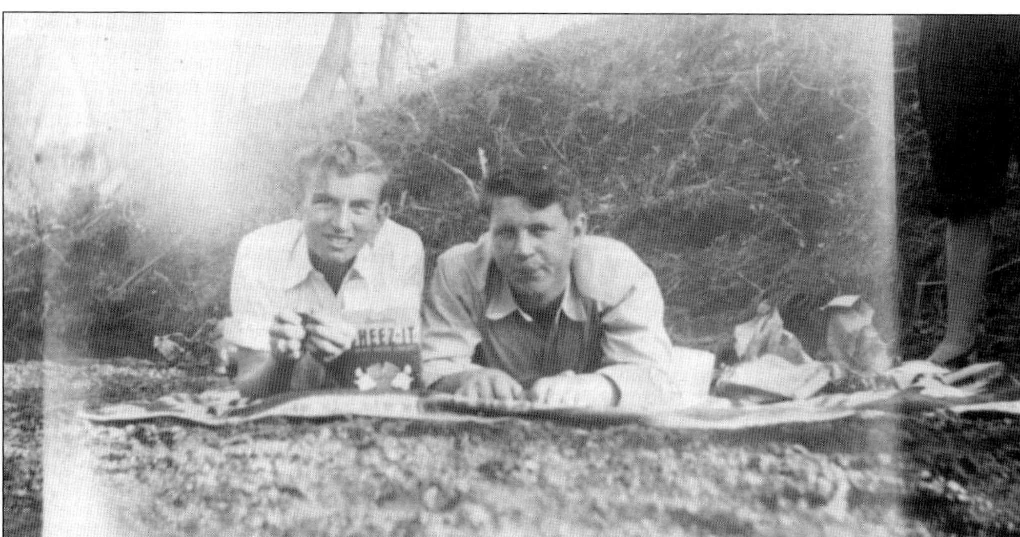

G.W. Roark (left) and Jack Mullins pose for the camera in the 1940s; two unidentified girls took the photograph while the four enjoyed a picnic. (Wayne and Cindie Vaughan.)

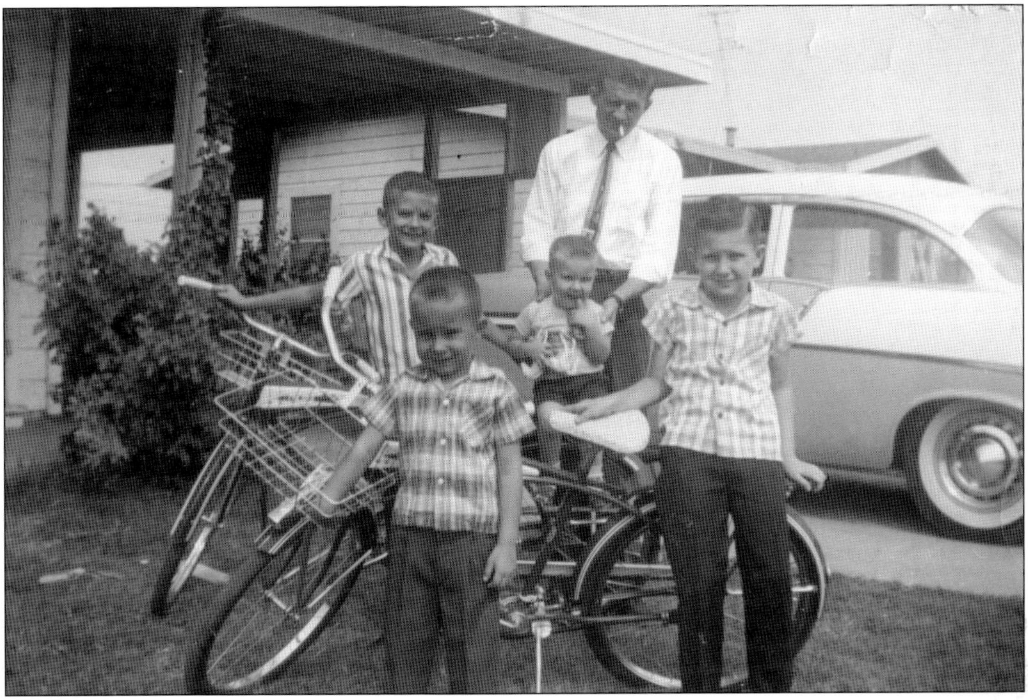

Dan McKnight Jr. and his sons pose for a photograph in 1958. Dan is holding son Jerry. The other sons are, from left to right, Bob, Donnie, and Jack Myers. (Arvella McKnight.)

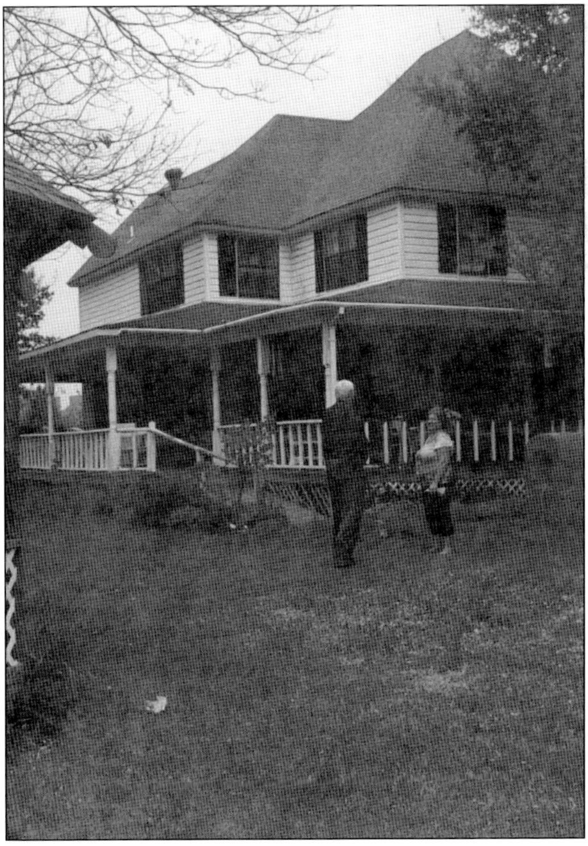

Don Davenport and Cindie Vaughan stand in front of the Willett-Vaughan home. Jim Willett, the great-uncle of current resident Wayne Vaughan, originally bought the house in the early 1900s. (Authors' collection.)

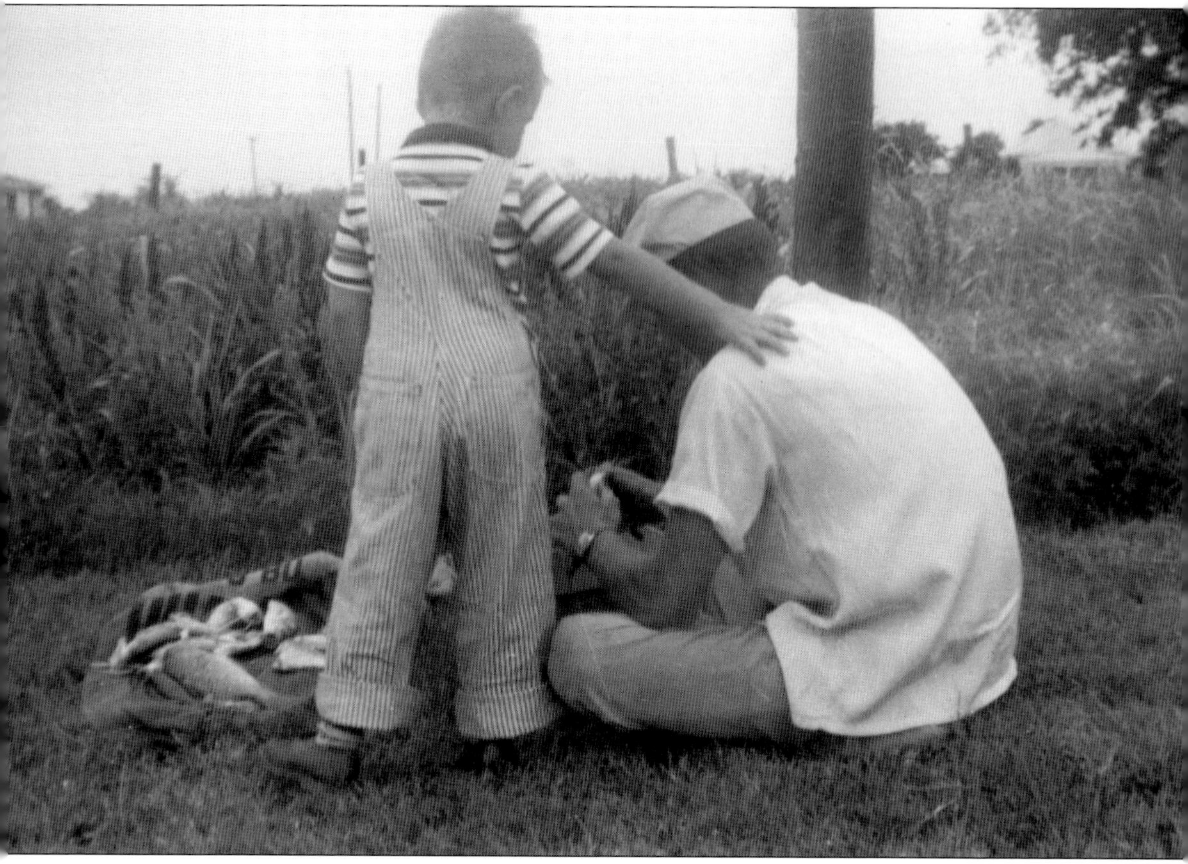

A father and his son share a moment in time while cleaning fish. Standing is Jerry McKnight and seated is Dan McKnight Jr. (Arvella McKnight.)

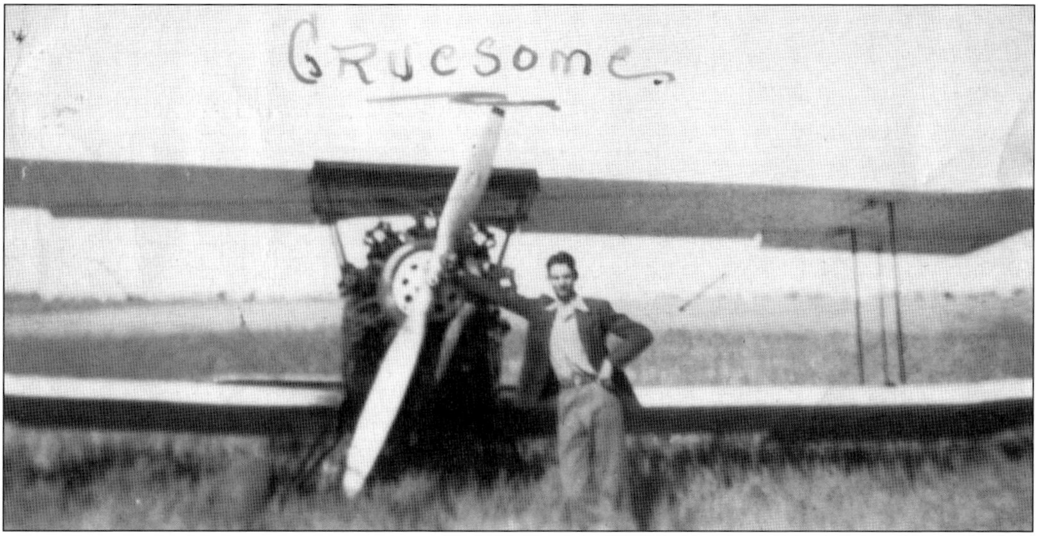

This photograph was in the collection of Laura Willett Vaughan. The pilot is unidentified, but he must have had some importance to Laura and Tioga. Curiously, the word "Gruesome" is written across the top of this 1930s image. (Wayne and Cindie Vaughan.)

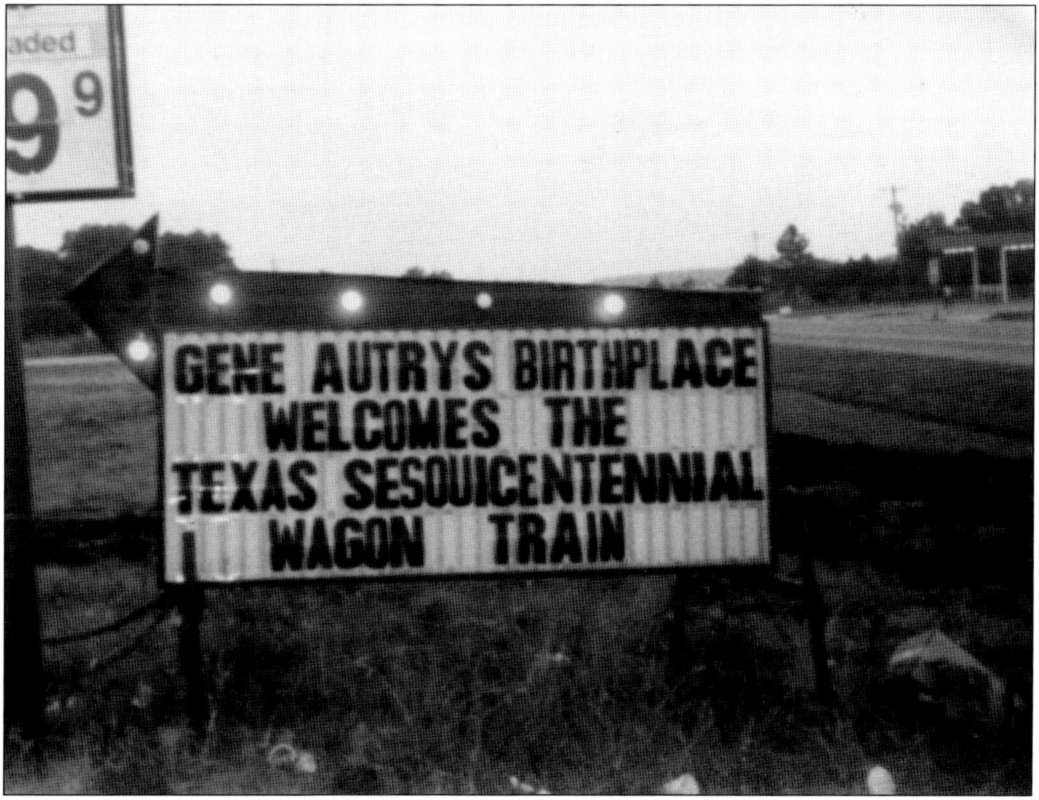

Tioga welcomes the 1986 Texas Sesquicentennial Wagon Train traveling across the state. Tioga had a parade in celebration of the occasion. Folks cooked food and met on the streets of Tioga, and a celebration of Texas's historic year brought much happiness all over the state. (Arvella McKnight.)

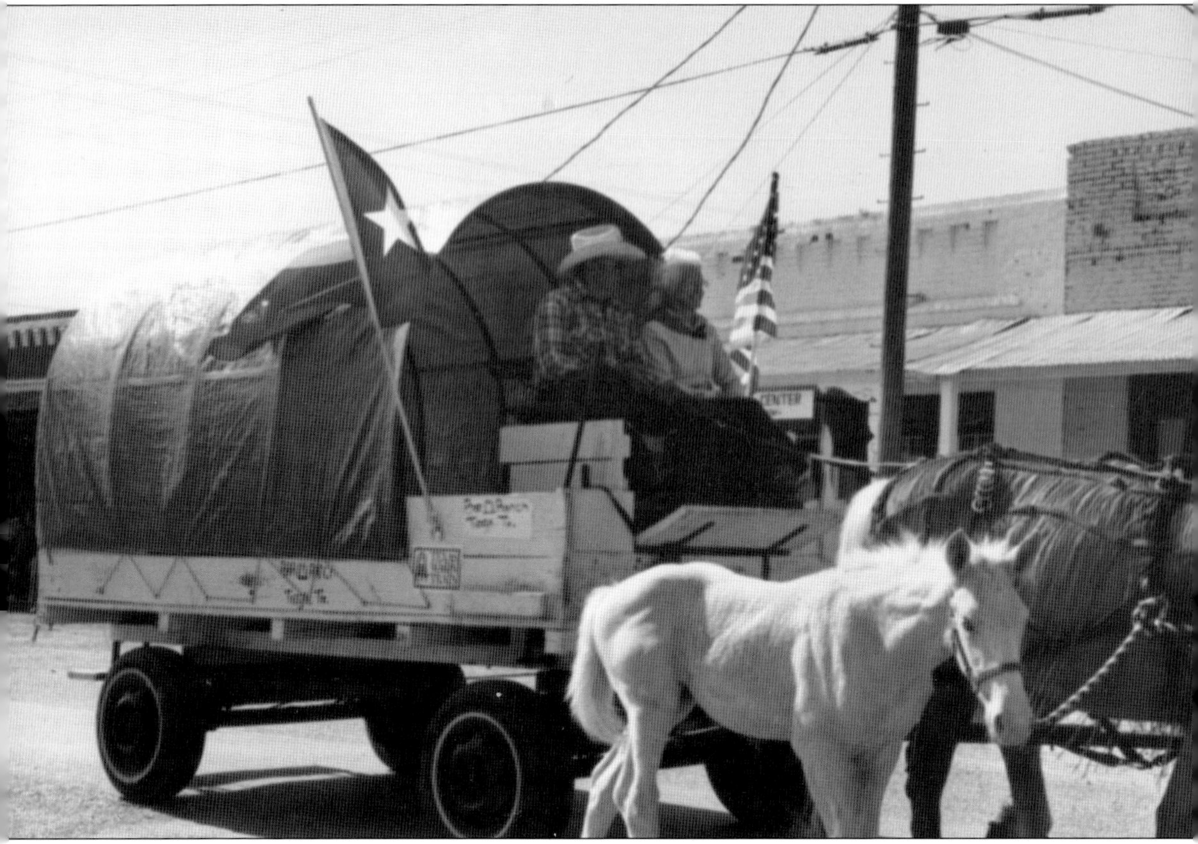

A wagon in Tioga's parade joins in the celebration of Texas's sesquicentennial. (Arvella McKnight.)

Two

TIOGA
SCHOOL DAYS

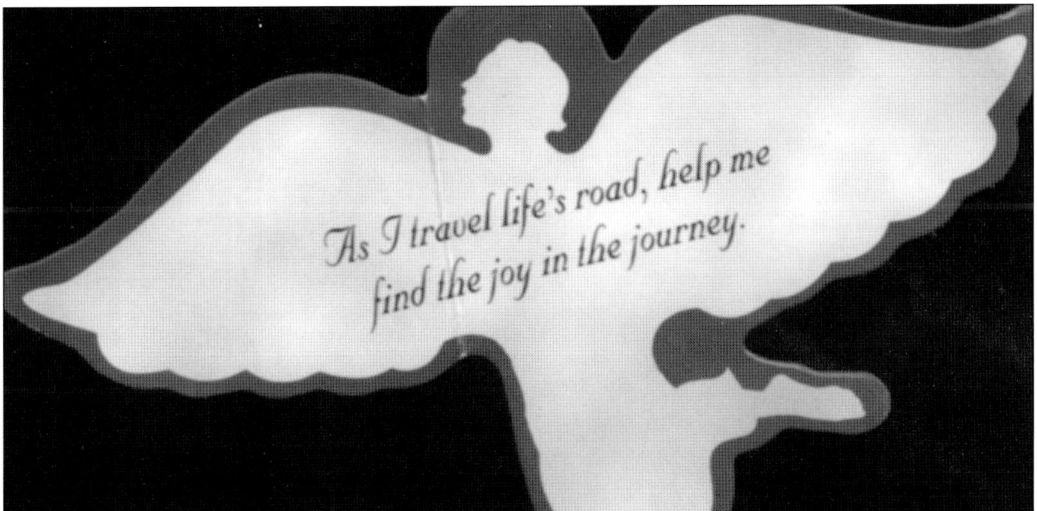

This was in Laura Willett Vaughan's belongings dating from her senior year of high school (1948). It was a testament to the life she lived—always looking for the joy in the journey. (Wayne and Cindie Vaughan.)

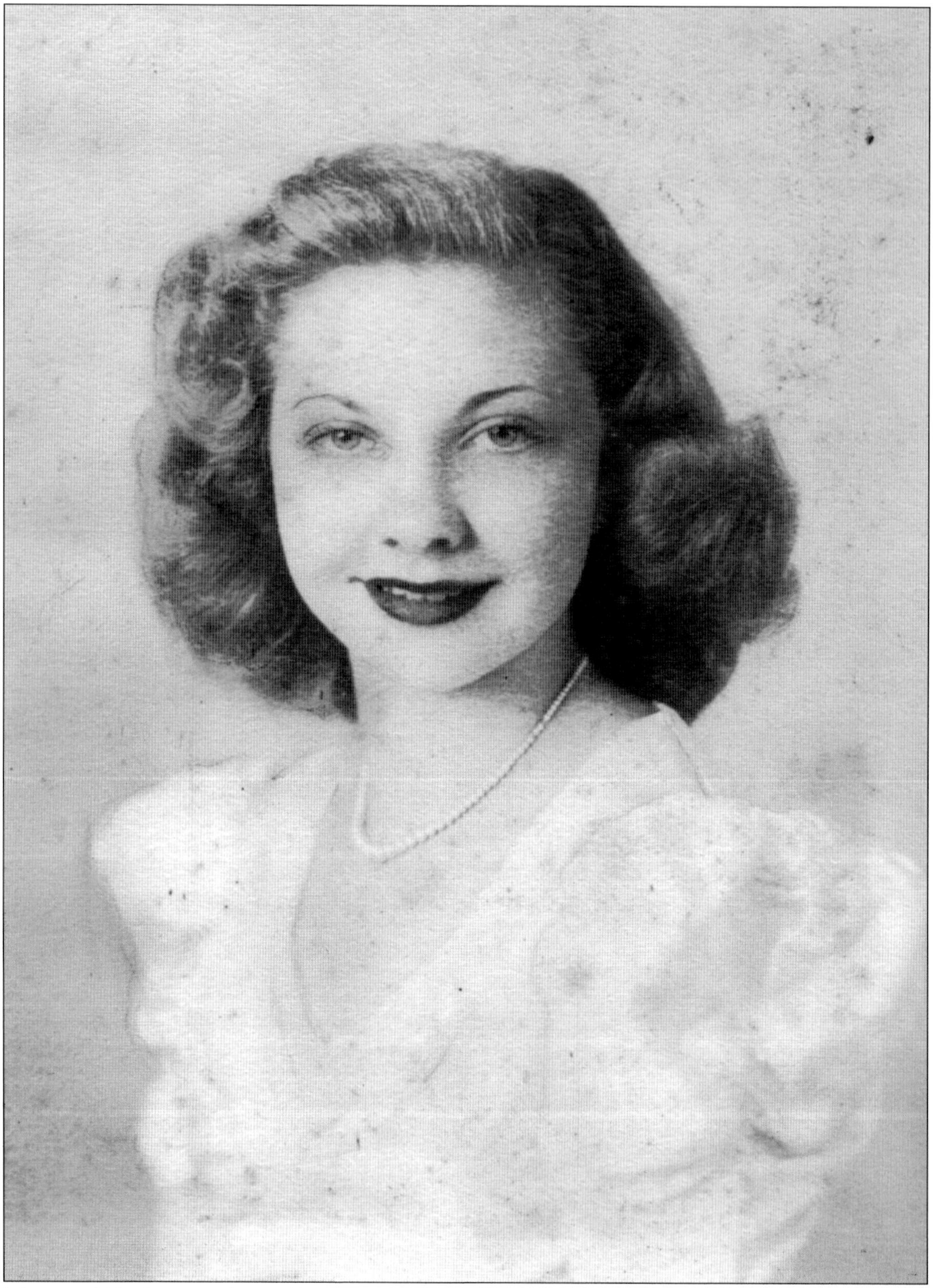

This c. 1948 photograph is of Laura Willett Vaughan as a senior at Tioga High School. Laura never forgot the town she grew up in. She was always ready to help serve on committees or do anything her beloved town needed. She raised her family and spent her last days in Tioga. (Wayne and Cindie Vaughan.)

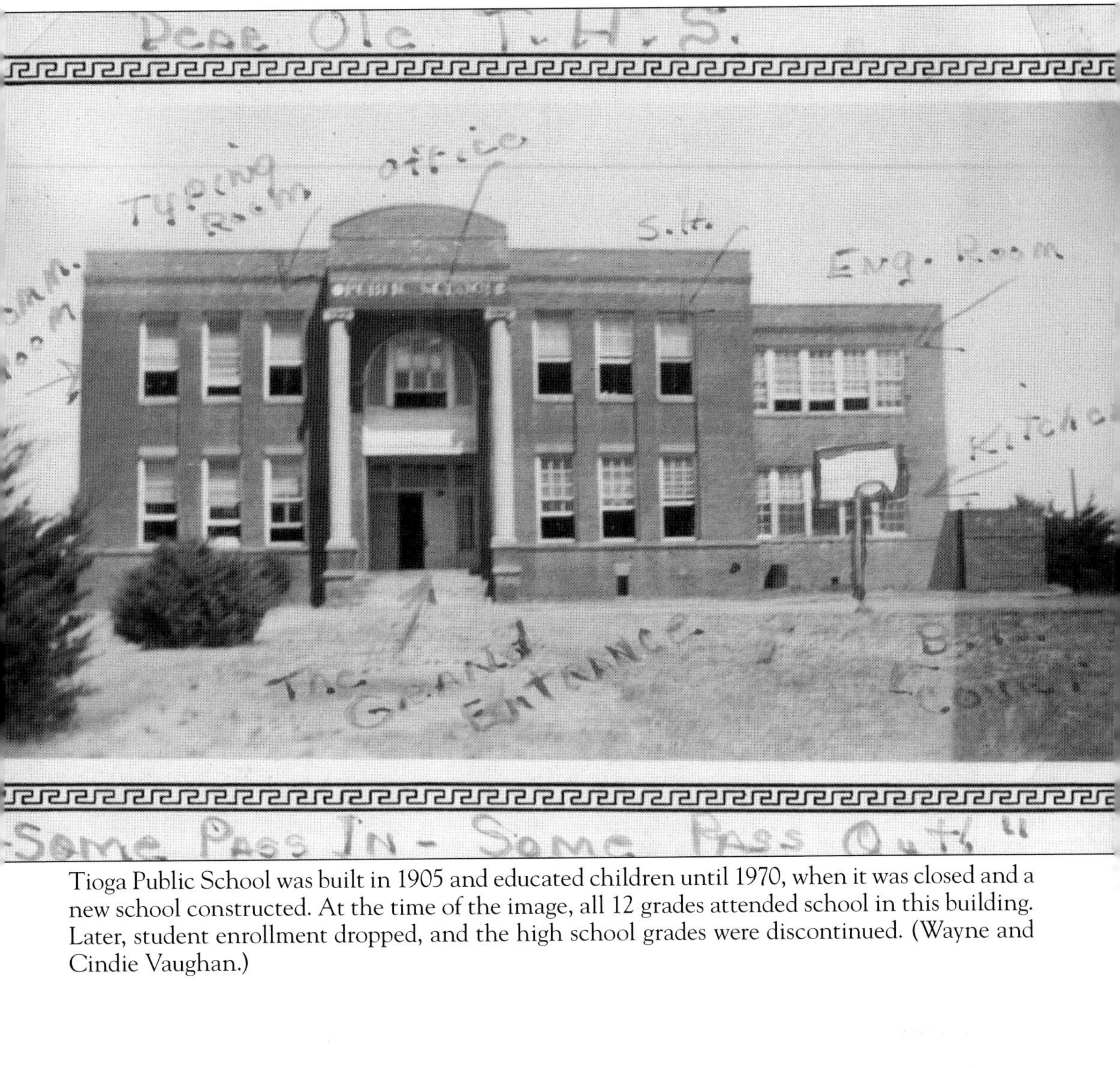

Tioga Public School was built in 1905 and educated children until 1970, when it was closed and a new school constructed. At the time of the image, all 12 grades attended school in this building. Later, student enrollment dropped, and the high school grades were discontinued. (Wayne and Cindie Vaughan.)

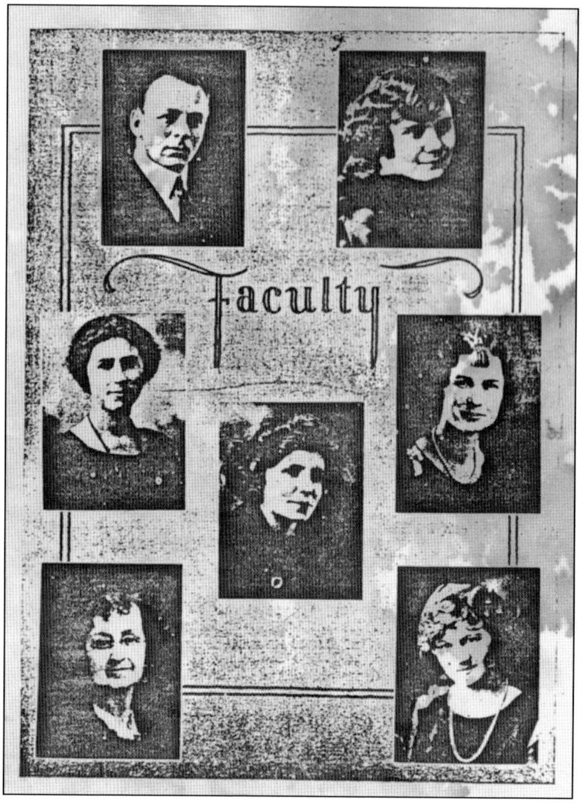

Here is a page right out of the 1924 annual of Tioga Public School that depicts the faculty. (James Hilliard.)

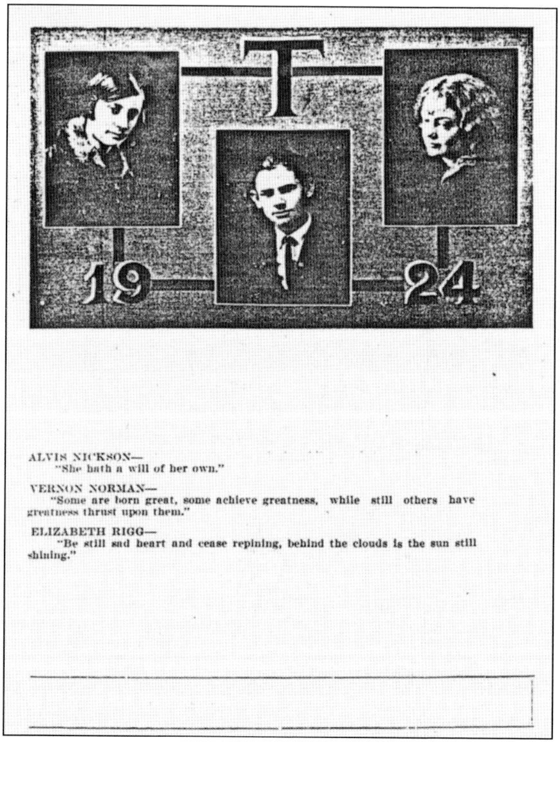

ALVIS NICKSON—
"She hath a will of her own."

VERNON NORMAN—
"Some are born great, some achieve greatness, while still others have greatness thrust upon them."

ELIZABETH RIGG—
"Be still sad heart and cease repining, behind the clouds is the sun still shining."

Also from the 1924 annual, the quotes seen here describe the personalities of 1924 seniors Alvis Nickson, Vernon Norman, and Elizabeth Rigg of Tioga Public School. (James Hilliard.)

The dedication in the 1924 annual of Tioga Public School reads, "As a manifestation of our high esteem fro her courtesy, her untiring efforts in behalf of the school, and in token of the affections that we all hold for her we respectfully dedicate this, our second annual, to Miss Velma Smith." (James Hilliard.)

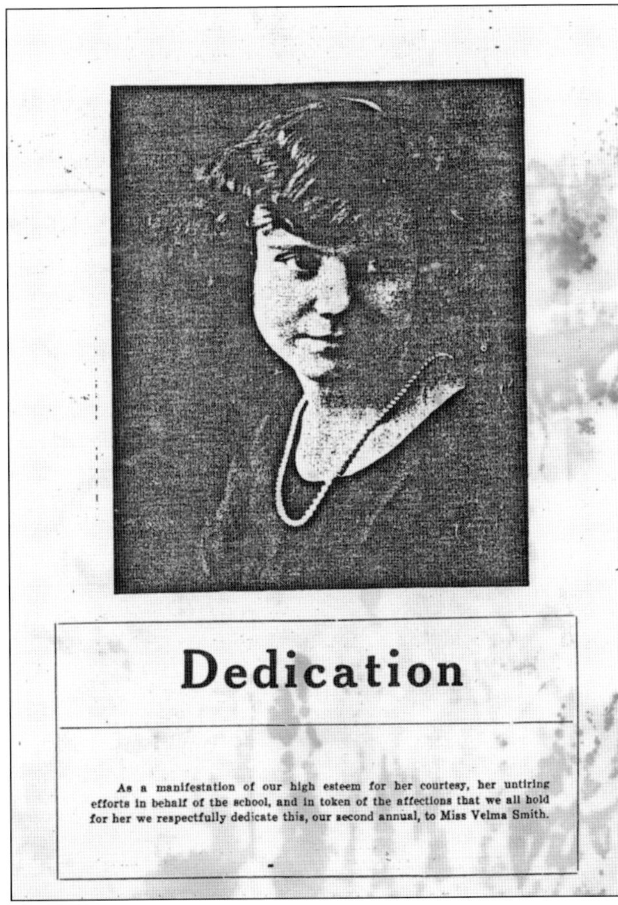

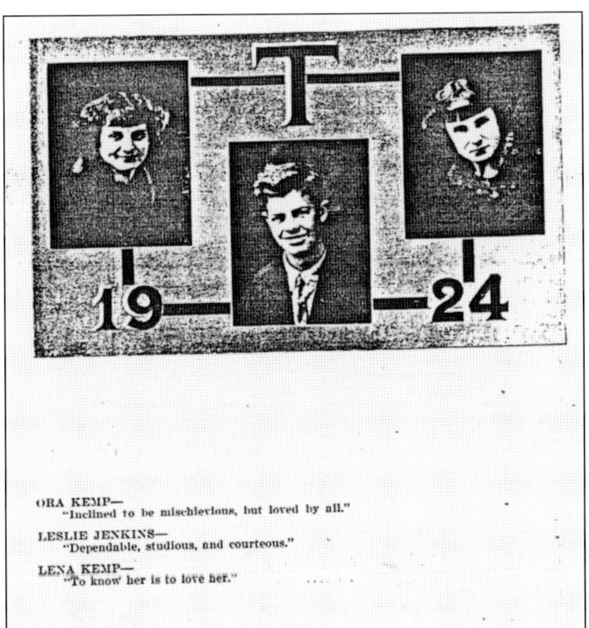

Here, more quotes describe the personalities of 1924 seniors Ora Kemp, Leslie Jenkins, and Lena Kemp of Tioga Public School. (James Hilliard.)

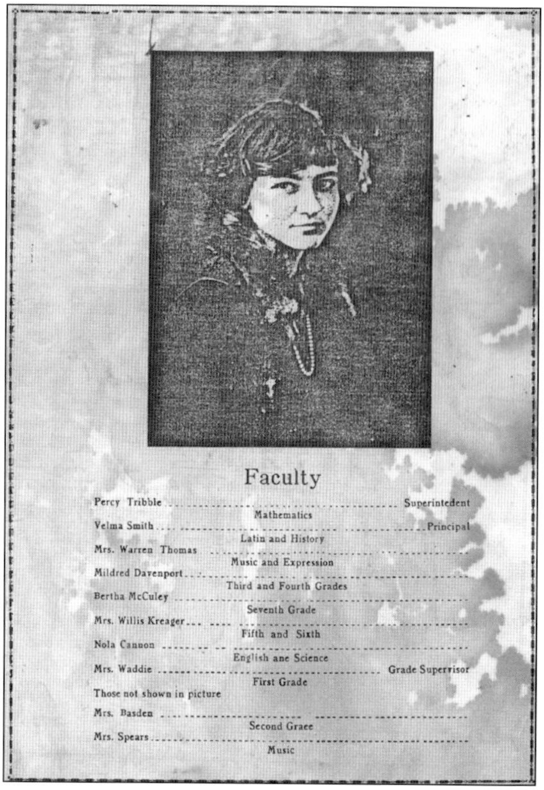

Faculty

Percy Tribble .... Superintedent
Mathematics
Velma Smith .... Principal
Latin and History
Mrs. Warren Thomas ....
Music and Expression
Mildred Davenport ....
Third and Fourth Grades
Bertha McCuley ....
Seventh Grade
Mrs. Willis Kreager ....
Fifth and Sixth
Nola Cannon ....
English ane Science
Mrs. Waddie .... Grade Superrisor
First Grade
Those not shown in picture
Mrs. Basden ....
Second Graee
Mrs. Spears ....
Music

The 1924 faculty members included Supt. Percy Tribble, mathematics; Principal Velma Smith, Latin and history; Mrs. Warren Thomas, music and expression; Mildred Davenport, third and fourth grades; Bertha McCuley, seventh grade; Mrs. Willis Kreager, fifth and sixth grades; Nola Cannon, English and science; Mrs. Waddie, first grade; Mrs. Basden, second grade; and Mrs. Spears, music. (James Hilliard.)

The 1945–1946 Tioga girls' basketball team is pictured here. The members are, from left to right, (first row) Helen Johnson and Laura Mae Willett; (second row) Janie Secrest, Billie Faye Dodson, unidentified, Dorothy Davenport, Betty Van Zandt, coach Drapper, Charlene Renfro, Patsy Davis, and Faye Fulmer. (James Hilliard.)

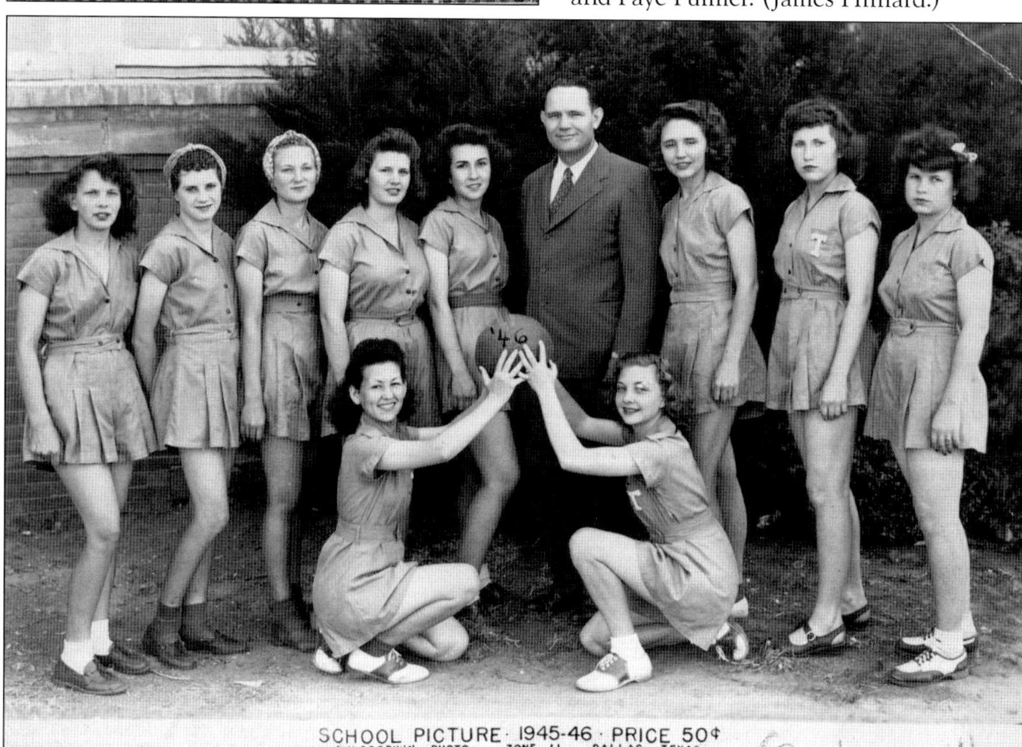

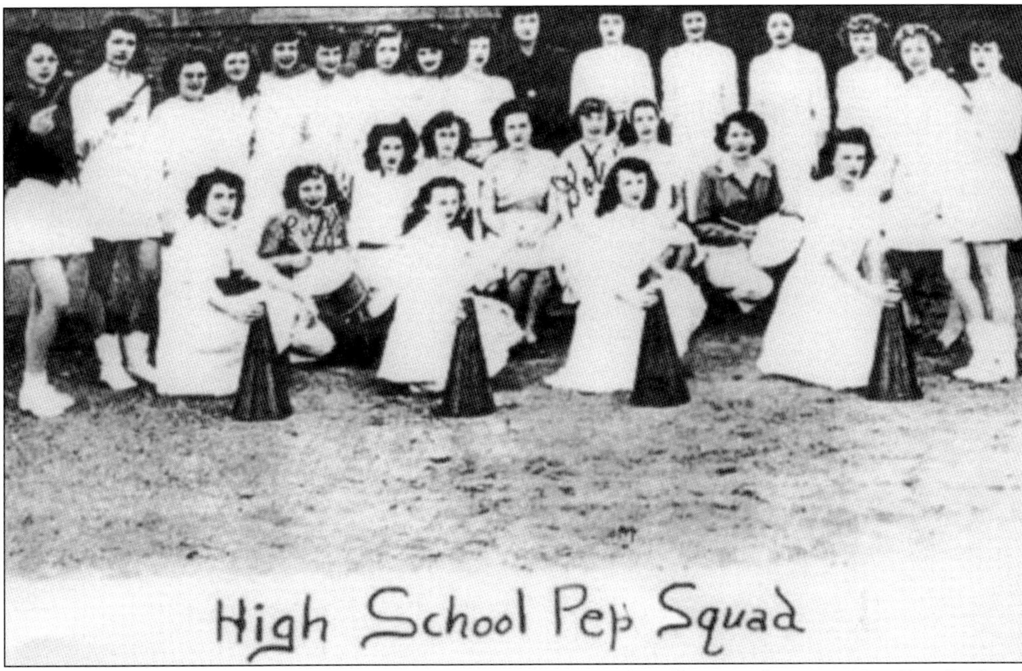

Members of the 1947 Tioga pep squad are, from left to right, (first row) Betty Van Zandt, Betty McKinley, Jackie Parks, and Dorothy Davenport; (second row) Laura Mae Willett, Nelda Cook, Letha Davidson, Dolores "Tommy" Bodovsky, Dorothy Suter, unidentified, and Janie Secrest; (third row) Inez Lubbers, Charlene Renfro, Mary Frances Foster, Cleo Hickman, Juanell Bodovsky, Joyce Cook, Ruby Hart, Margaret Norriss, unidentified, Mrs. Sanders, Waldene Midgett, Dorothy Clark, Geraldean Clark, Loretta Suter, Anna Draper, and Faye Fulmer. (James Hilliard.)

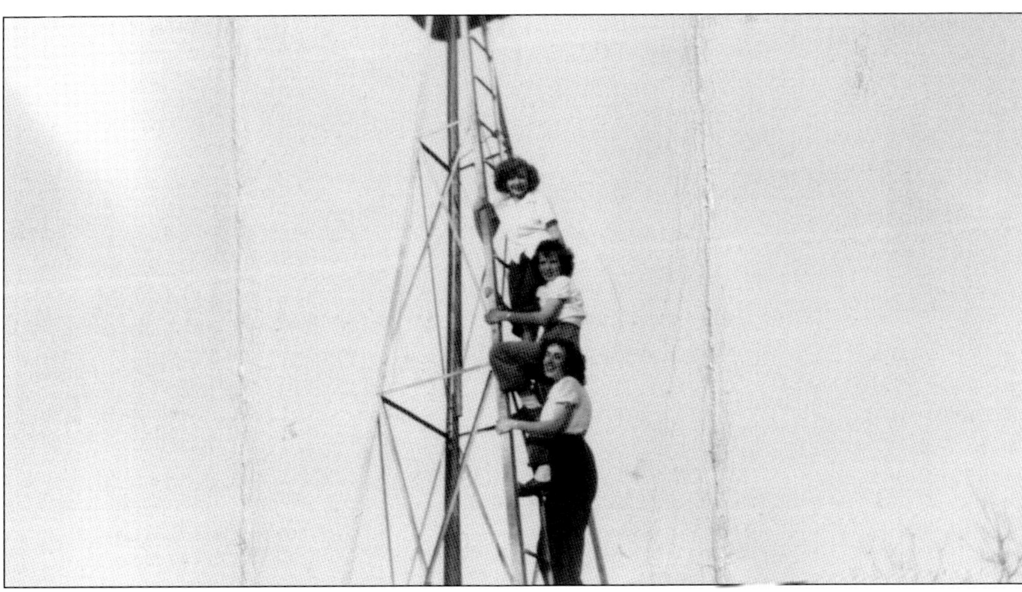

Climbing a windmill in 1948 are, from top to bottom, Laura Mae Willett, Janie Secrest, and unidentified. (Wayne and Cindie Vaughan.)

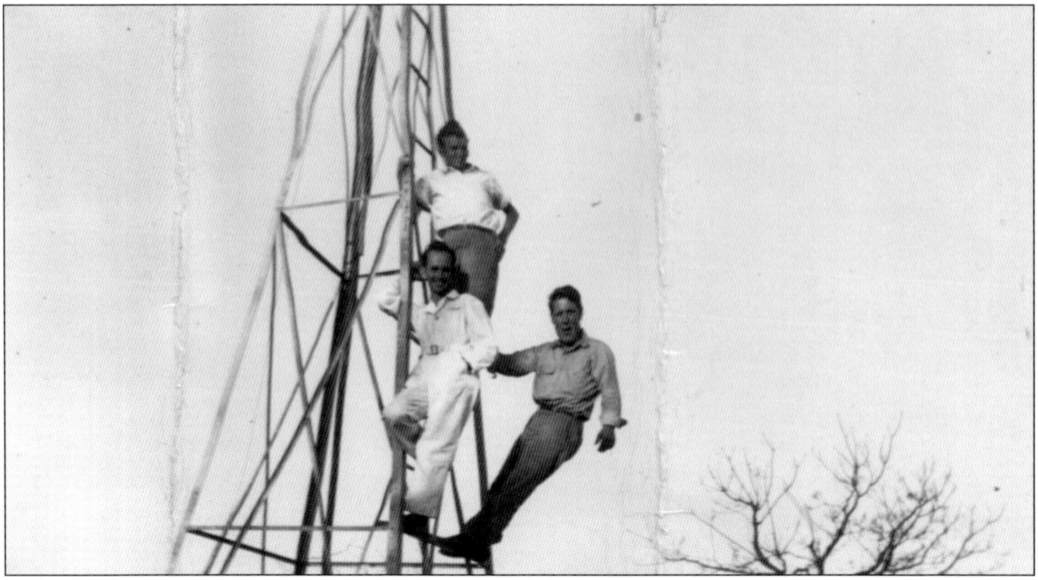

If the girls could do it, so could the boys. The only participant here who can be identified is G.W. Roark (top). The location of windmill is unknown. (Wayne and Cindie Vaughan.)

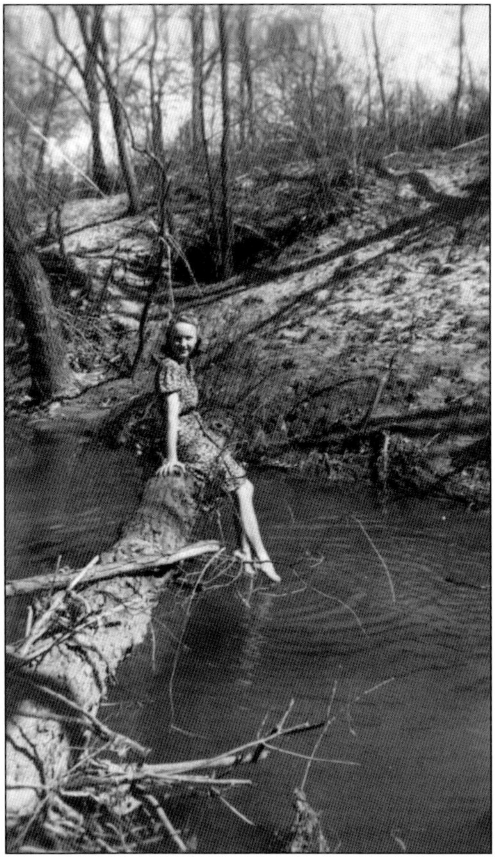

Laura Mae Willett relaxes on a tree trunk that crosses a creek. She paused to soak her feet in the cool water. This photograph was taken about 1948. (Wayne and Cindie Vaughan.)

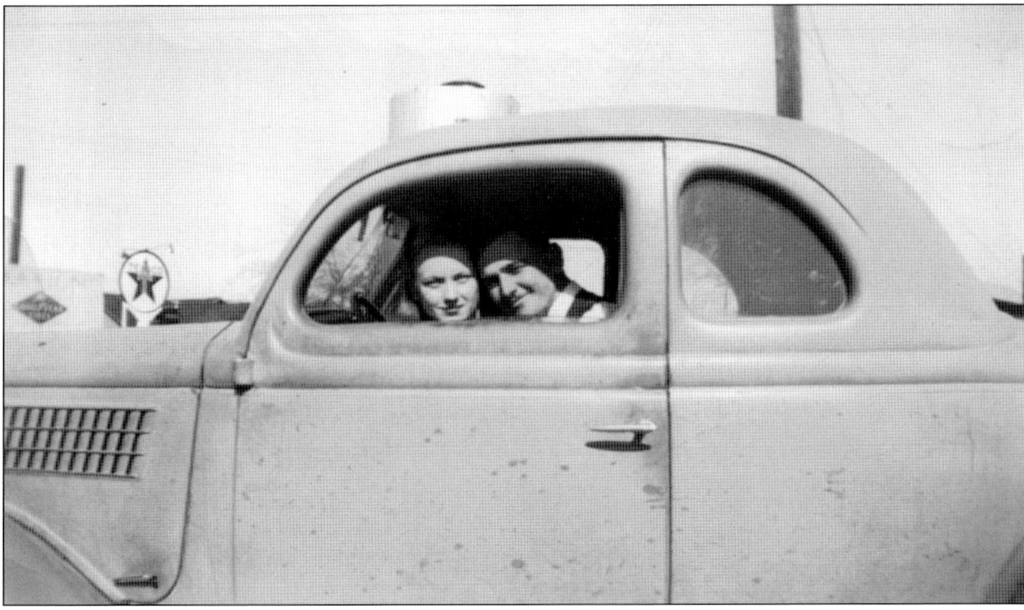

A couple is having fun on a sunny day in Tioga. This image was taken around 1948. (Wayne and Cindie Vaughan.)

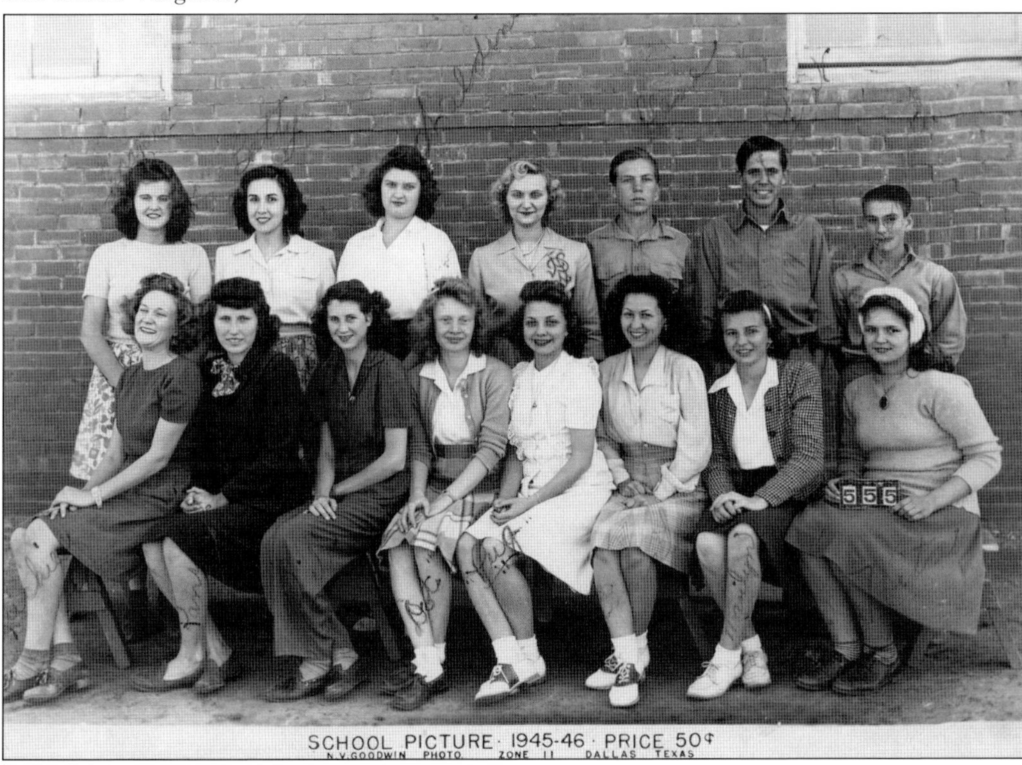

Pictured is the 1945–1946 sophomore class of Tioga Public School. The students are, from left to right, (first row) unidentified, Patsy Davis, Billie Faye Dodson, Dorothy Suiter, Laura Mae Willett, Helen Johnson, and two unidentified; (second row) Imogene Norris, Betty Van Zandt, Waldine Midgett, Mrs. King, Gene Myers, Junior Norris, and Kenneth Self. (James Hilliard.)

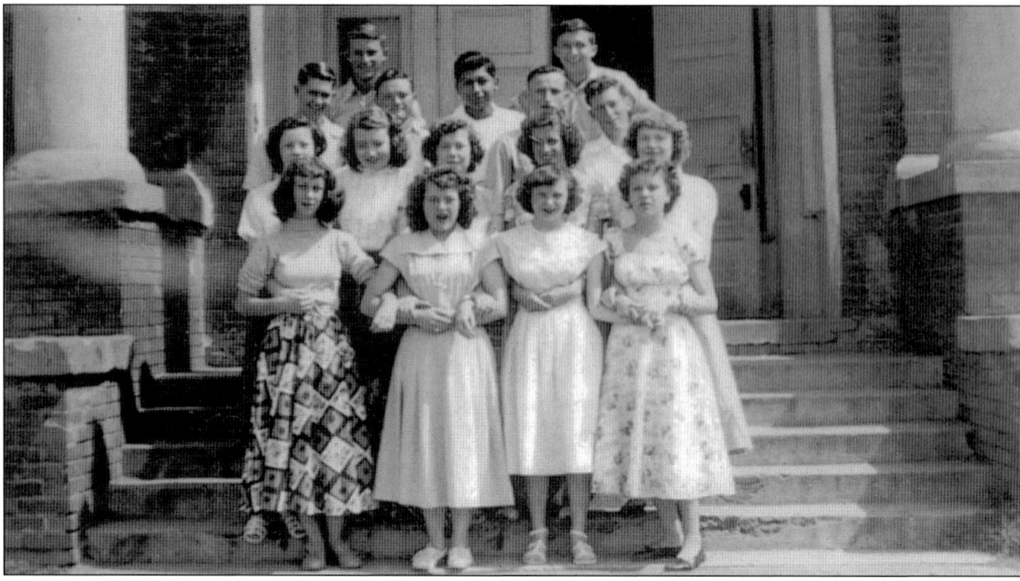

Pictured is the senior class of 1949–1950. The students are, from left to right, (first row) Letha Davidson, Mary Frances Foster, and two unidentified; (second row) Marine Hickman, two unidentified, Nelda Cook, and unidentified; (third row) Leon Clark, Barney Wayne Hall, John Rameriz, Walter Finley, and Bobby Jack Scoggins; (fourth row) David White and Dennis Baughman. (James Hilliard.)

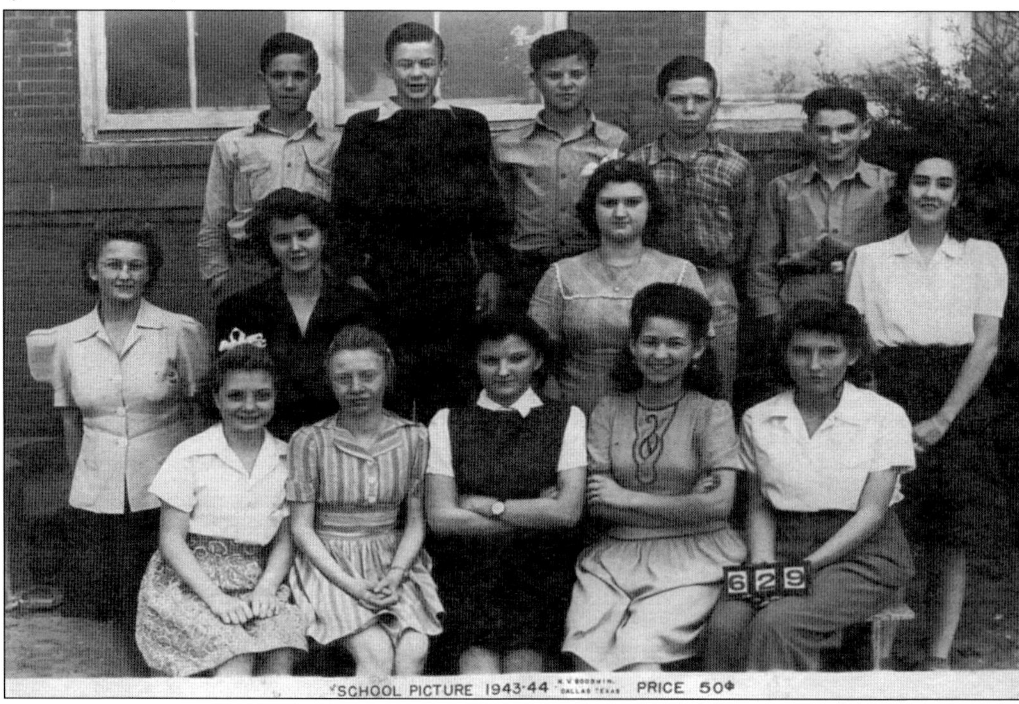

These students from 1943-1944 are, from left to right, (first row) Laura Mae Willett, Dorothy Suter, unidentified, Helen Johnson, and unidentified; (second row) Mrs. Velma Willett, Imogene Norris, Waldine Midgett, and Betty Van Zandt; (third row) Junior Norris, unidentified, Frank Norris, Gene Myers, and Kenneth Self. (James Hilliard.)

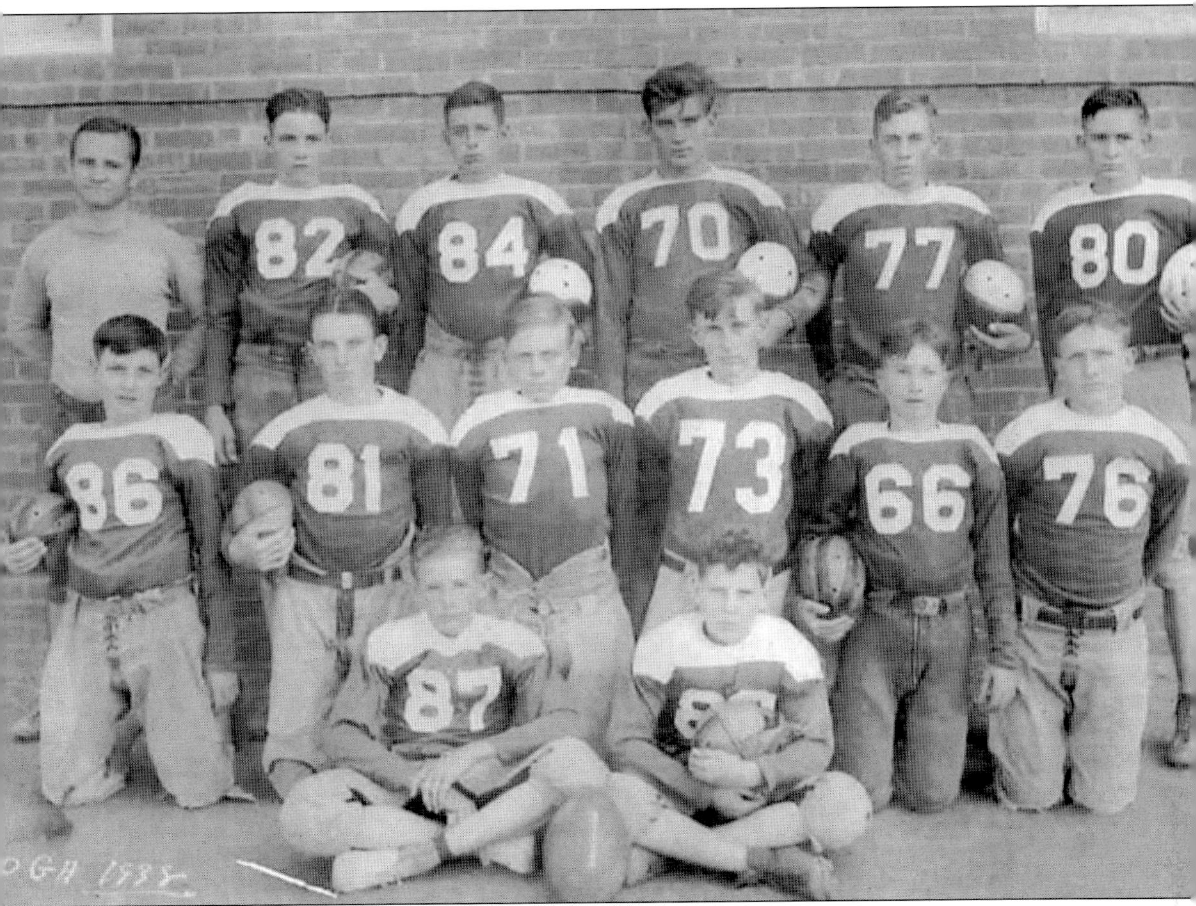

This is the 1938 Tioga football team. They played 11-man football at the time. (James Hilliard.)

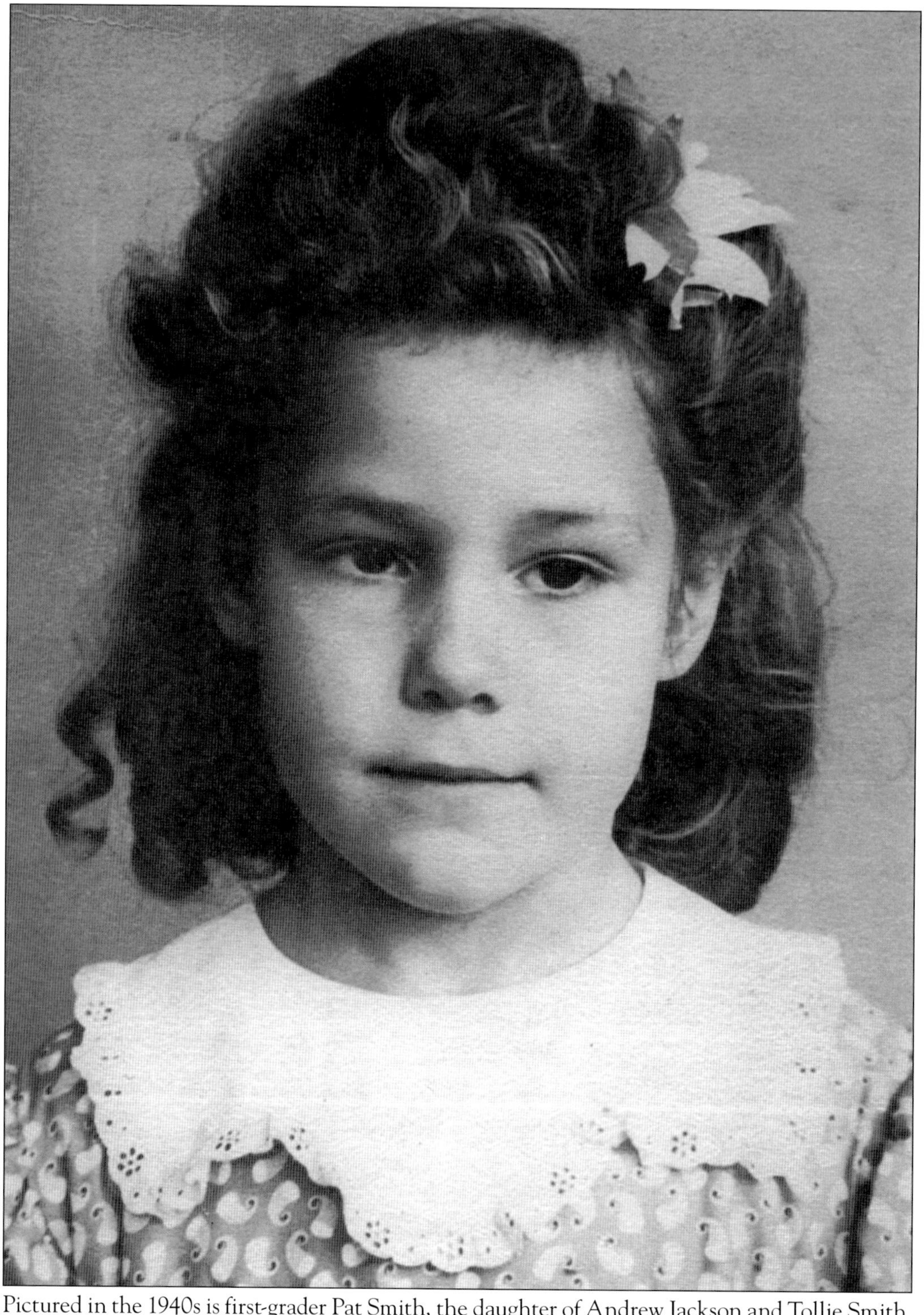

Pictured in the 1940s is first-grader Pat Smith, the daughter of Andrew Jackson and Tollie Smith. Pat later married a Smith and did not have to even change her name. Her son Brent Smith and his wife, Sherri, still reside in Tioga. (Pat Smith.)

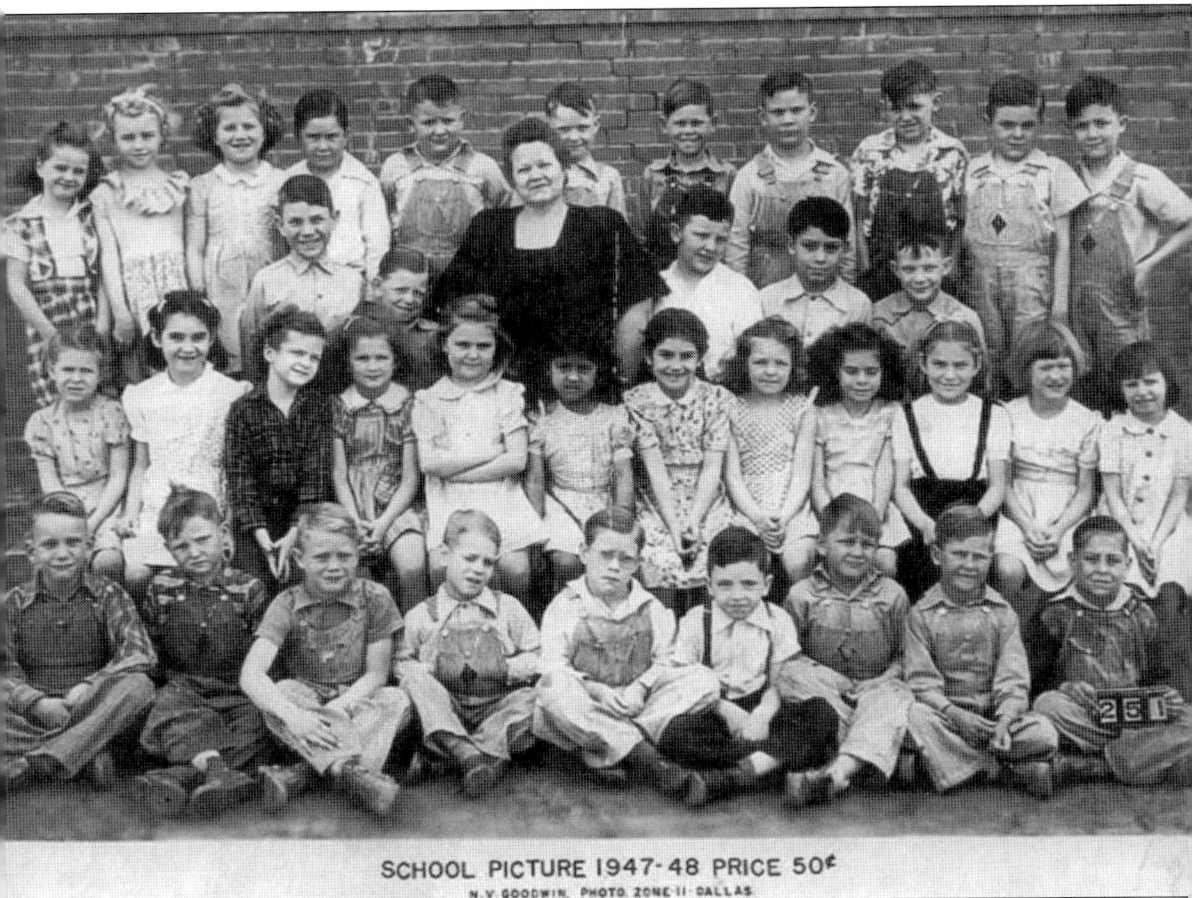

Students pose for the camera in this 1947–1948 Tioga Public School picture. (James Hilliard.)

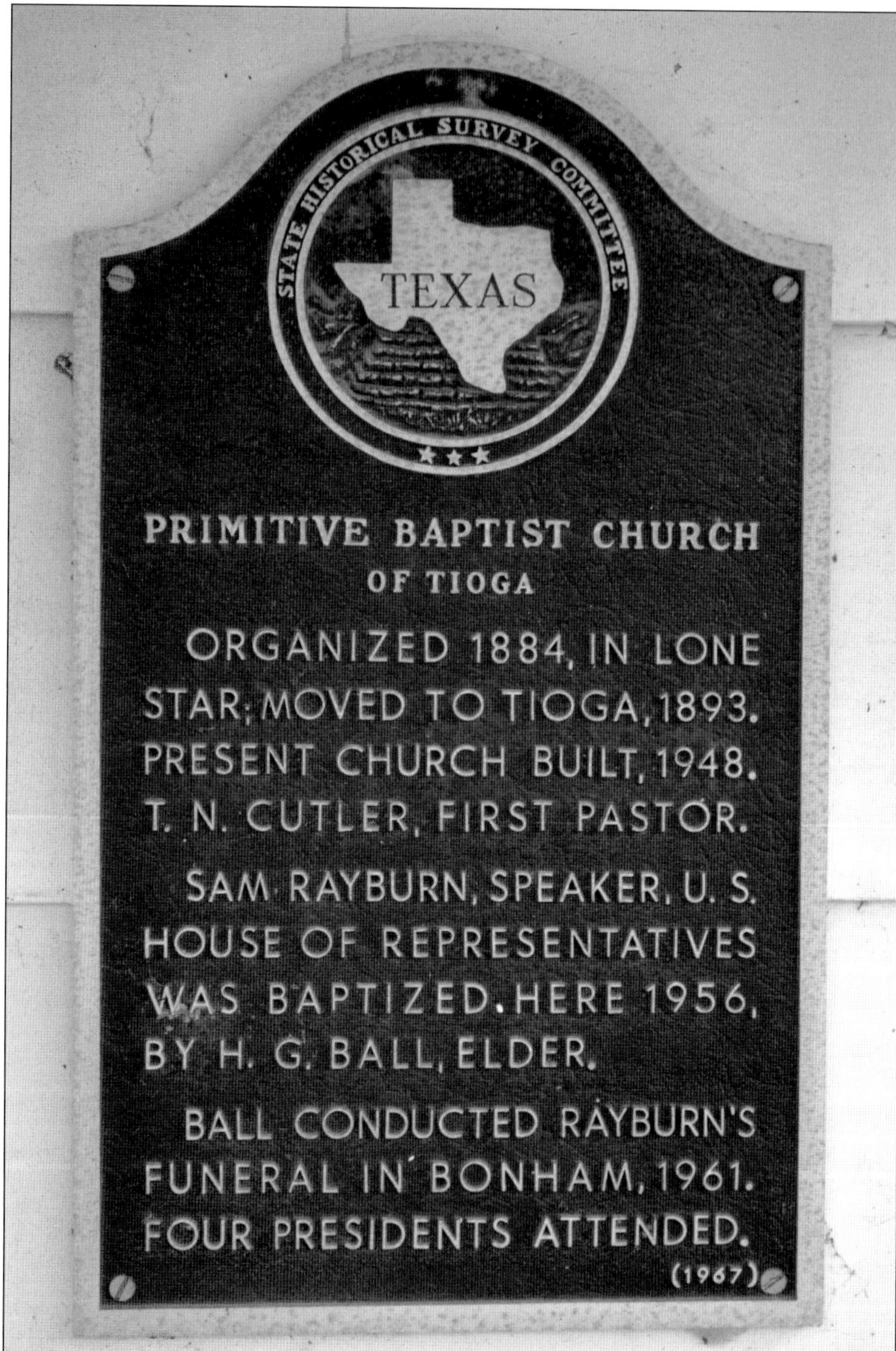

This plaque is on the church where Henry Ball was pastor. His good friend Sam Rayburn was speaker of the US House of Representatives. Rayburn was saved and baptized in this church by Elder Ball in 1956. This was a very big honor for a small town. (Authors' collection.)

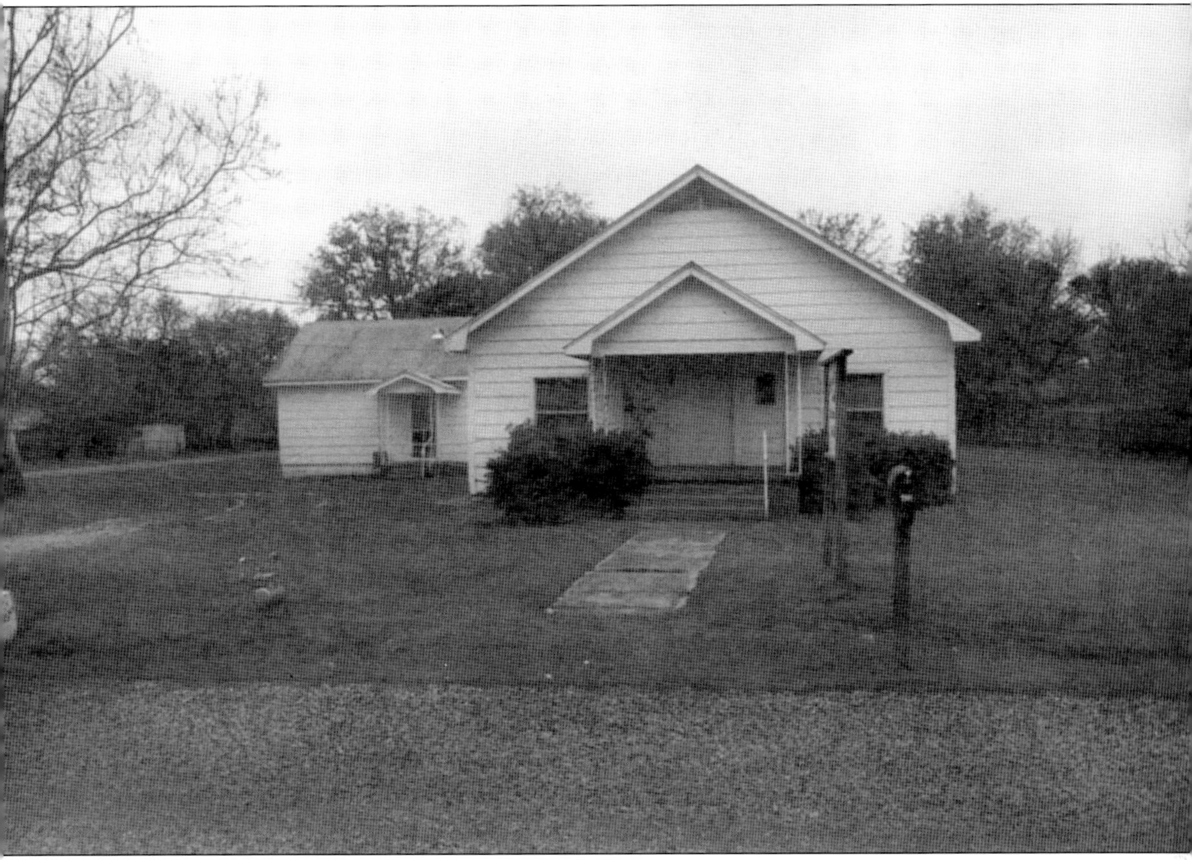

This is the Primitive Baptist Church where Elder Ball baptized Sam Rayburn, who was speaker of the US House of Representatives in 1956. When Rayburn passed away, Elder Ball presided at his funeral with four US presidents in attendance: John Kennedy, Lyndon Johnson, Dwight Eisenhower, and Harry Truman. (Authors' collection.)

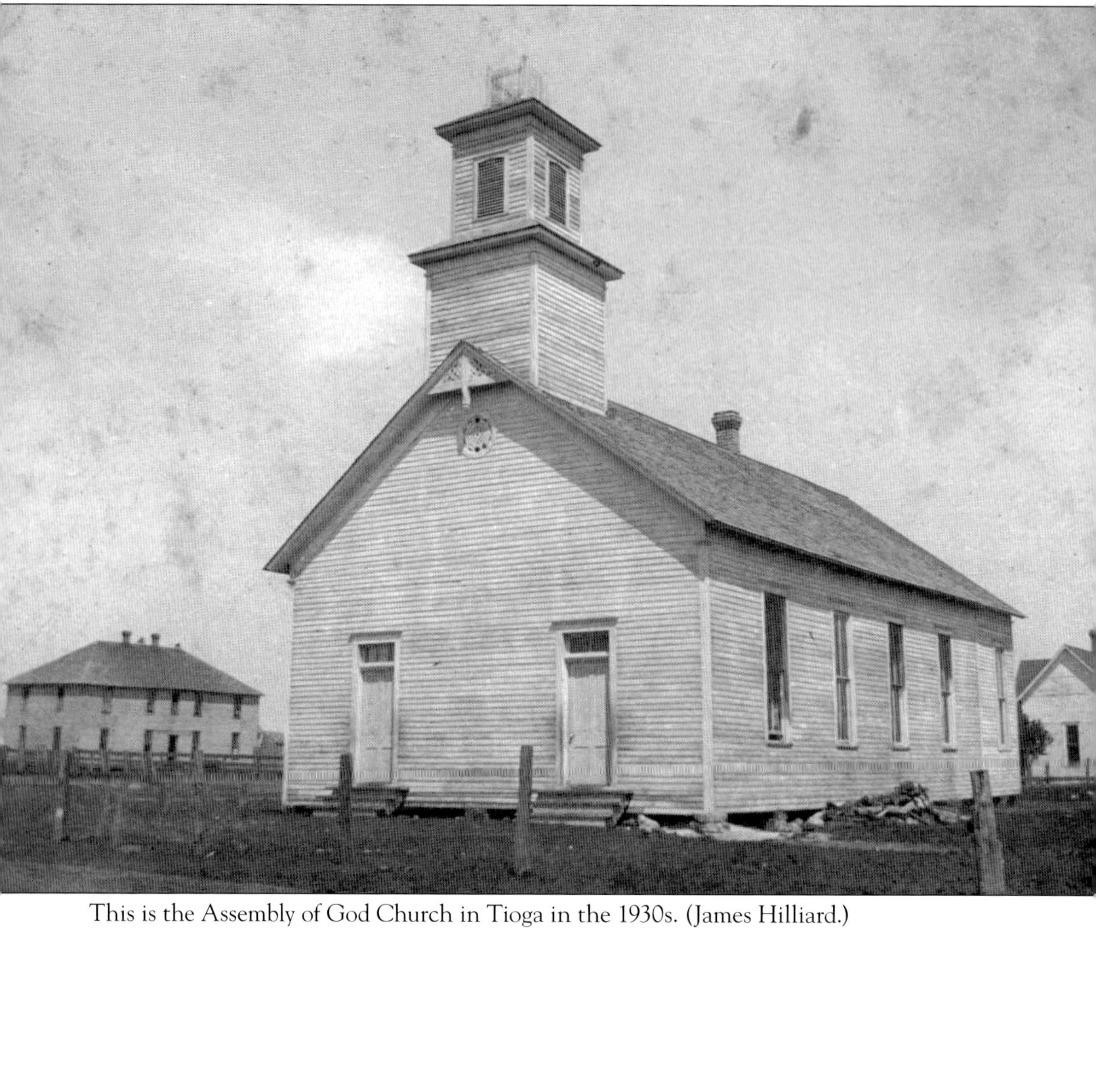

This is the Assembly of God Church in Tioga in the 1930s. (James Hilliard.)

Three

Tioga
The Healing Waters

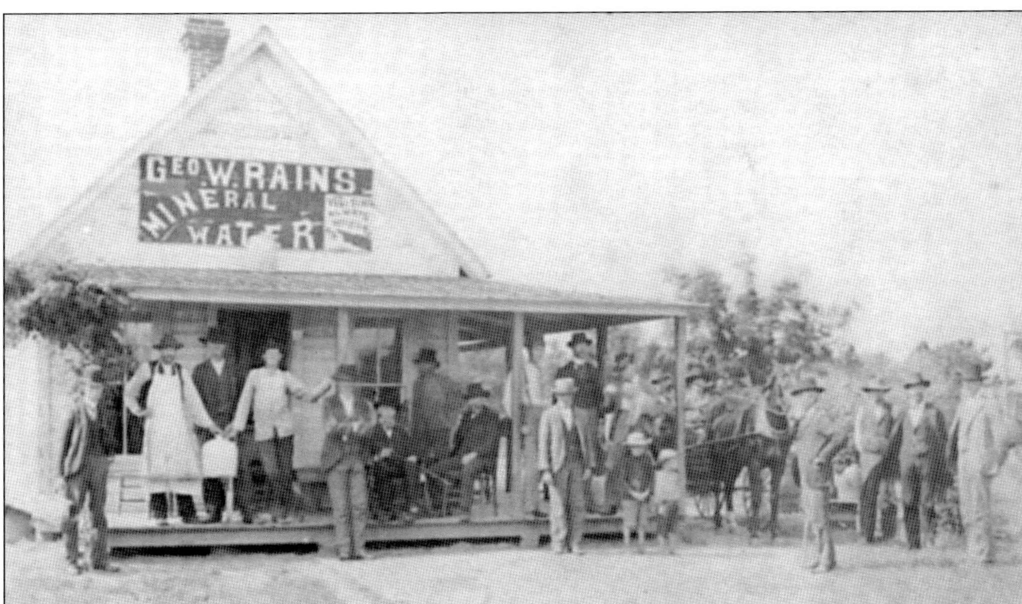

Here are some Tioga residents in late 1800s to early 1900s standing in front of a very popular store at the time. It seemed as if folks were always anxious to have their picture taken. It was still a novelty of sorts, and so they gladly posed for the photographer. (James Hilliard.)

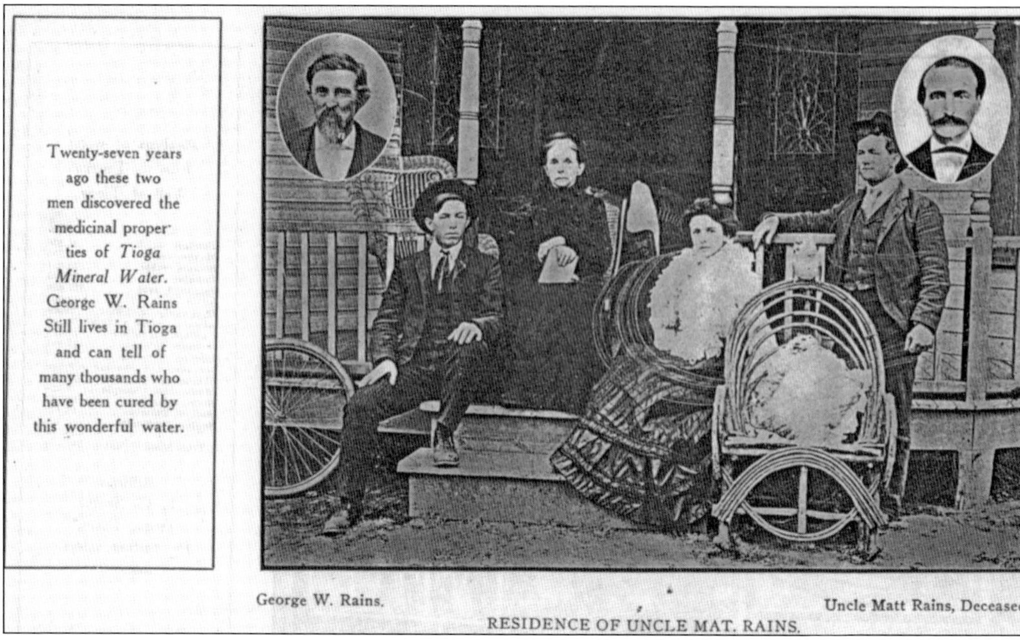

Legend has it that blacksmith Matt Rains was the first to discover the healing properties of mineral water. He had burned his hand and washed it off with water from a well on his property. In a few days, he noticed the hand had healed. Of course, he told his friends and neighbors, and soon other wells were being dug in Tioga for the healing properties of the mineral water. Salves and ointments were made, and water was bottled and shipped to faraway destinations. Hotels were built, and mineral bathhouses were opened. The town bustled with enthusiasm for the newfound bounty of mineral water. In all, eight wells or more were dug seeking the healing properties of this bad-tasting water. (James Hilliard.)

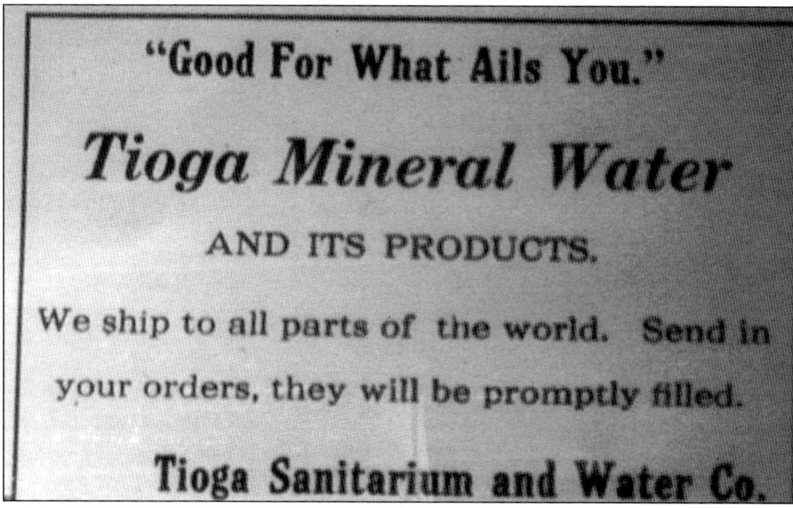

Ads like this ran in the *Tioga Herald* explaining all about the healing powers the area's water possessed. Many people visited, and many claimed they were totally healed by the mineral waters. (Tioga Museum and Cultural Center.)

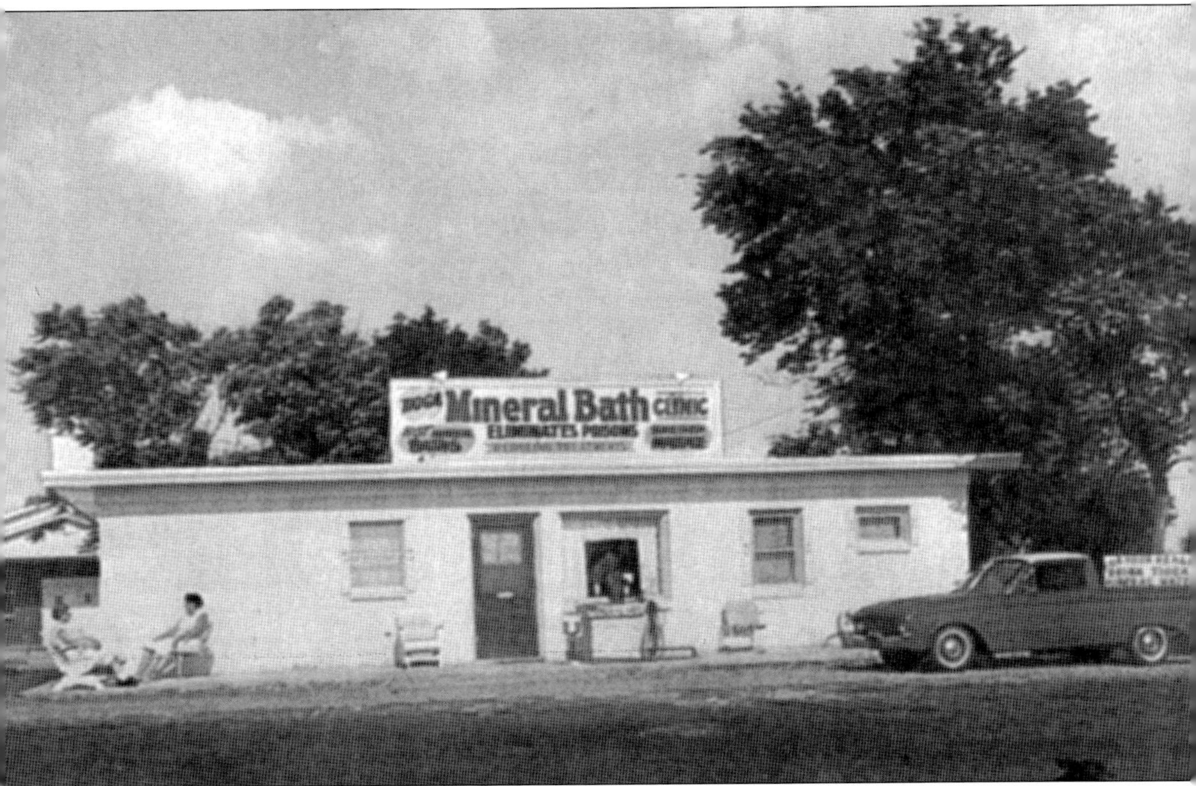

A few mineral bathhouses were still operational in the 1960s. Though many had closed and crowds no longer filled the streets of Tioga with visitors from all over the world, the town still reaped the benefits from past years of selling the precious mineral water. The Tioga Museum and Cultural Center, highlighting the Gene Autry Museum, is now housed in the building seen here. (James Hilliard.)

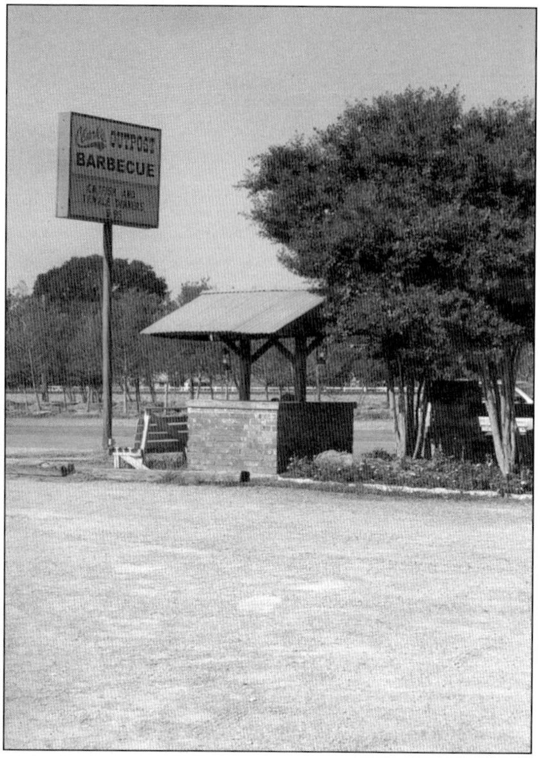

This is supposedly the first mineral well in Tioga. In the 1800s, as stated on page 56, the blacksmith burned his hand and washed it in water from his well, and its healing qualities became apparent. (Authors' collection.)

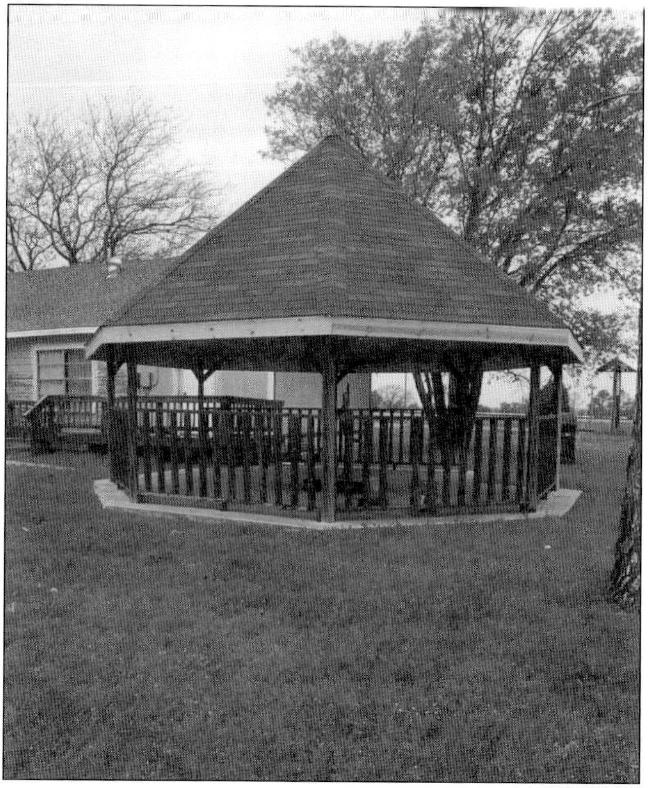

Pictured is an arbor covering an old mineral well. The pump inside sits quietly waiting for an eager hand and strong back to once again bring up the water that waits just beneath the surface. Someone apparently chose to protect and preserve this once precious commodity. It is said W.T. Spears owned it originally. (Authors' collection.)

Four

Tioga
Colorful Residents

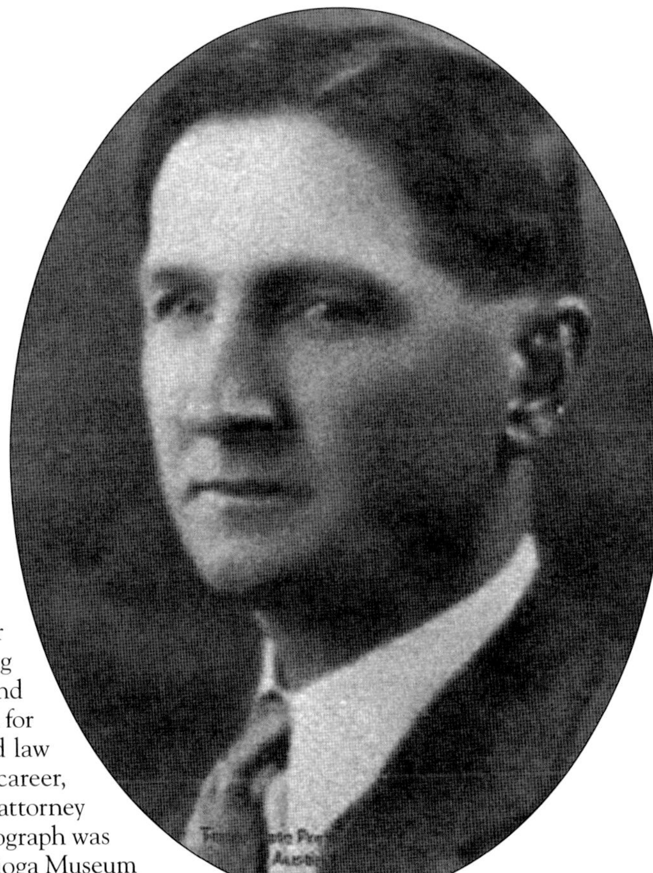

Sen. Olan R. Van Zandt was first a representative and then a senator in the Texas Legislature, spanning 16 years. Van Zandt was blind, and his father insisted he go to a school for the blind and then to college and law school. After he left his political career, Van Zandt spent many years as an attorney in Tioga and Sherman. This photograph was taken between 1926 and 1929. (Tioga Museum and Cultural Center.)

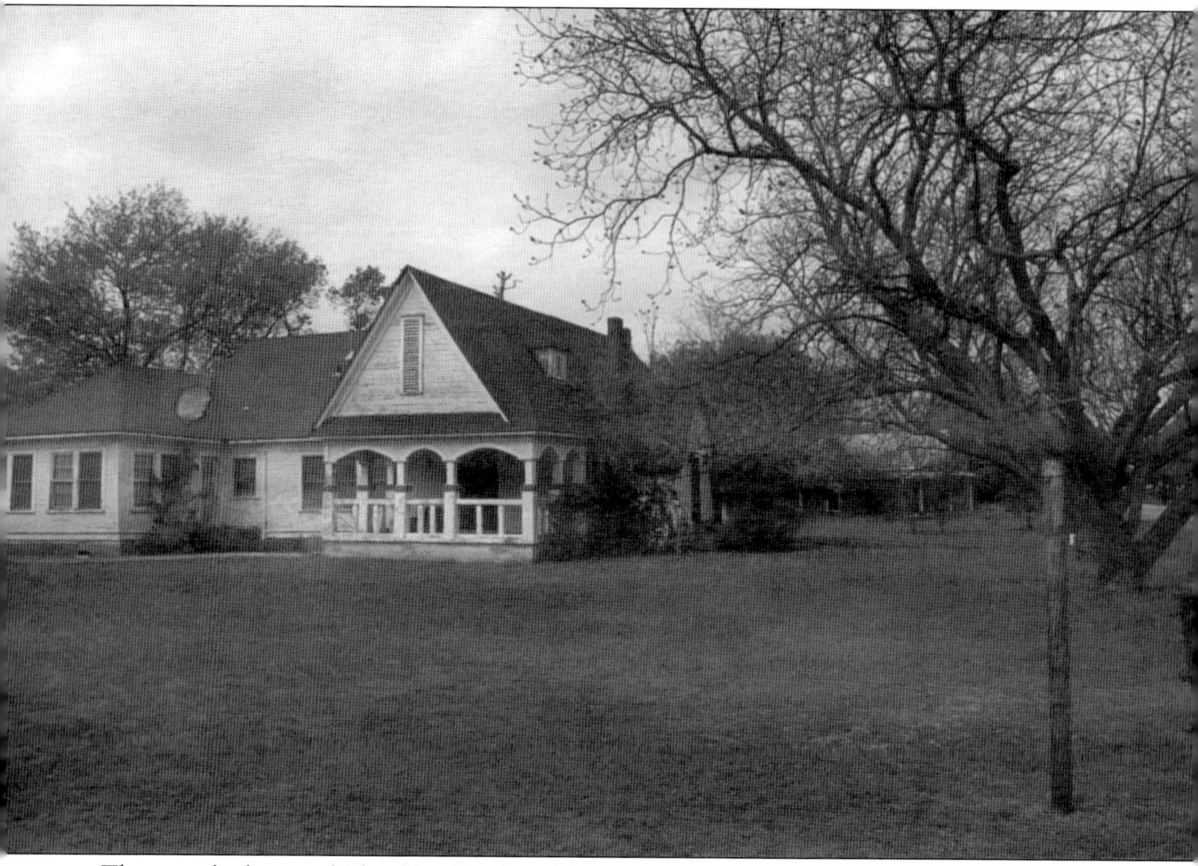

This was the home of Olan Van Zandt. Although Van Zandt was blind, he could make his way around Tioga without assistance. Kids would often try to fool him by moving things around in a store that he frequented. Much to their surprise, he always found them out and would tell them "to move that out of the way before someone gets hurt." Van Zandt was blinded when he was a child. The first eye he lost was to a rock from a slingshot, and the other eye was lost to a stick that broke when he hit a cow while moving it to another pasture. This house was the only one in Tioga to have a basement. (Authors' collection.)

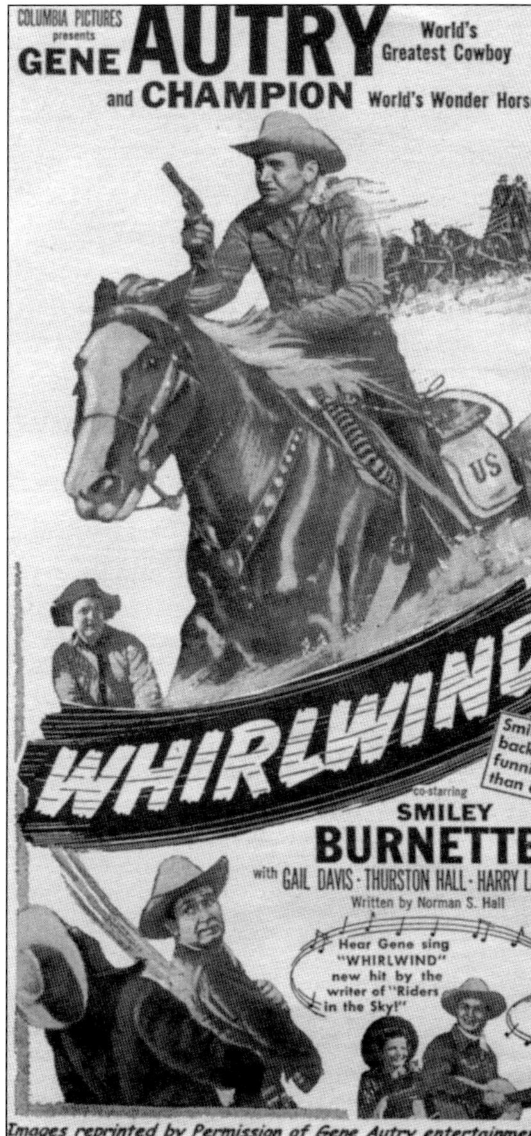

Gene Autry was raised in Tioga by his uncle Cal and attended Tioga Public School. Gene would sing to anyone who would listen, and he worked in Sam Anderson's barbershop as a shoe-shine boy to earn his spending money. He also made tips for serenading disembarking train passengers. A radio show out of Oklahoma that highlighted yodeling cowboys got the attention of a Hollywood producer, and Autry pole-vaulted into fame. He was a straight-shooting cowboy who never forgot his roots in Tioga. (Tioga Museum and Cultural Center.)

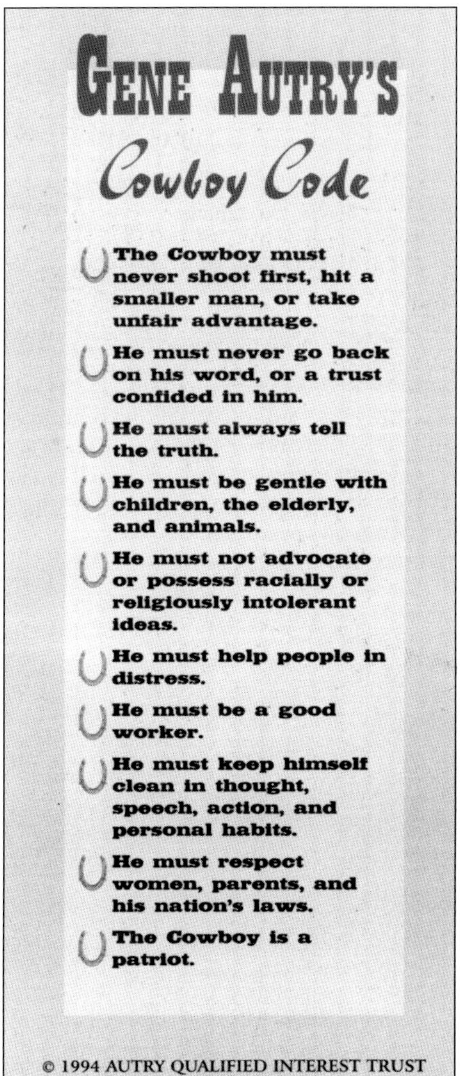
GENE AUTRY'S

Cowboy Code

- The Cowboy must never shoot first, hit a smaller man, or take unfair advantage.
- He must never go back on his word, or a trust confided in him.
- He must always tell the truth.
- He must be gentle with children, the elderly, and animals.
- He must not advocate or possess racially or religiously intolerant ideas.
- He must help people in distress.
- He must be a good worker.
- He must keep himself clean in thought, speech, action, and personal habits.
- He must respect women, parents, and his nation's laws.
- The Cowboy is a patriot.

Gene Autry's "Cowboy Code" could still be followed today. Autry pretty much lived by this code his entire life. He made millions of dollars as a singing star, and many of his songs are still hits today. "Rudolf the Red Nose Reindeer" is sung every Christmas around the world. He was a shrewd businessman, and at one time he owned the Los Angeles Angels major-league baseball team. (Tioga Museum and Cultural Center.)

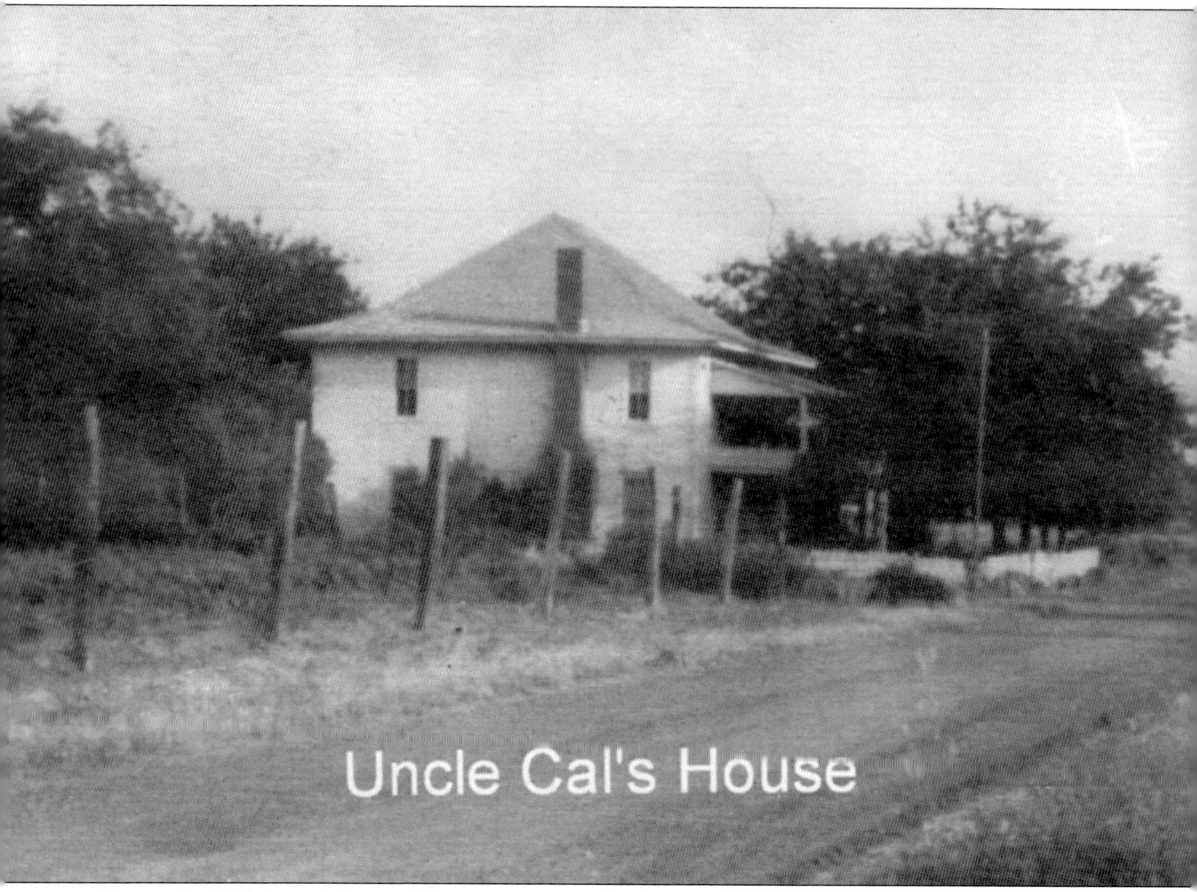

Pictured is Cal Autry's home. Gene grew up in this house and attended Tioga Public School. The house has since been torn down. This image was taken in the 1940s. (James Hilliard.)

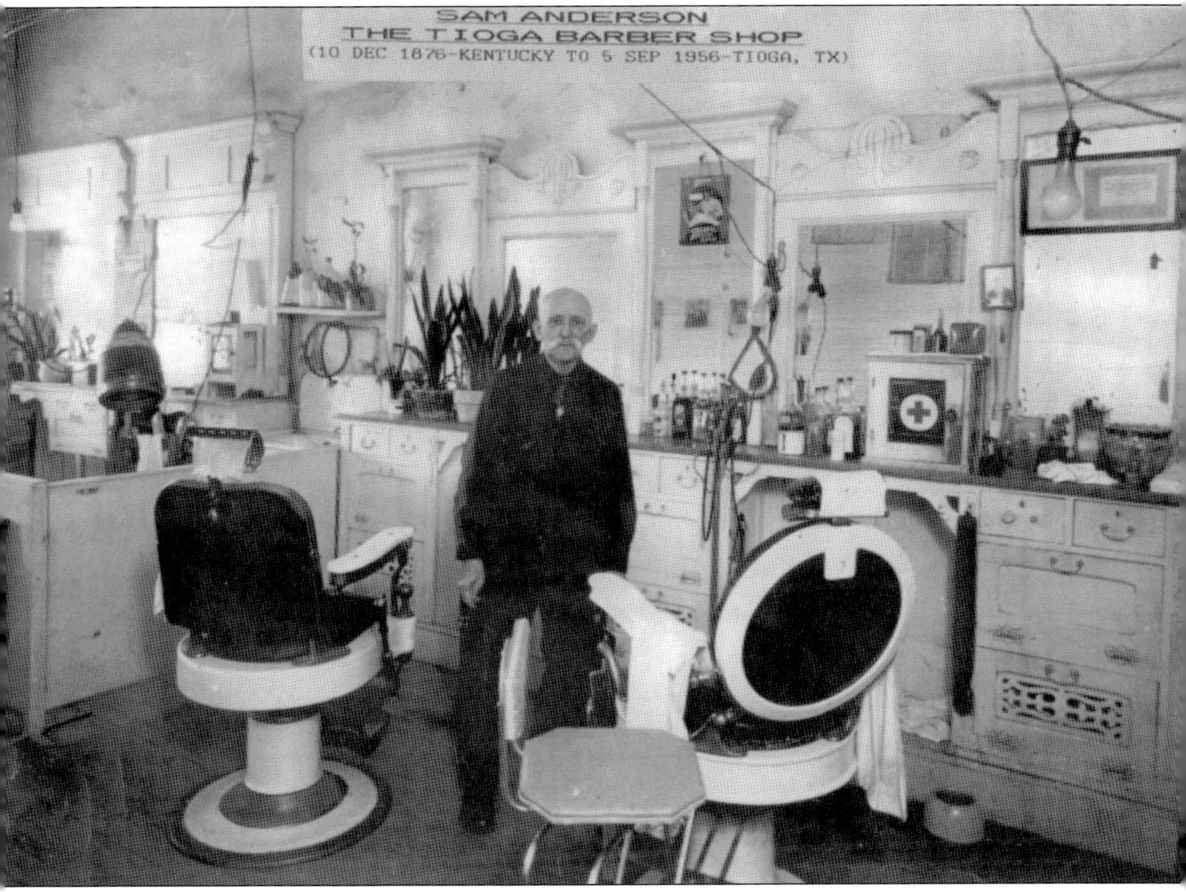

Sam Anderson is seen in his barbershop. It was here where Gene Autry shined shoes as a boy. Autry and Anderson remained friends all of their lives. (James Hilliard.)

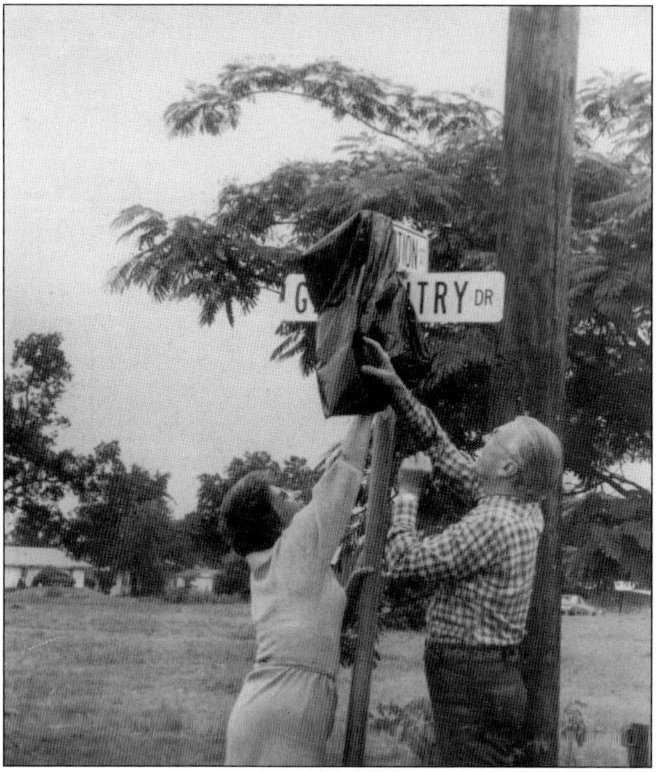

Lifetime Tioga resident Arvella (née Bodovsky) McKnight and Judge Roland C. Vaughan of Grayson County unveil the Gene Autry Drive street sign in Tioga in the 1980s. Years before, Autry had tried to get Tioga to change its name to Autry Springs, but at the time most citizens opposed the idea. They did, however, allow a street to be named after him. (Arvella McKnight.)

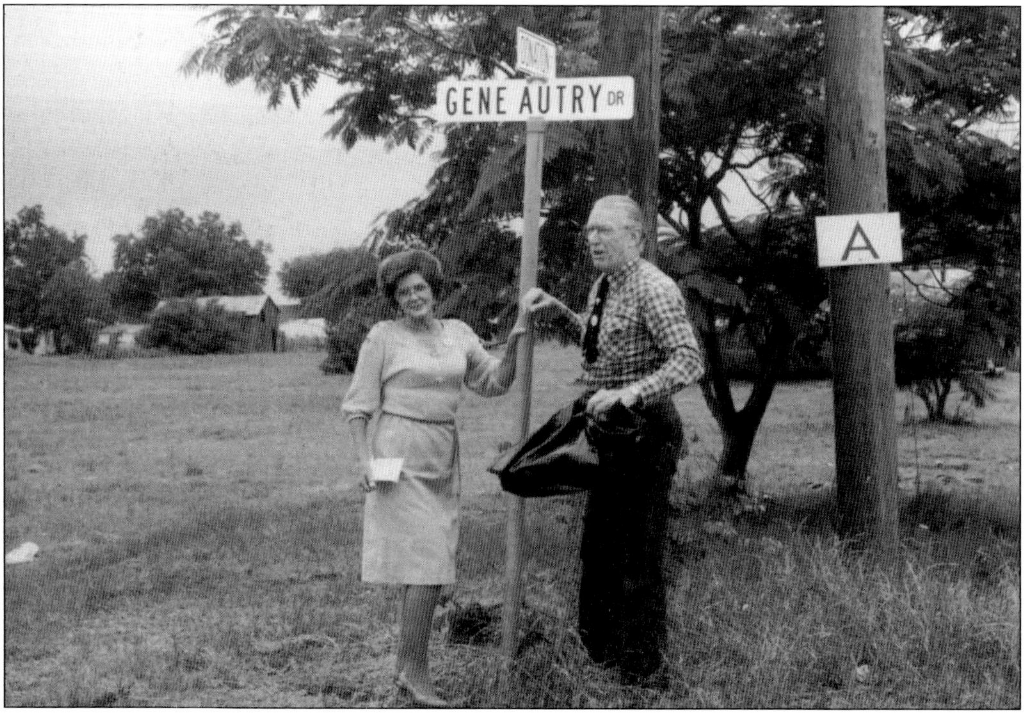

Arvella McKnight (left) and Judge Vaughan of Grayson County complete the unveiling of Gene Autry Drive street sign in this 1980s photograph. (Arvella McKnight.)

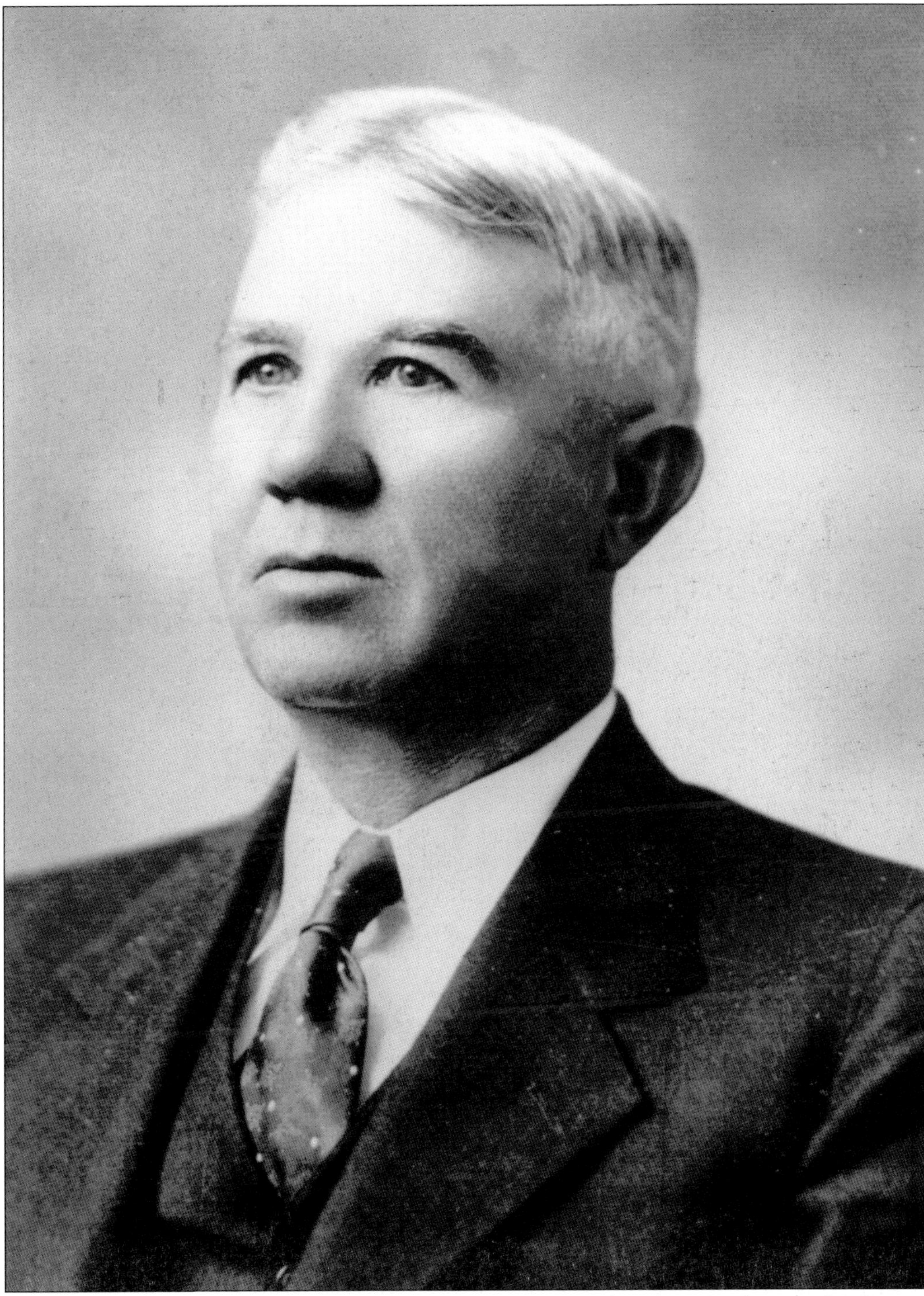

Dr. E.E. Ledbetter was a physician in Tioga for many years. This photograph was taken around 1920. During his time in Tioga, Dr. Ledbetter delivered many babies—one was Gene Autry. Supposedly, Dr. Ledbetter was instrumental in blocking the name change in Tioga to Autry Springs because he had never been paid for the delivery of Autry. (James Hilliard.)

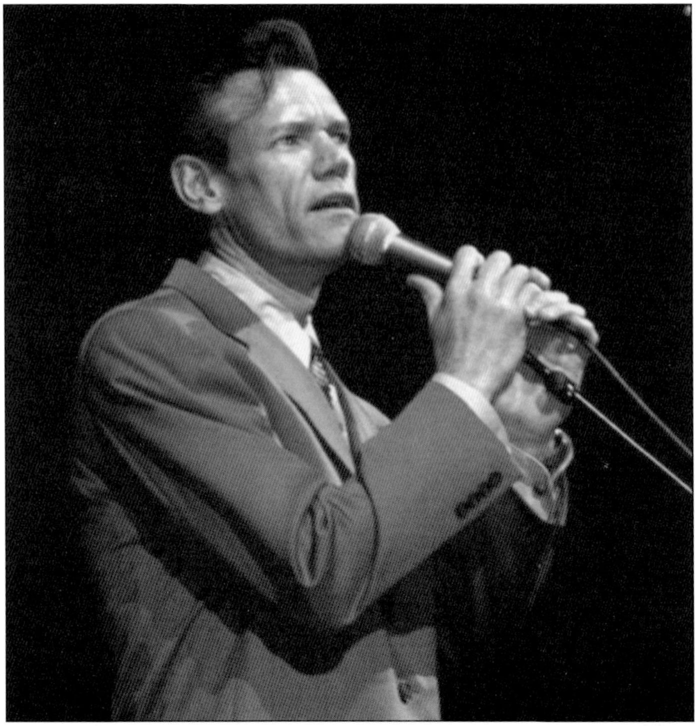

Randy Travis, famed singer and songwriter, now calls Tioga home. His health has declined recently, and the folks in town pray he soon will be well. He attends school events frequently in Collinsville and always is friendly and willing to give an autograph.

Shortly after Randy Travis became ill, some Tioga residents posted this sign on Highway 377 that runs through town. The community unites in praying for his recovery. They look forward to seeing him once again in the local establishments he so often frequented. (Authors' collection.)

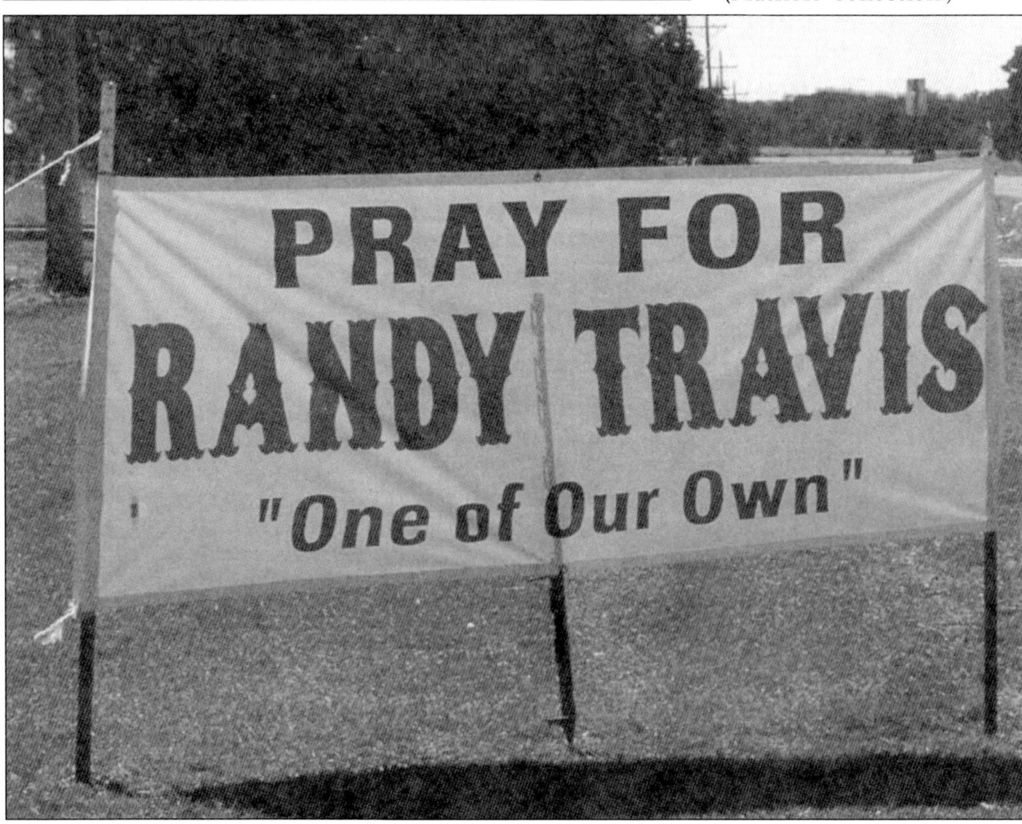

Five

Tioga
Changing Times

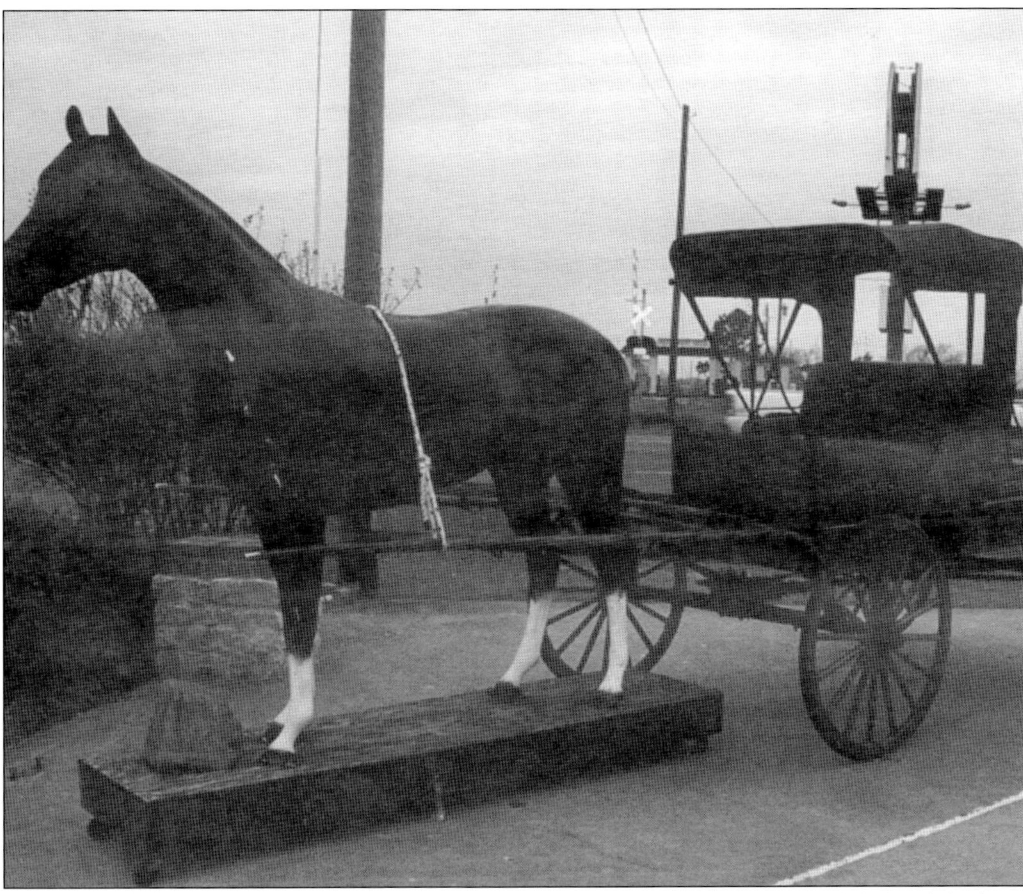

This horse-drawn buggy display stands in front of the local bank in Tioga. Directly behind the horse and buggy, across the highway, is where the beautiful train depot once stood. For many years, Tioga's growth was at a standstill, but now it is experiencing a growth spurt. (Authors' collection.)

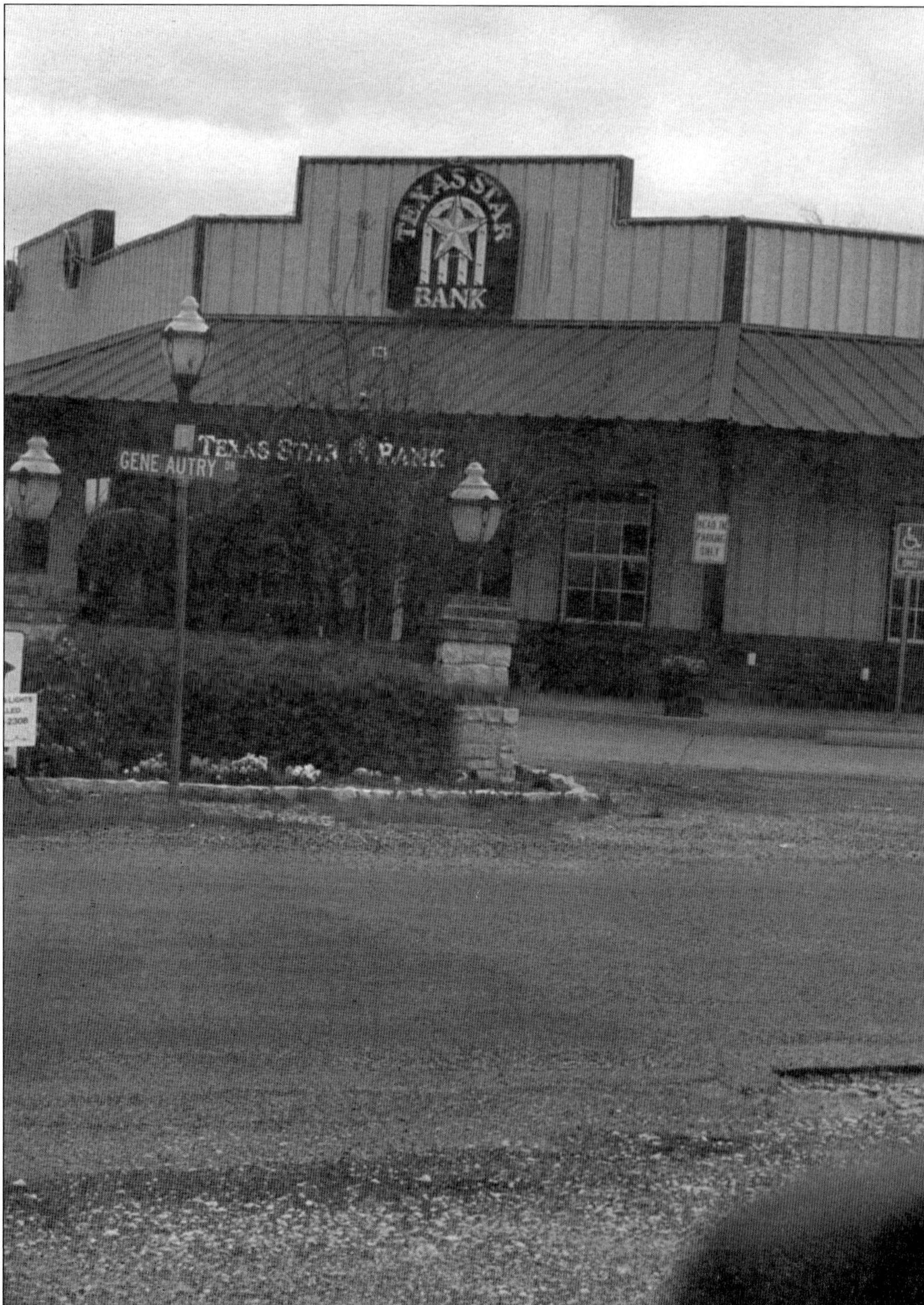

The present bank in Tioga is the Texas Star, located on Gene Autry Drive. It is the only one now, but at one time Tioga had six banks. (Authors' collection.)

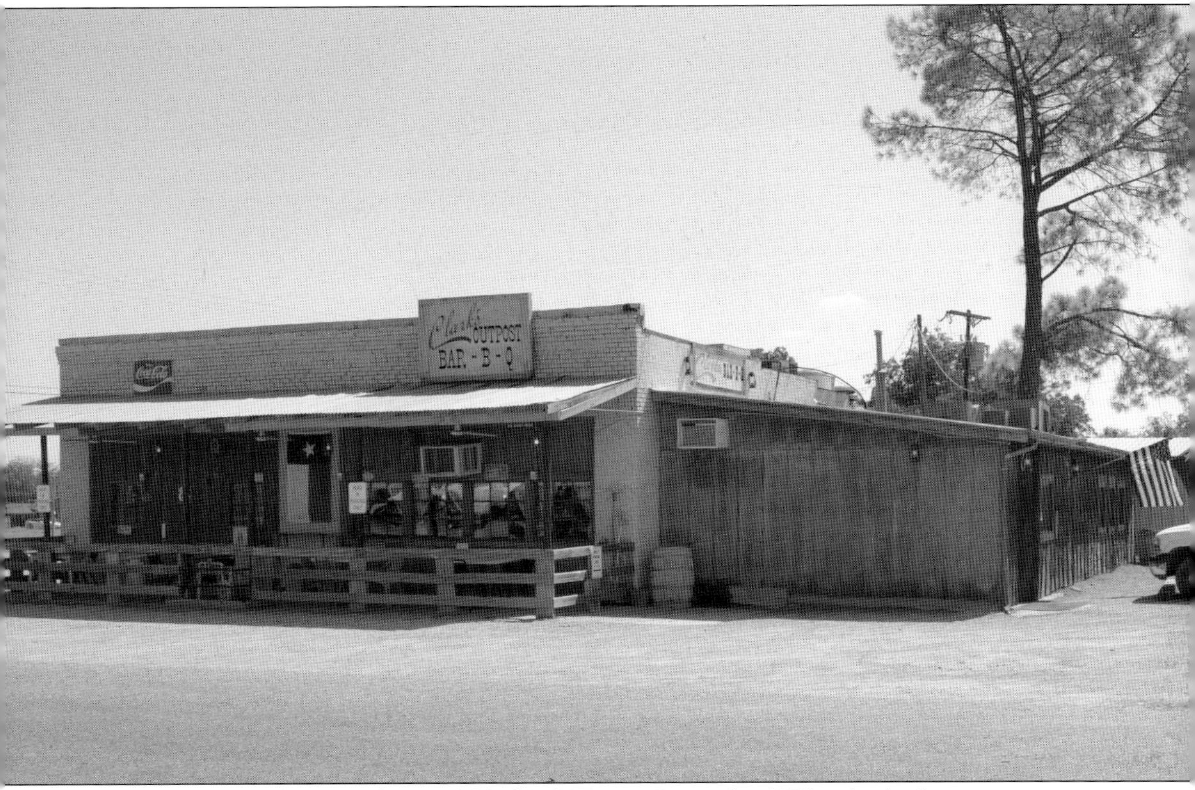

The flag is always flying in front of Clark's Outpost. Since the 1970s, the barbecue restaurant has called to people all over the country. Celebrities and common folk alike come to enjoy the food. On any given summer Saturday, there may be 15 motorcycles and 20 cars parked in front of the eatery. Inside the establishment, pictures are on display of Tioga's past and present. The ambiance is one of friendliness, and the smell of the food cooking stirs one's very soul. Clark's Outpost is located directly behind what some say was the first mineral water well in Tioga, and its fondness of the past is emulated in the decor. Folks passing by on Highway 377 or turning onto Gene Autry Drive are invited to come in and join the revelry. (Authors' collection.)

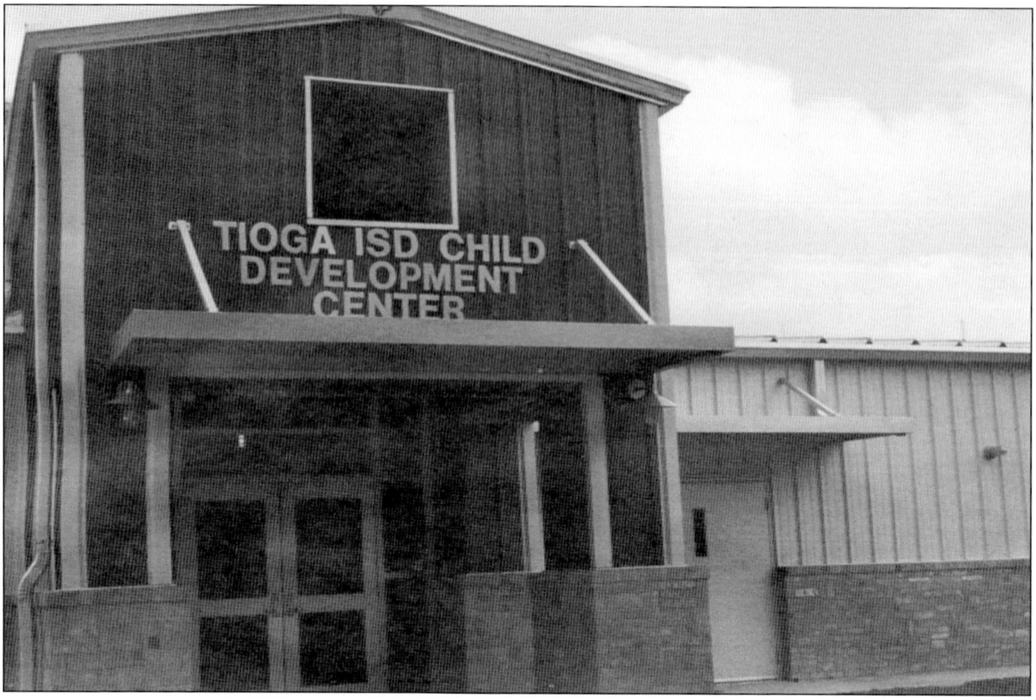

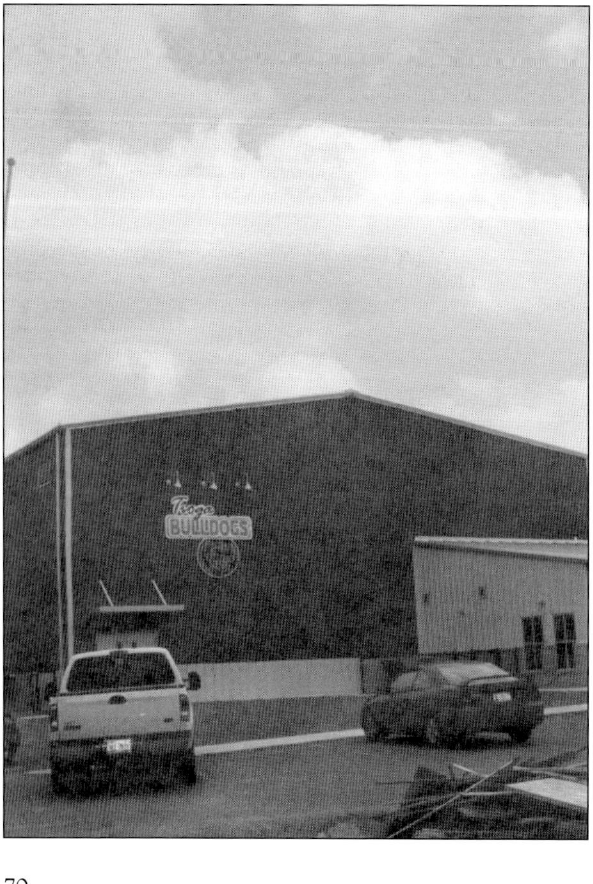

The Tioga Independent School District Child Development Center is the first of its kind in Tioga. It boasts of the care and concern it offers to all who enter. The laughter of children rings throughout the building, and smiles are seen on small faces as they eagerly await their teacher's attention. (Authors' collection.)

The Tioga Bulldogs pledge allegiance to their school and faculty. Once again, the football team takes the field, as a new football field with bright lights and warm greetings await the players. Tioga's heart has always been with the school and its activities. For years, the school went only to the eighth grade. Since 2012, a high school–level grade has been added every year and will continue to do so until all four years of high school are offered. As the school expands its boundaries, the excitement in town grows too, thanks in part to superintendent Dr. Charles Holloway. (Authors' collection.)

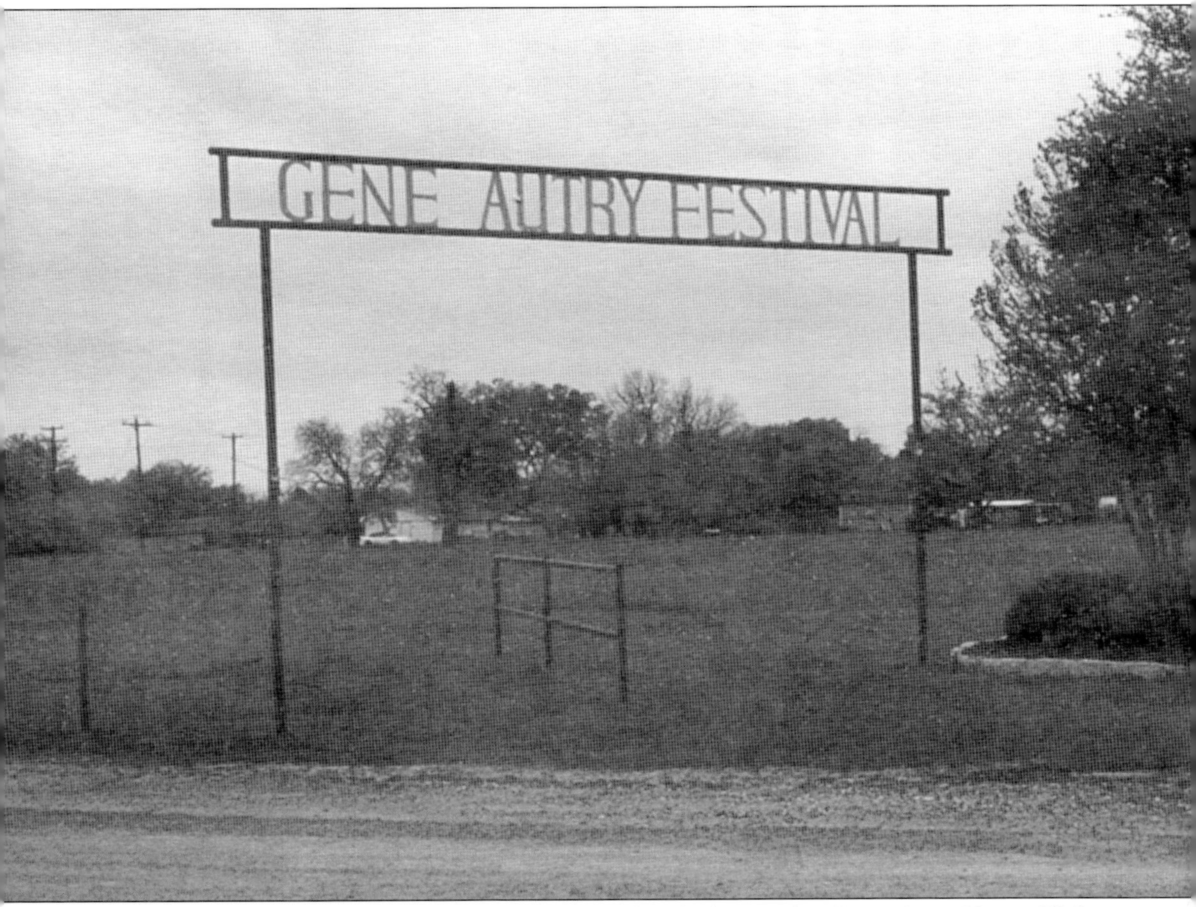

A vacant lot in the heart of town supports the metal arch that reads, "Gene Autry Festival." On this huge lot directly in front of the Gene Autry Museum, a yearly festival is held. Folks come from all over to enjoy the fun, food, and festivities. Tioga proudly claims its heritage of being the home of Gene Autry. (Authors' collection.)

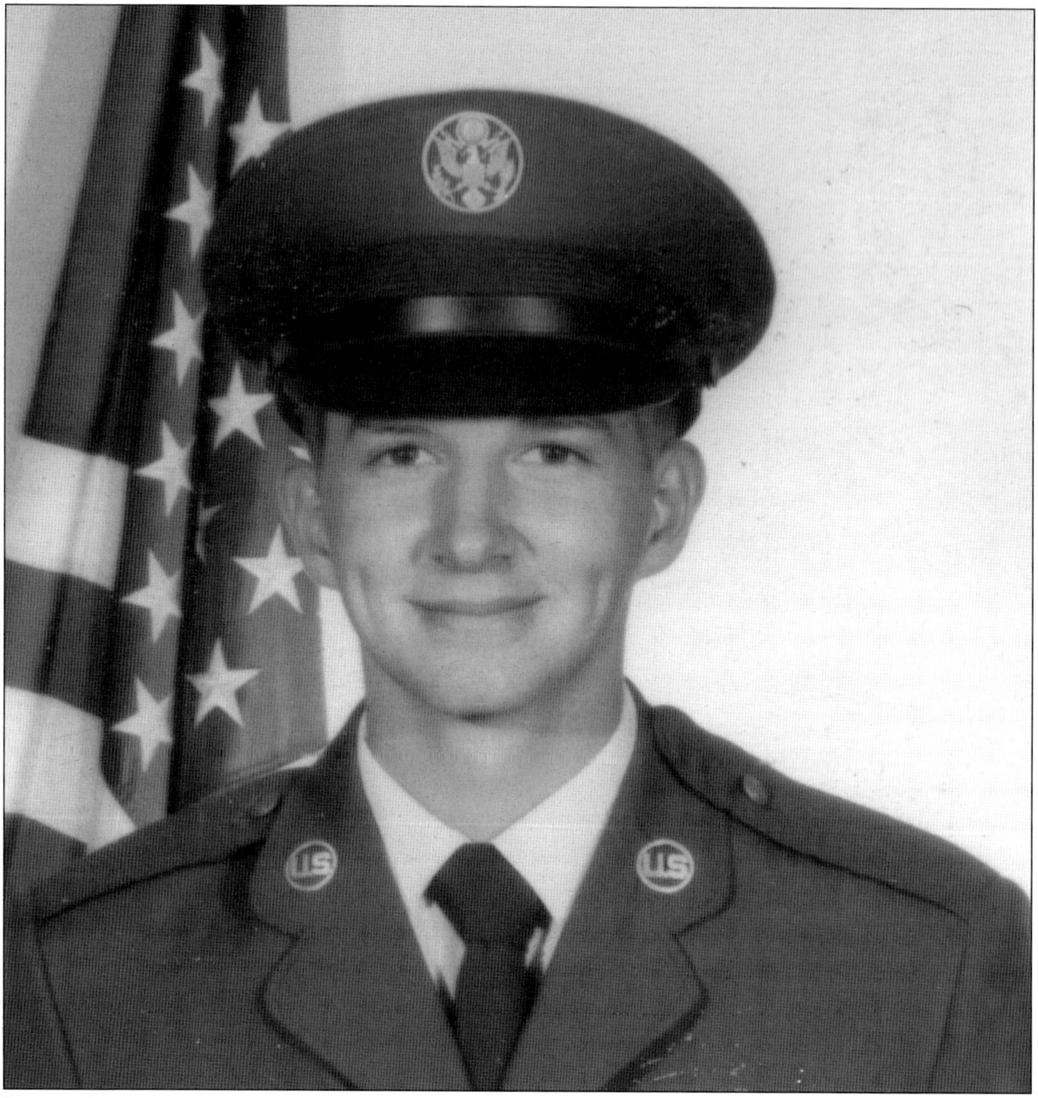

Pictured is serviceman Jerry McKnight. Tioga and the surrounding areas have sent many men into the armed services. Most of them came home, but there were those who did not. Some of Jerry's family still resides in Tioga. He left the Air Force in 1978. (Arvella McKnight.)

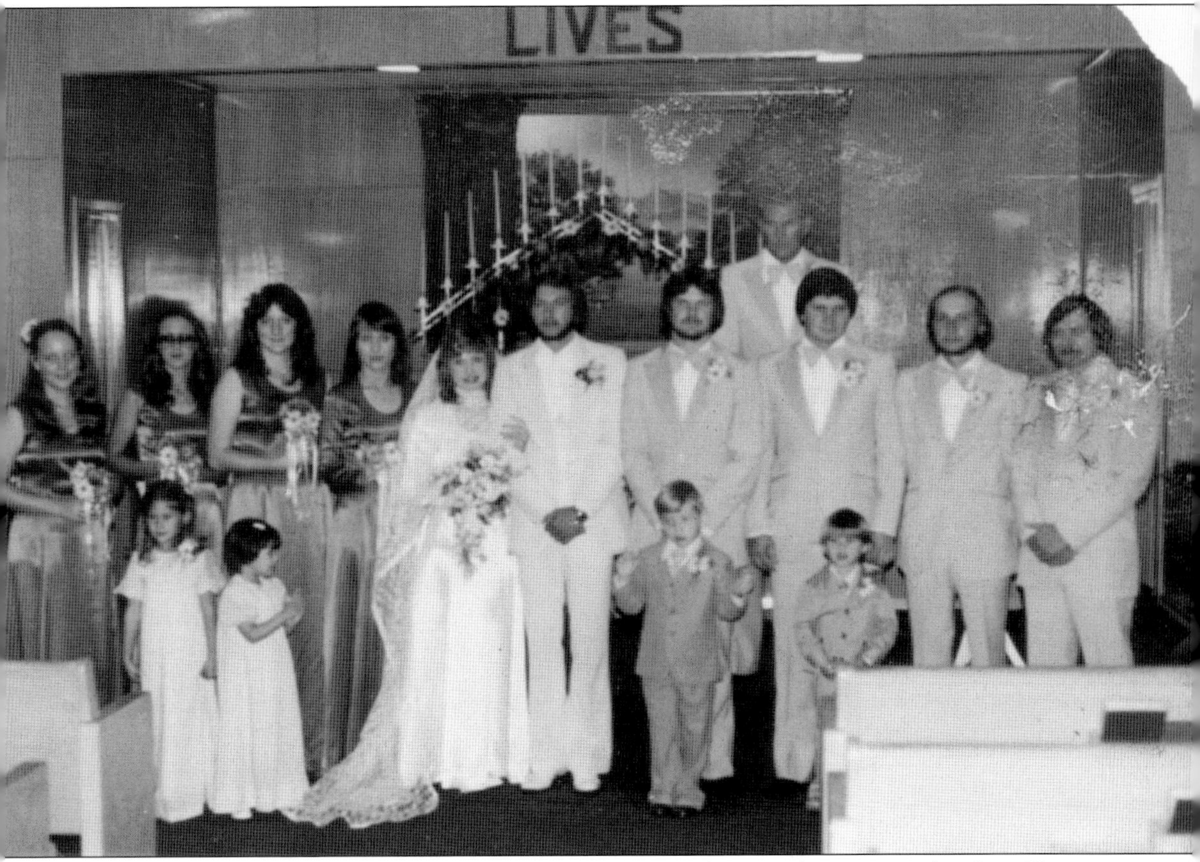

In 1979, the marriage of Carol Mitchell and Jerry McKnight united two Tioga families. Having grown up in Tioga, Carol attended high school in Collinsville, and Jerry went to work at a service station in Collinsville when he returned home from the Air Force. They decided to live and raise their family in Collinsville, Tioga's sister city. Many Tioga residents have married Collinsville people and vice versa. The two towns in Texas share bloodlines; each has kinfolk in the other town. Members of this wedding party include Jack, Donnie, and Bob McKnight, Danny Litner, Susan Hickman, and Pam and G.G. Cox. (Arvella McKnight.)

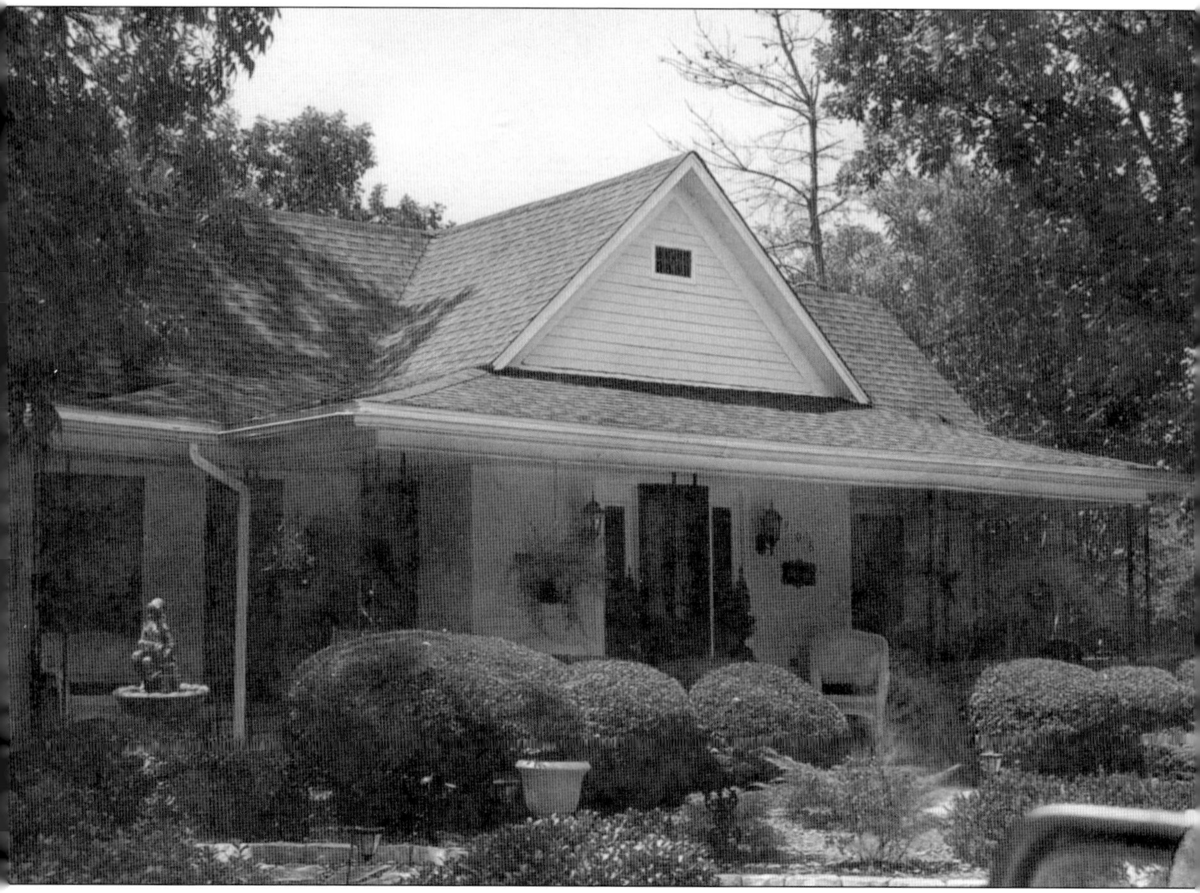

This was originally Bob and Sophie Spears's home. "Uncle Bob" and "Aunt Sophie" owned a drugstore in Tioga. The house was built in the early 1920s, and the Spearses lived there until the 1960s. It is a beautiful home today and displays the owners' pride in preserving such a lovely piece of history. (Authors' collection.)

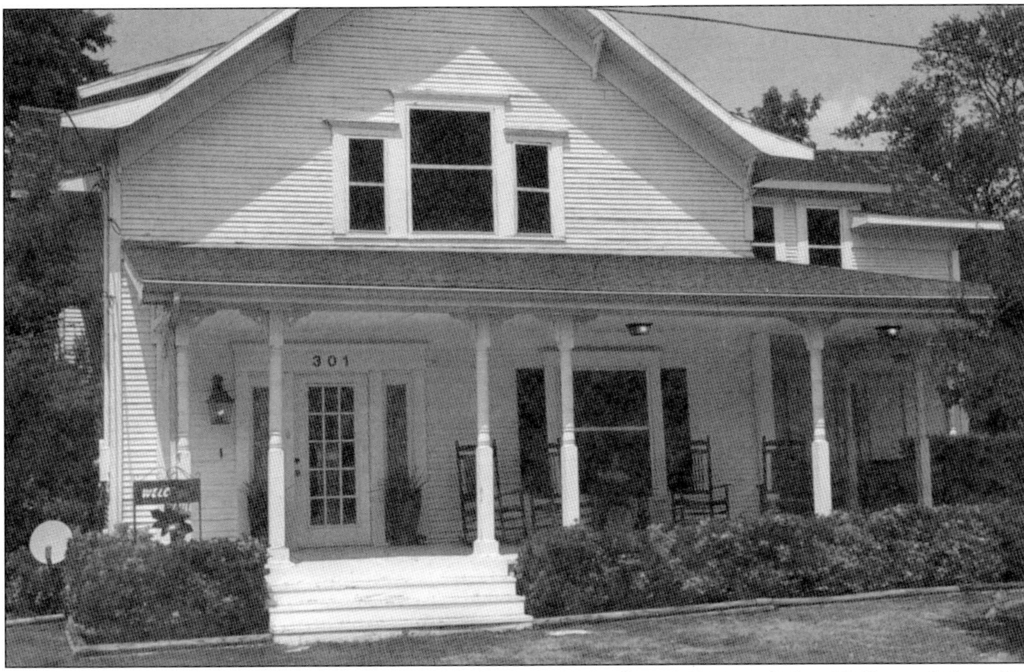

This home first belonged to Dr. Eugene Ledbetter from the 1920s until the 1940s and then Dr. John D. Harvey from the 1940s until the 1960s. It has been lovingly restored and sits on display for all to see. (Authors' collection.)

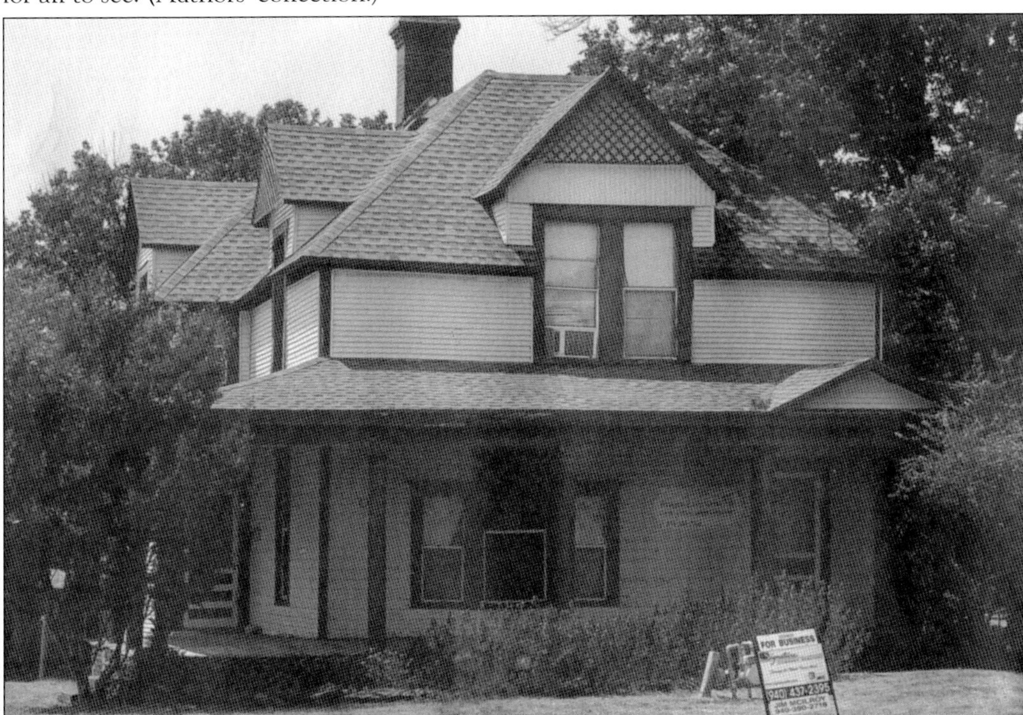

The old Secrest home still stands tall and proud as hundreds of cars pass by daily on Highway 377. The Secrests first occupied this house around 1939. (Authors' collection.)

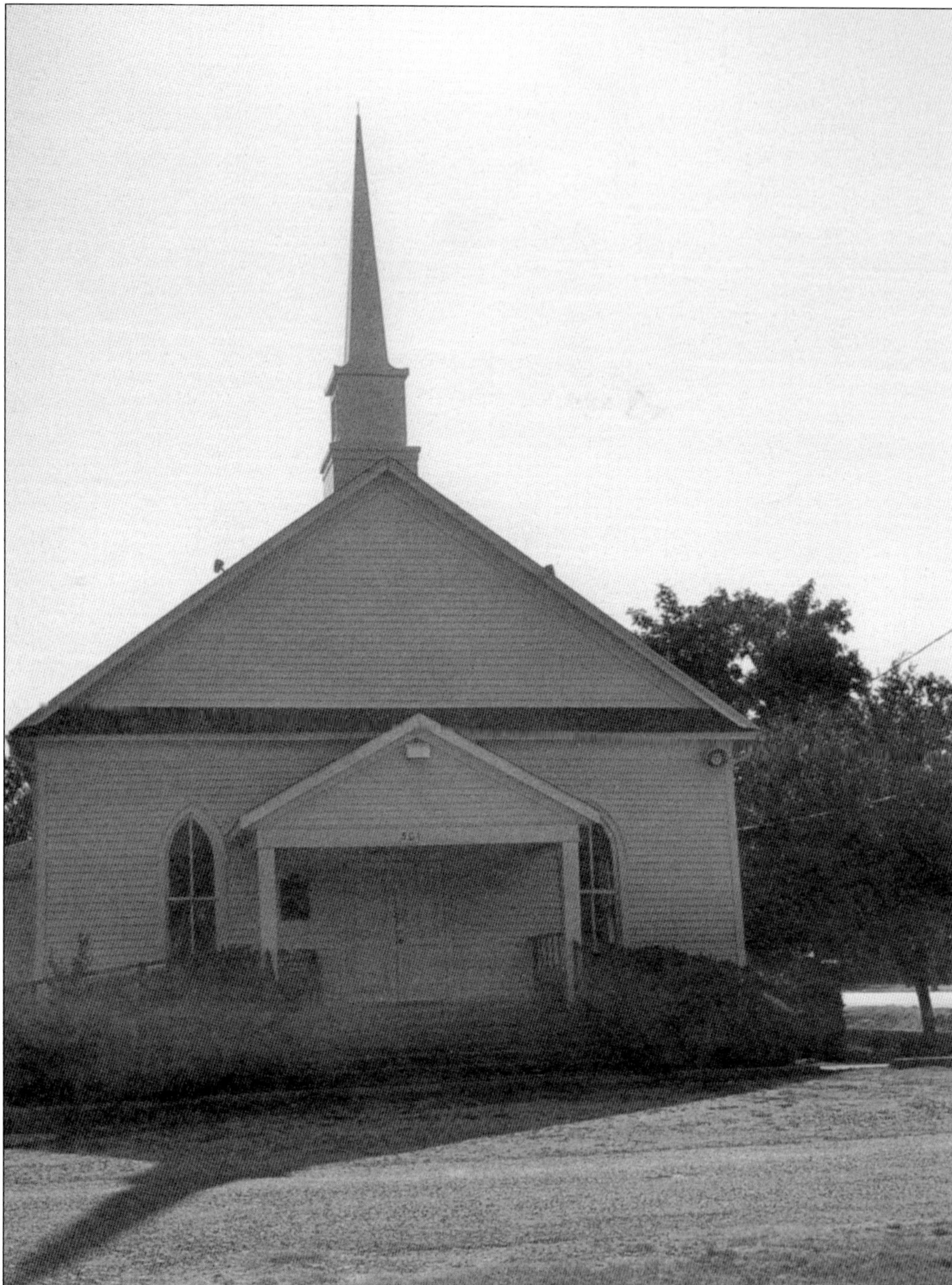

The First United Methodist Church of Tioga was first organized in 1887. It was called the Shiloh Methodist Church and was on a corner of land east of Tioga owned by Olan Van Zandt's grandfather John Rogers. After Tioga was founded, the congregation moved into town and established the Methodist church that is still being used today. The original building was erected in 1893. This church has faithfully served Tioga for over 100 years. (Authors' collection.)

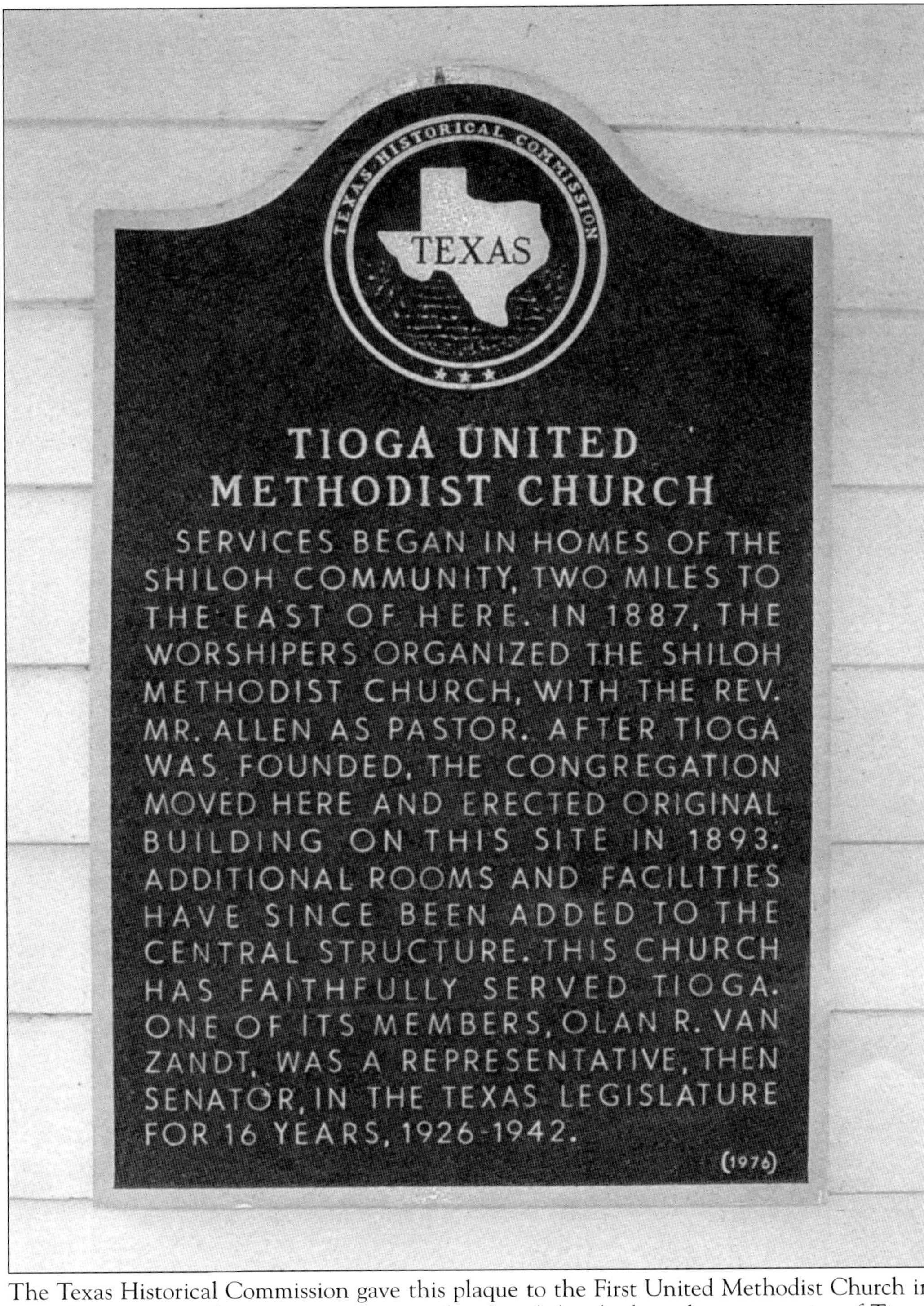

The Texas Historical Commission gave this plaque to the First United Methodist Church in 1976. It recognizes the positive influence the church has had on the community of Tioga. (Authors' collection.)

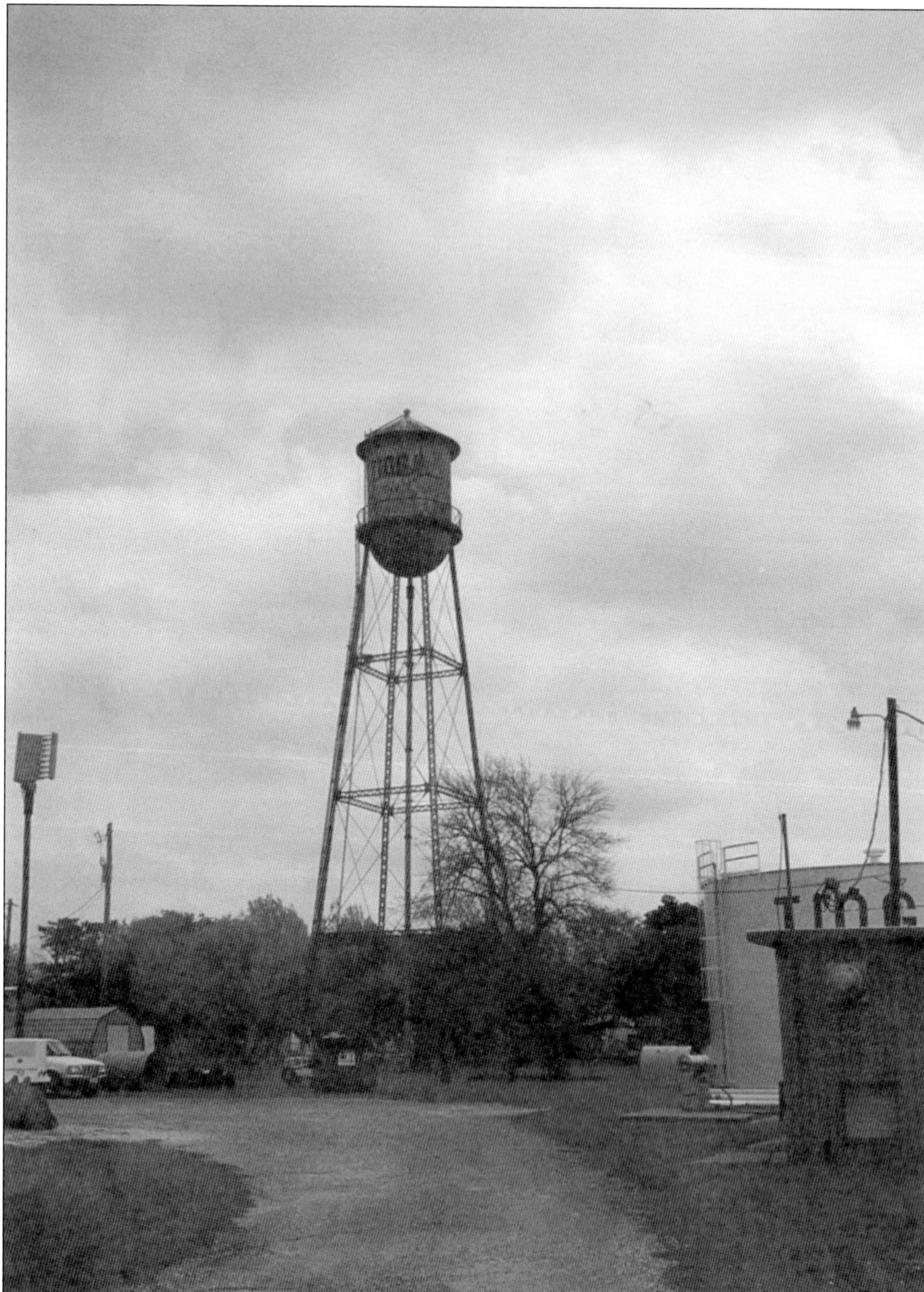

Tioga's water tower of today stands tall as it has for many years. The old wooden water tower was replaced with this more modern one; however, this is the same tower that has stood since the author was a small boy in the 1940s. (Authors' collection.)

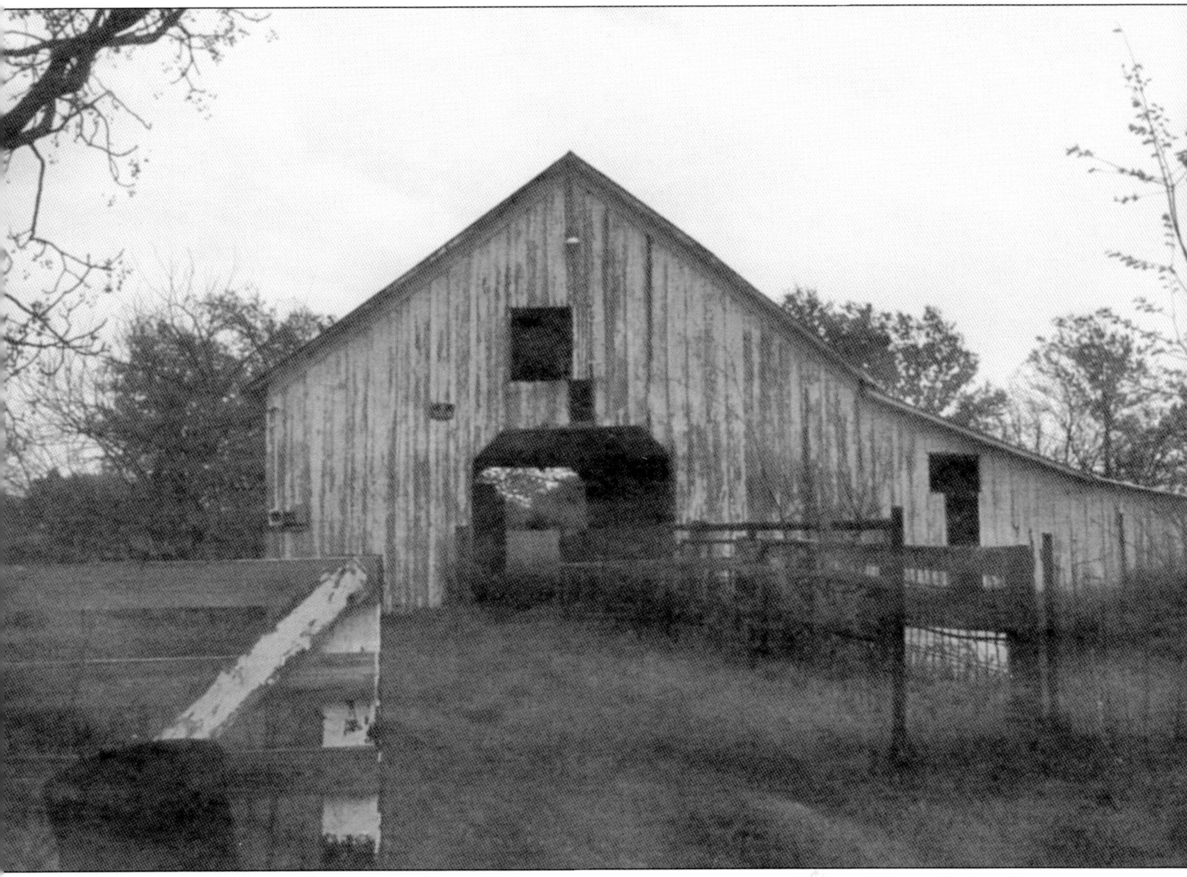

Woodall's old barn still is in good condition as it continues its watch over Tioga. It has been on Van Zandt Street since the early 1920s. Clarence Woodall owned the Chevrolet dealership in Tioga from the 1920s to the 1970s. (Authors' collection.)

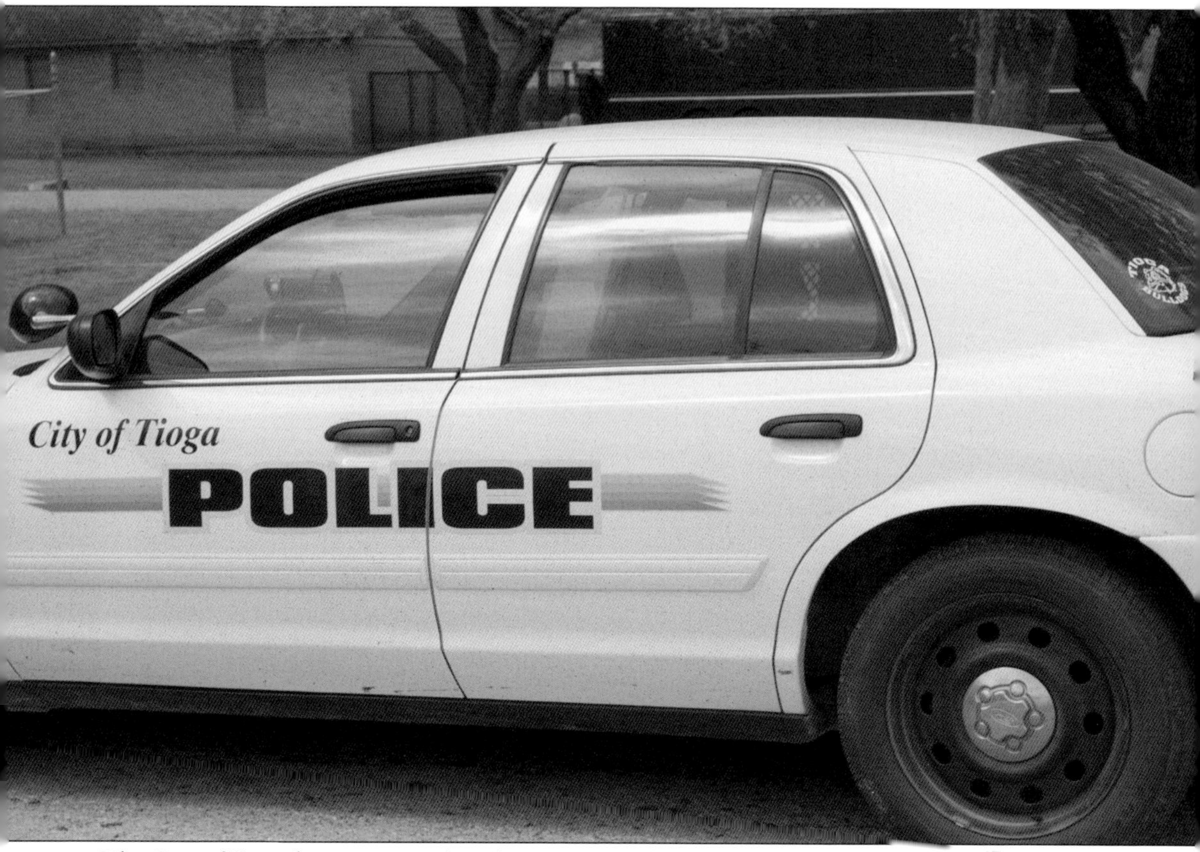

The City of Tioga has its own police department. Lake Ray Roberts and Highway 377 bring many visitors to the area, and the presence of law enforcement is appreciated. (Authors' collection.)

Six

Collinsville
The Early Years

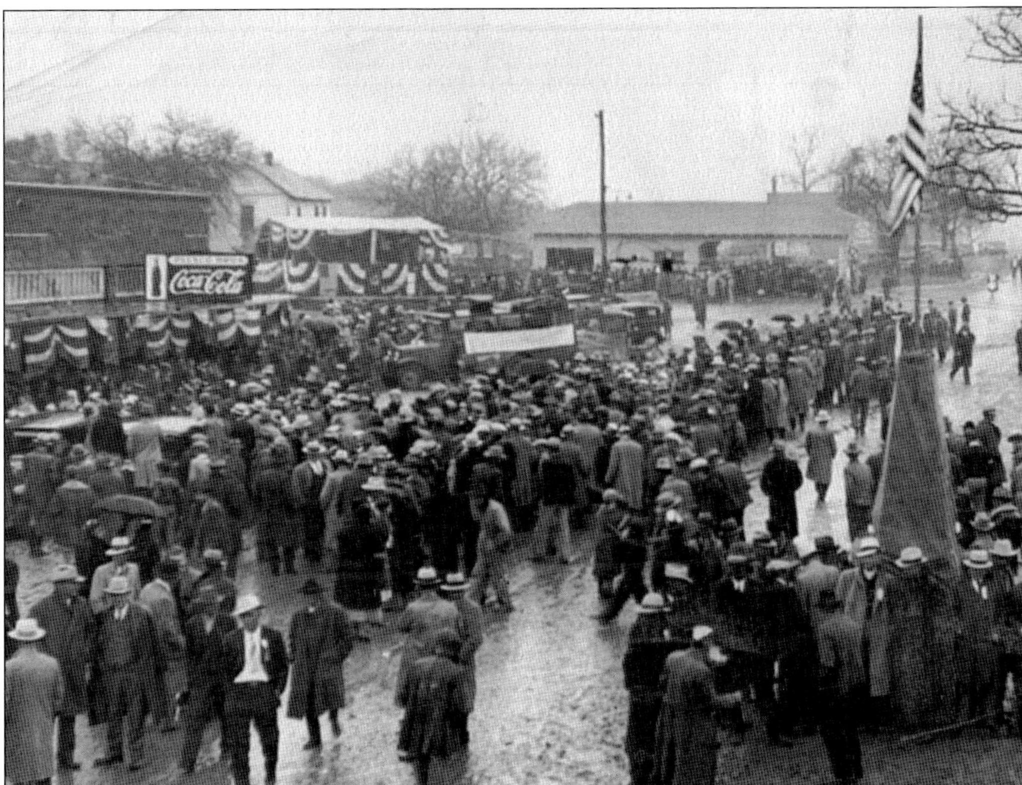

The citizens of Collinsville, formerly called Toad Suck, decked out the town for the arrival of their native son William Henry Davis Murray. Murray was running for governor of Oklahoma in 1932 and had promised to come through his town of birth and greet his admiring supporters. Even if they could not vote for him, they could help him in many other ways. Though it appears to be raining the photograph, the townsfolk tried to make Bill Murray's brief homecoming special. Food had been prepared, and it is said that the Order of the Eastern Star had quilted a special quilt just for Murray. (Cox Land Survey.)

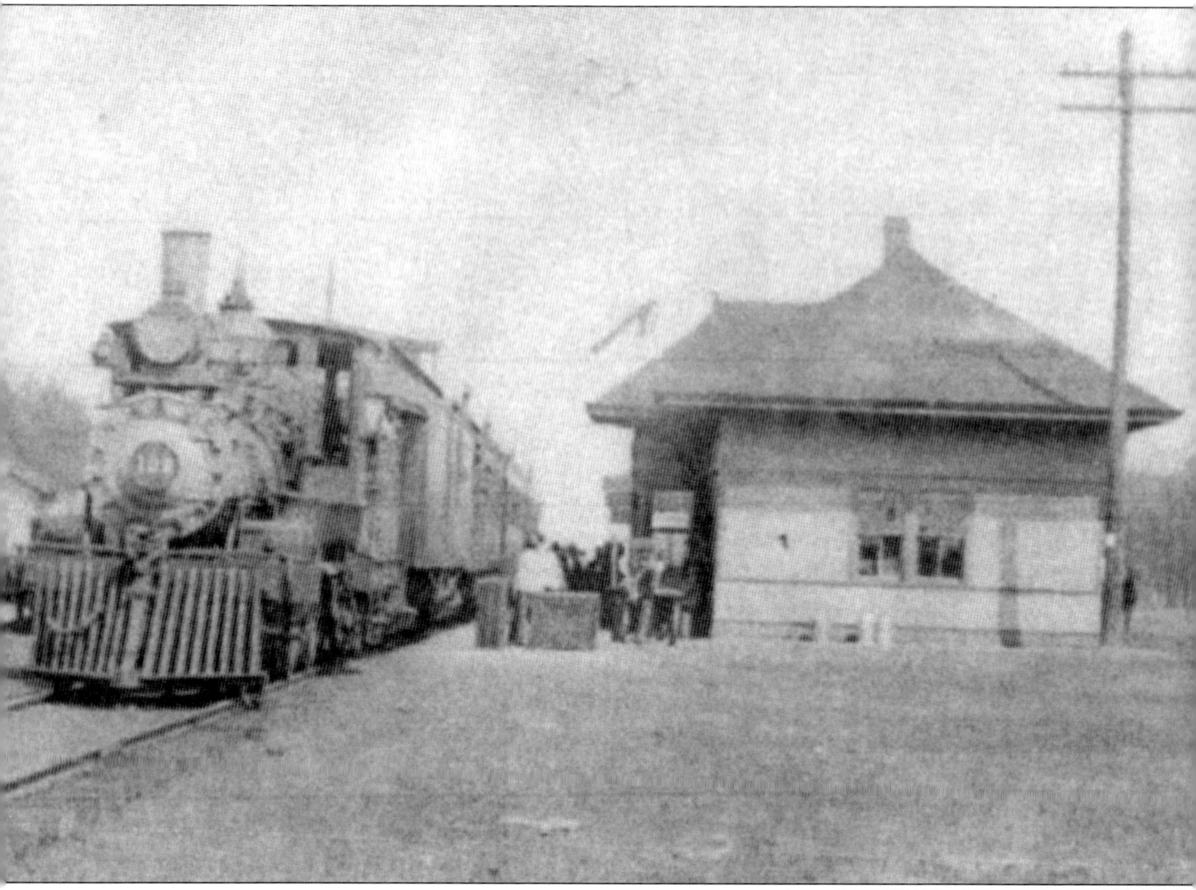

Here is Collinsville's train depot, and Bill Murray arrived here in the 1930s for the festivities in his honor set forth by the city. (Cox Land Survey.)

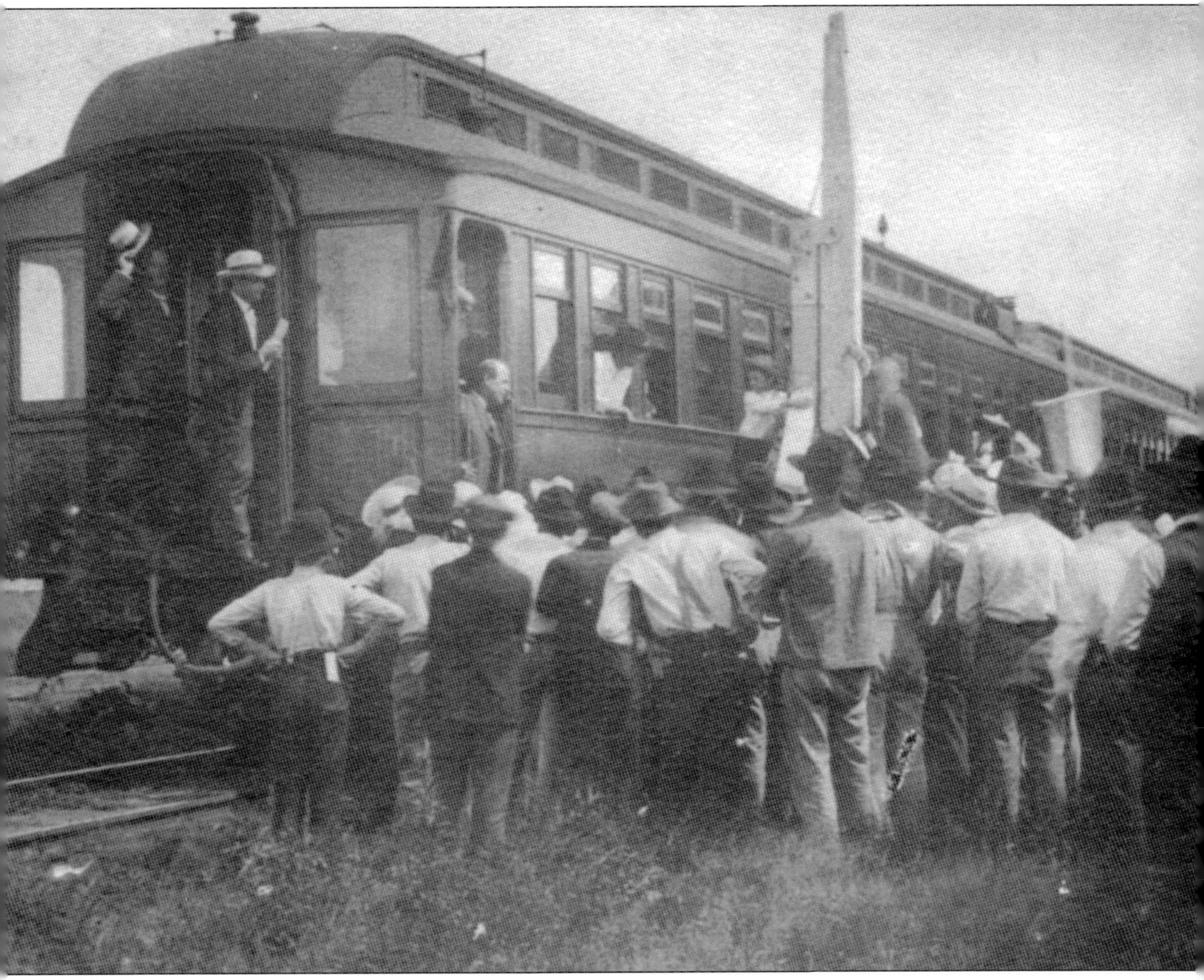

This could have been the train Bill Murray rolled in on while visiting Collinsville. Supposedly, when he arrived in town, political aides tried to get him off the train. To their dismay, unfortunately, he was too inebriated to disembark. Legend has it that then Murray, after lighting up his big cigar and placing his thumbs in his vest, told his helpers that he was not even from Collinsville. Word quickly spread back to those anxiously awaiting his arrival. It probably started with a whisper, but it ended in a roar. (James Hilliard.)

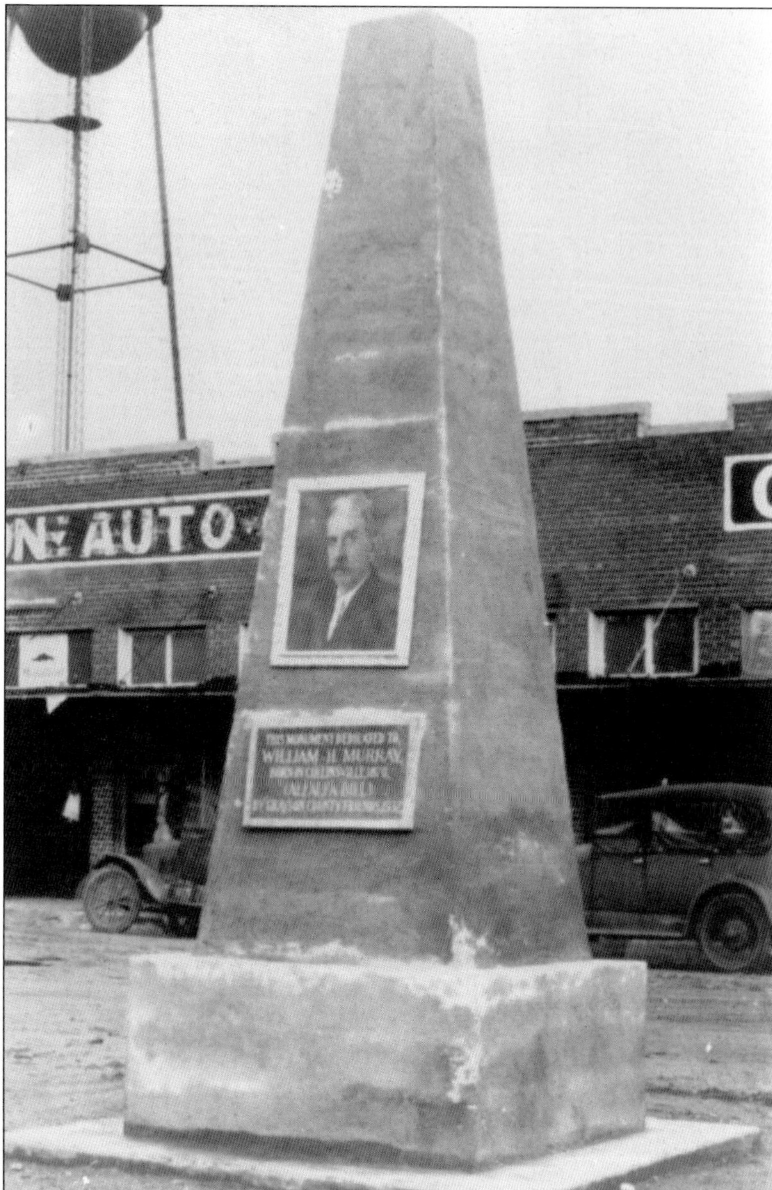

Pictured is the monument citizens of Collinsville had erected in Bill Murray's honor. It was draped and was to be unveiled upon his arrival. On the monument, it had his picture, and under it was written: "This monument dedicated to / William H. Murray, / born in Collinsville, 1870. / (Alfalfa Bill) / by Grayson County Friends, 1932." When residents found out what Murray had said on the train and that he was going to be a no-show for the festivities, they put ropes around the monument, hooked it to several teams of horses, and pulled it down. They then dug a hole and buried the monument upside down on Main Street with its base above ground. Legend has it that city officials used it for years as a place on which to stand while speeches and announcements were made. There are several tales about this fateful day in Collinsville, and the truth is bound to rest somewhere in the middle. The only way a person can mention Bill Murray's name in Collinsville is if he or she spits afterwards. (Cox Land Survey.)

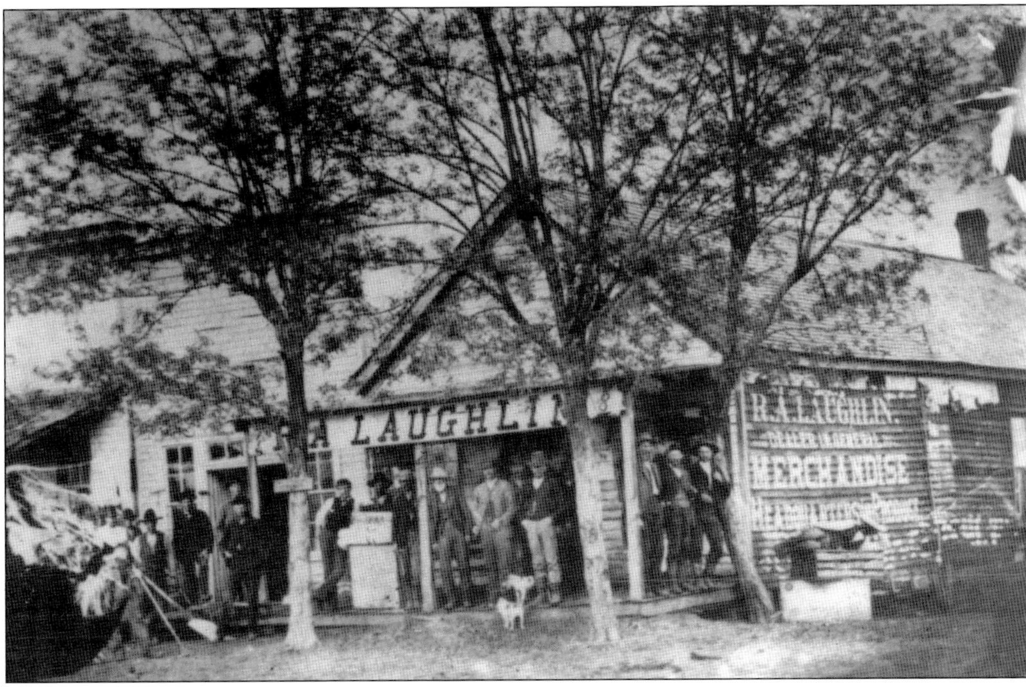

This general store could have been in the original town of Toad Suck. Toad Suck was not changed to Collinsville until the 1890s. (Cox Land Survey.)

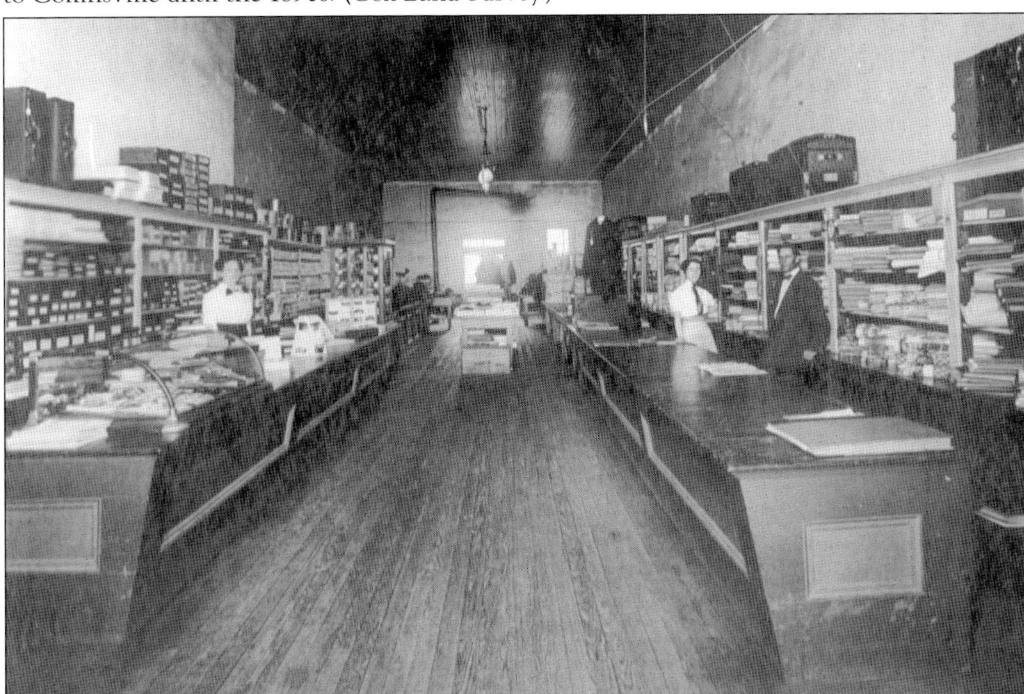

Here is a dry goods store in Collinsville in the early 1900s. Dry good stores prided themselves on having the latest in haberdashery, as well as shoes and other essentials. Note the steamer trunks on the top shelf. (Cox Land Survey.)

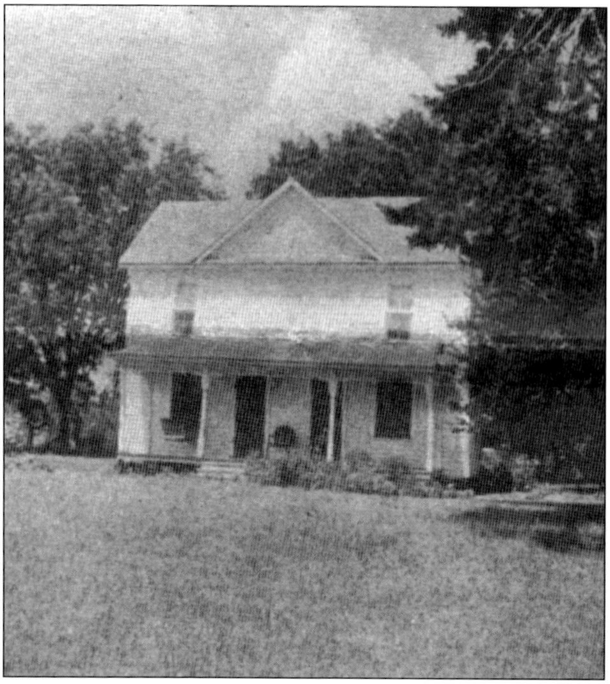

This was said to be the structure once called Toad Suck Hotel. The original house layout had just two rooms and was built by Lou Neatherly in 1872. J.Q. Adamson bought it from Neatherly and added more rooms and an outside staircase and turned it into a hotel for the cowboys who traveled the nearby Chisholm Trail. Joe Huffaker bought it about 1900 and turned it back into a home. Huffaker was Hattie Light's father. In 1975, Ms. Light still owned the house. It is said that the home was on the first street in Collinsville, which was named Main Street (now Broadway). Because of its location, it could have been the Toad Suck Hotel. This photograph was taken in the 1950s; the house has since been torn down. (Jacquita Lewter and *Whitesboro News*.)

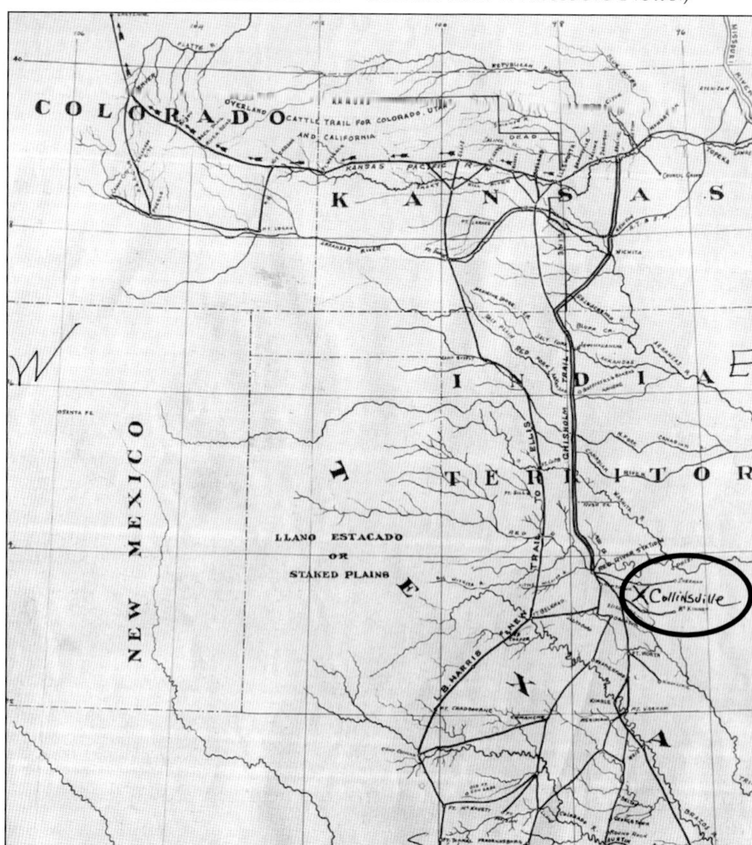

It is noteworthy that the Chisholm Trail mentioned was very close to Collinsville, as shown on this map. Since Toad Suck with its saloons and hotels was so close to the trail, dusty cowboys looking for a bath and a strong drink would have frequented the area often, and they could find both in Toad Suck. (Authors' collection.)

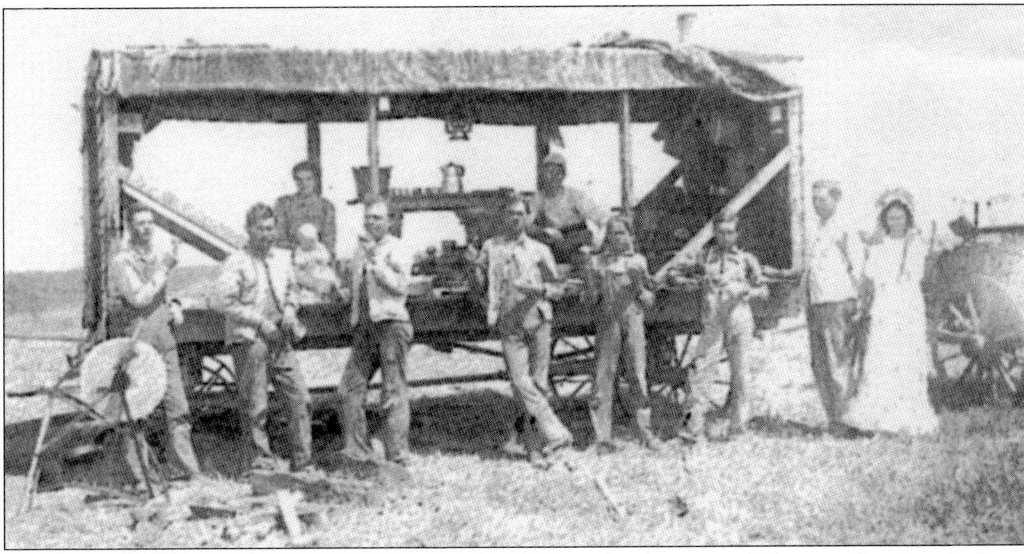

This photograph is of farmhands taking a break at a chuck wagon. The people identified are, from left to right, (standing) George Culpepper, W.A. Young, Ben Stein, Noah Hulsey, Charlie Bryan, Ernest Bryan, W.S. Culpepper, and unidentified wife; (sitting on the wagon) Effa Bryan, an unidentified baby, and the cook, Neaser Leath. The image originally belonged to Cindy Butler. (Ken Kemp.)

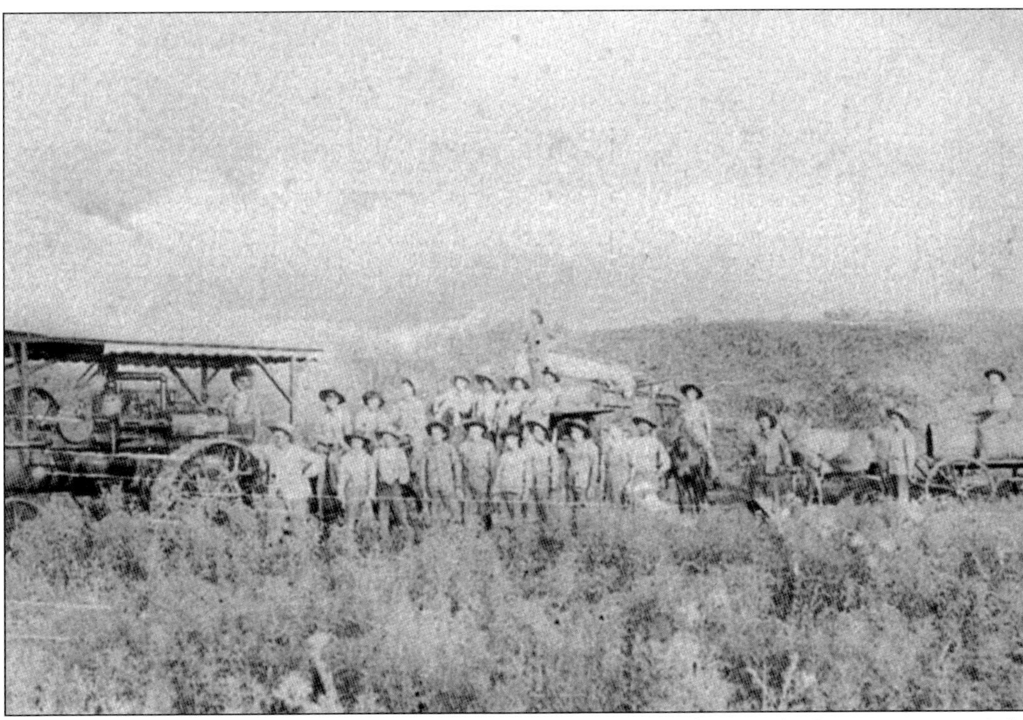

Pictured is a farm southeast of Collinsville near Hogstown Road. Note the huge tractor and the round water container pulled by mules or horses. The workers appear to be young, attesting to the fact that children had to work the farm as well in the 1800s. (Ken Kemp.)

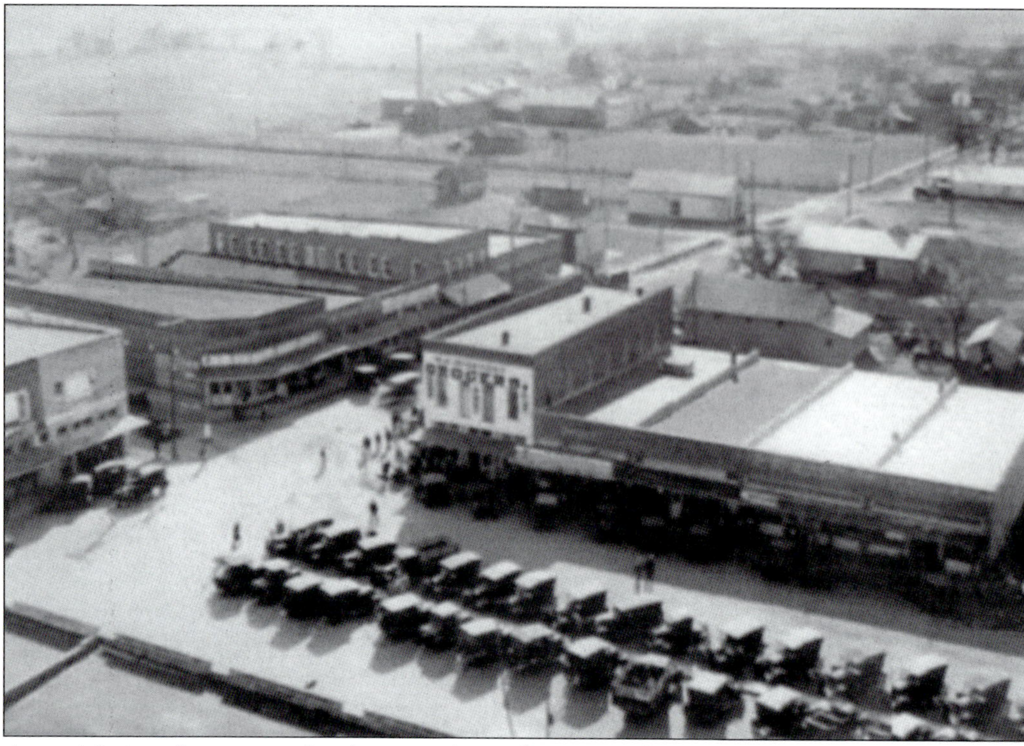

An aerial view of a town was hard to come by in the 1930s. This is one of Collinsville's downtown taken from the top of the water tower. (Ken Kemp.)

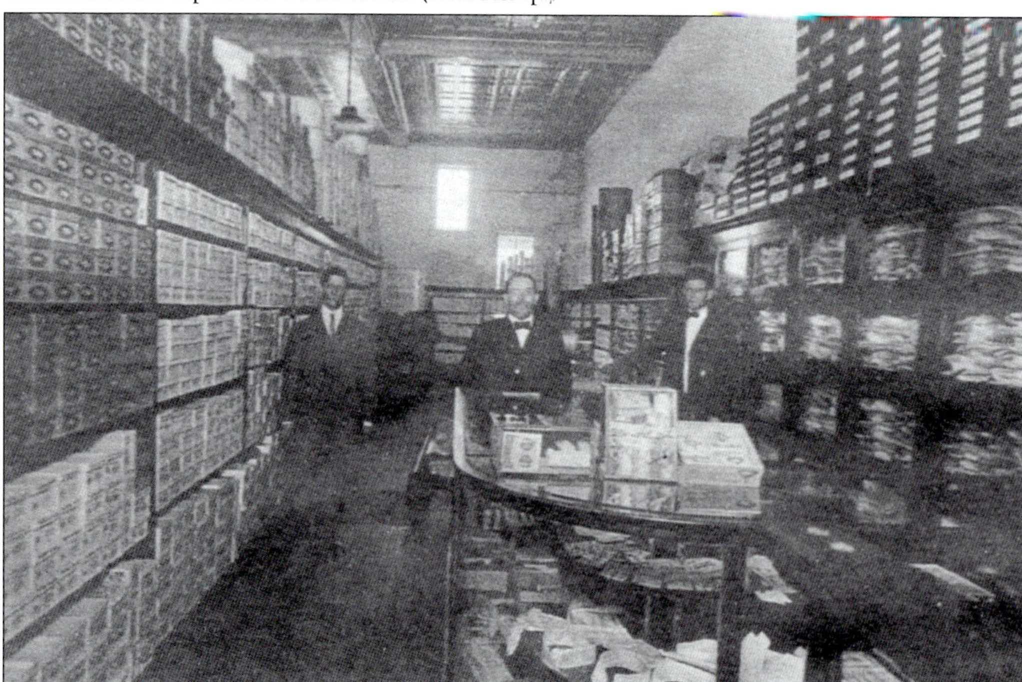

A c. 1905 Collinsville dry goods store appears well stocked. (Cox Land Survey.)

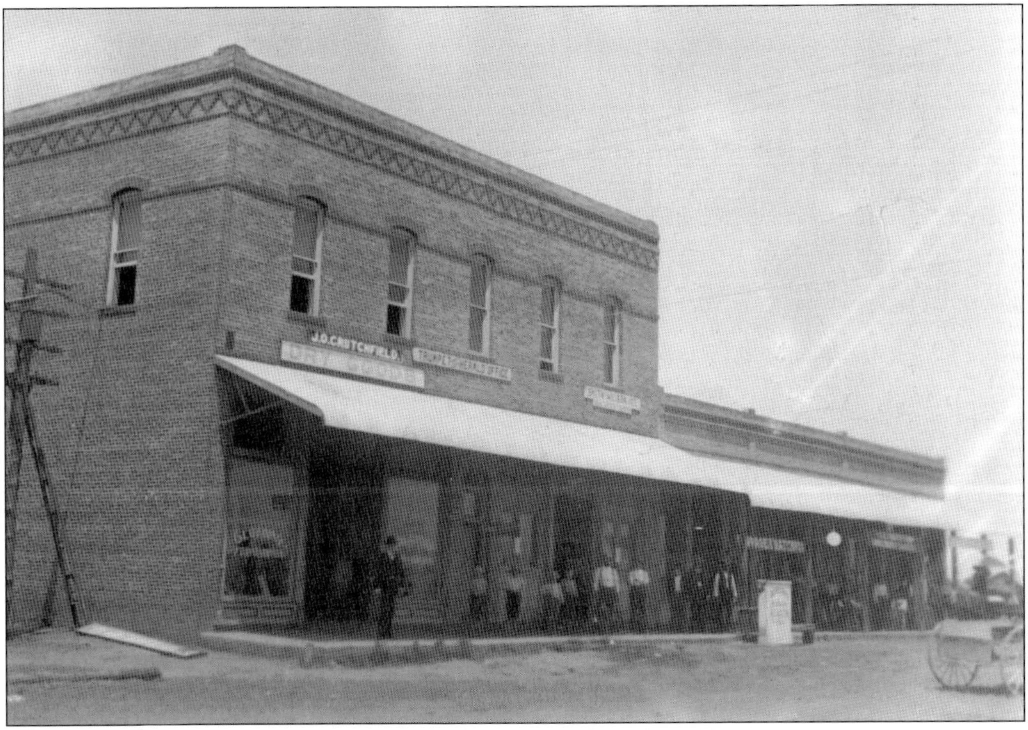

Pictured is Collinsville's downtown in the late 1800s. (Ken Kemp.)

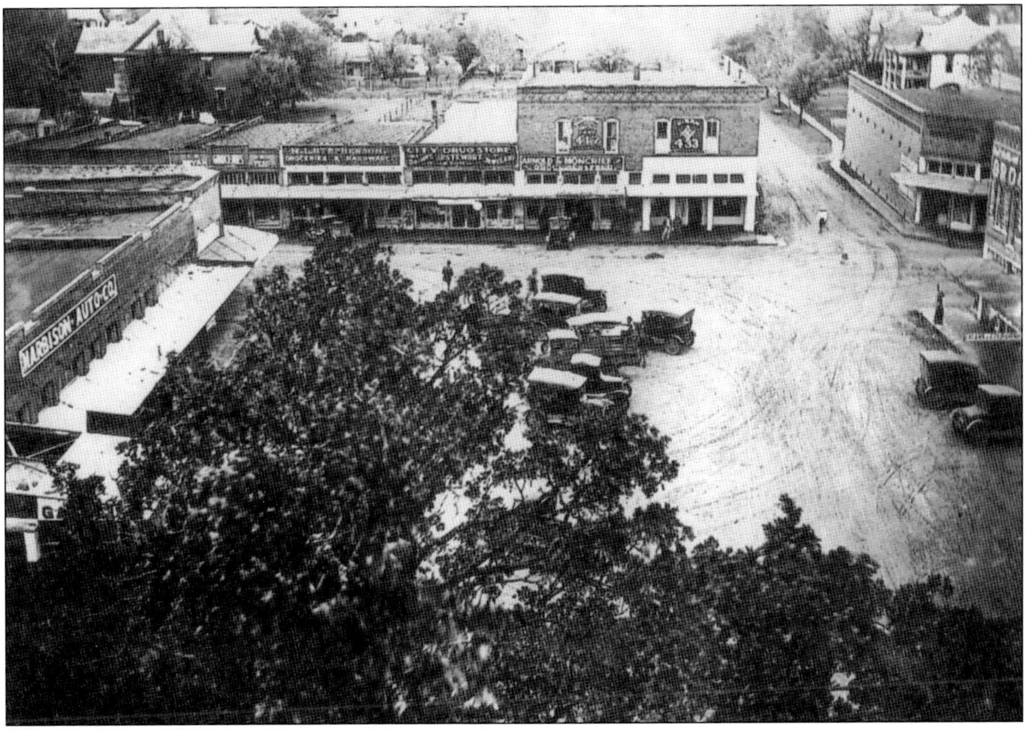

Here is another photograph of downtown Collinsville in the 1920s. It appears to have been taken from the water tower as well. (Ken Kemp.)

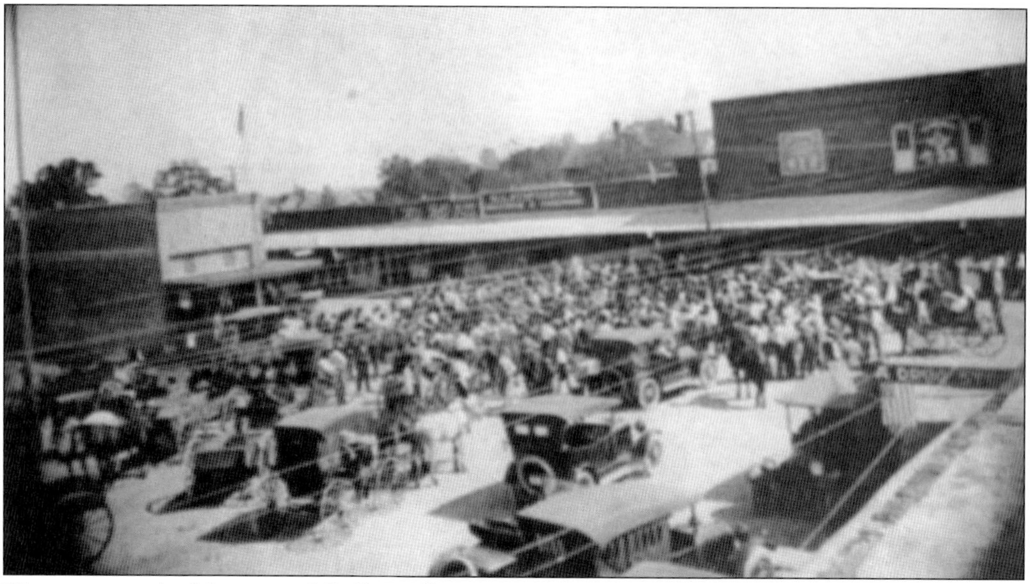

This is a wonderful scene of Collinsville's Main Street in the mid-1920s. It must have been a Saturday, as that was when everyone came to town to buy groceries and visit one another. Note that buggies and cars are sharing the street. (Ken Kemp.)

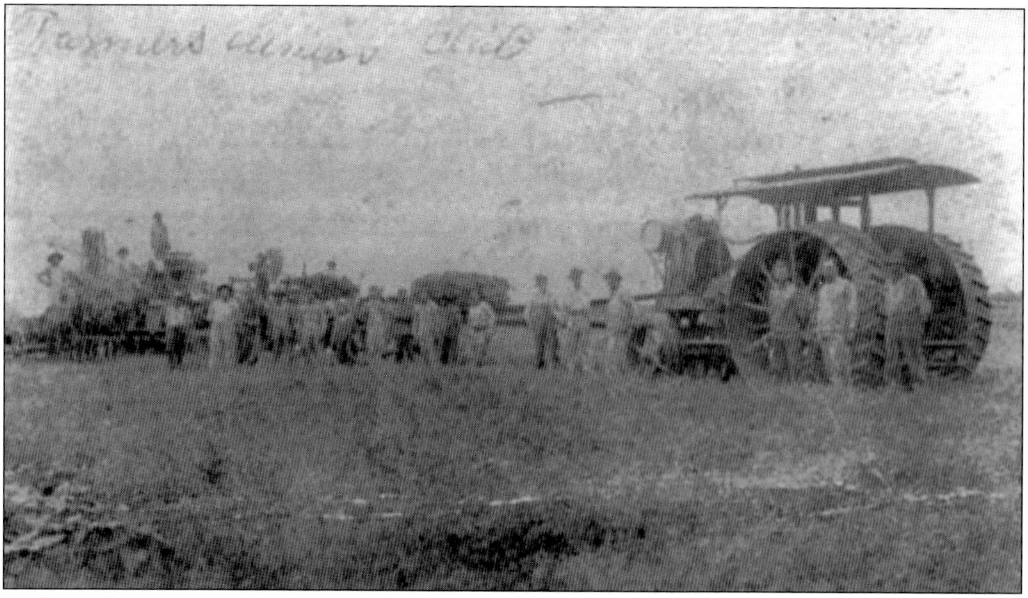

Collinsville Texas Farmers Union Club has gathered in Fel Grahams's field to have a photograph taken in 1917. The image originally belonged to John Davis. (Ken Kemp.)

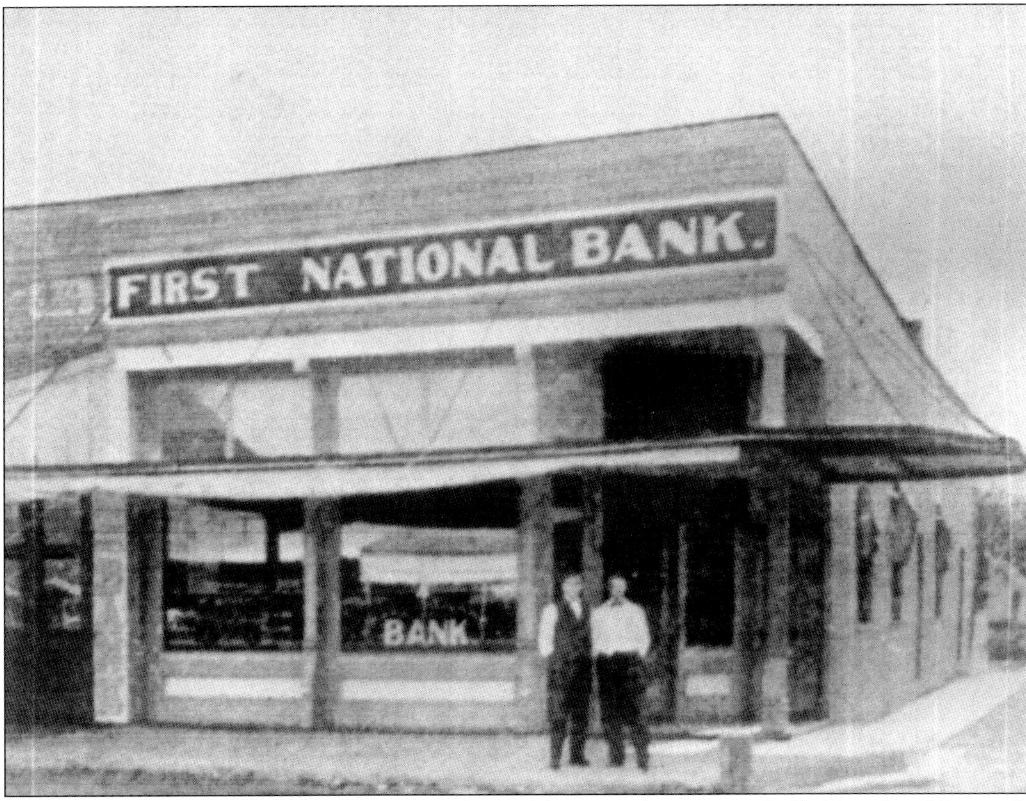

The Collinsville State Bank is seen here. The building now houses city hall. (Cox Land Survey.)

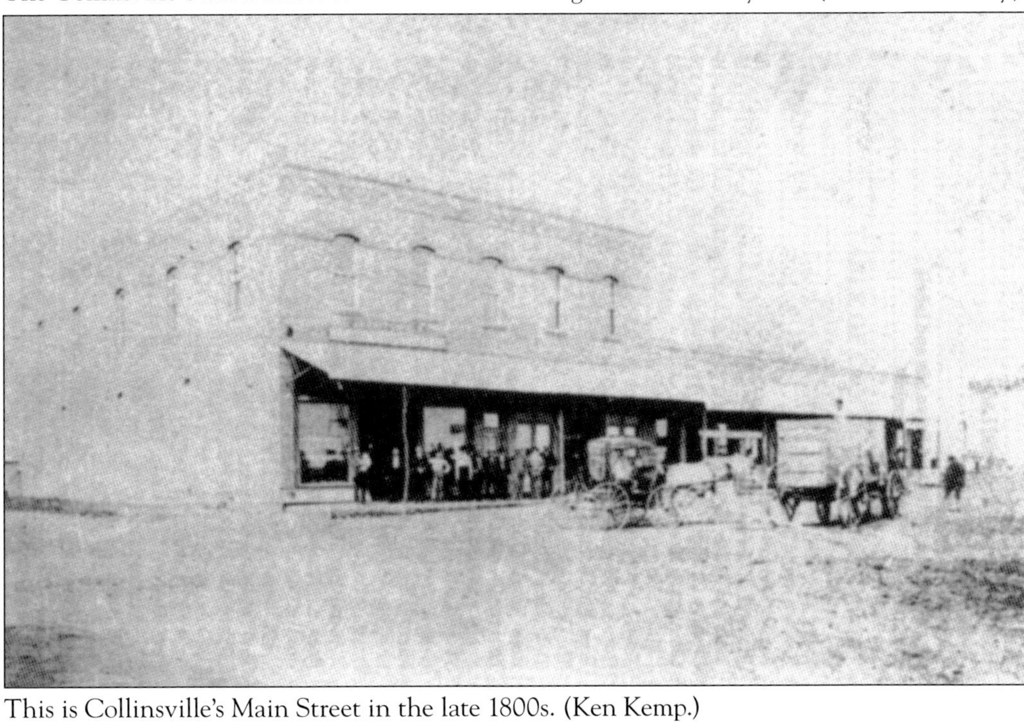
This is Collinsville's Main Street in the late 1800s. (Ken Kemp.)

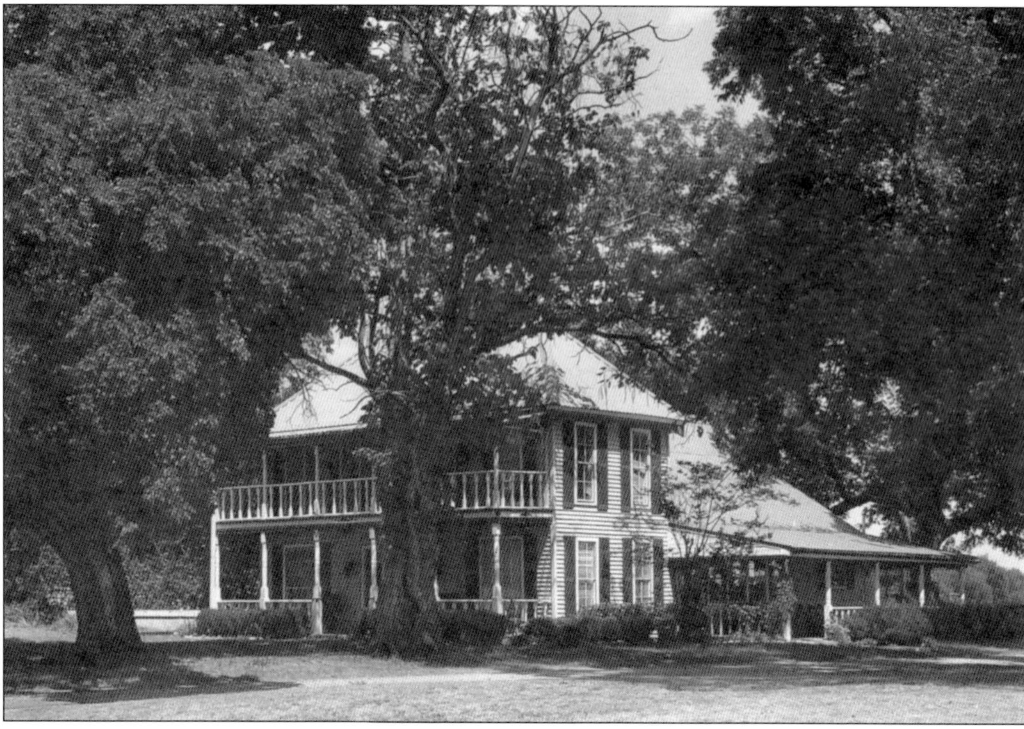

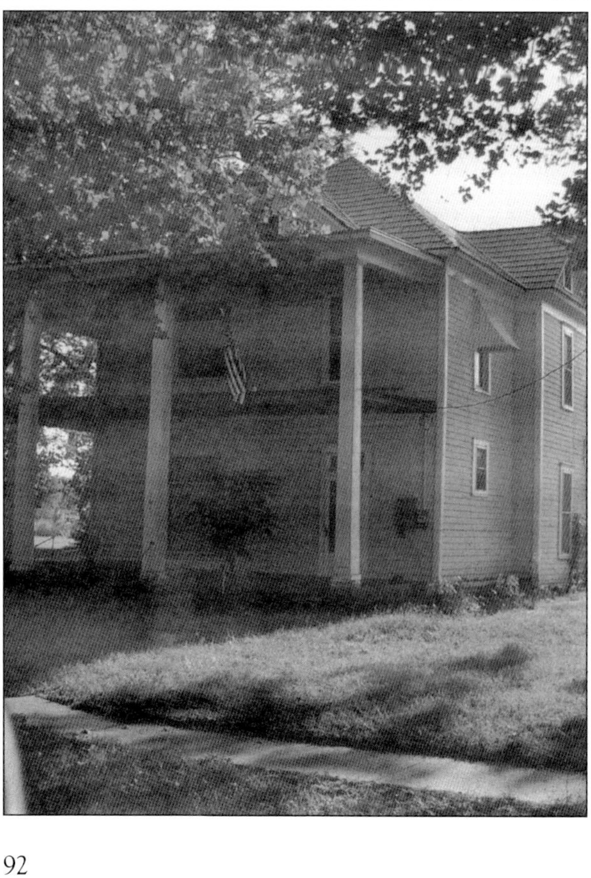

Pictured is the old Bates house in the early 1900s. Noel Lewter, featured in chapter eight, lived in this home when he came to Collinsville as a child. Now, it is a beautiful cutting horse ranch. (Authors' collection.)

The Pelphrey house on what was called Silk Stocking Avenue (now Main Street) was believed to have been built around a log cabin constructed by William deCordova, who previously owned the property site. deCordova sold the property between 1879 and 1883 to A.T. Pelphrey and his wife, Louisa. (Authors' collection.)

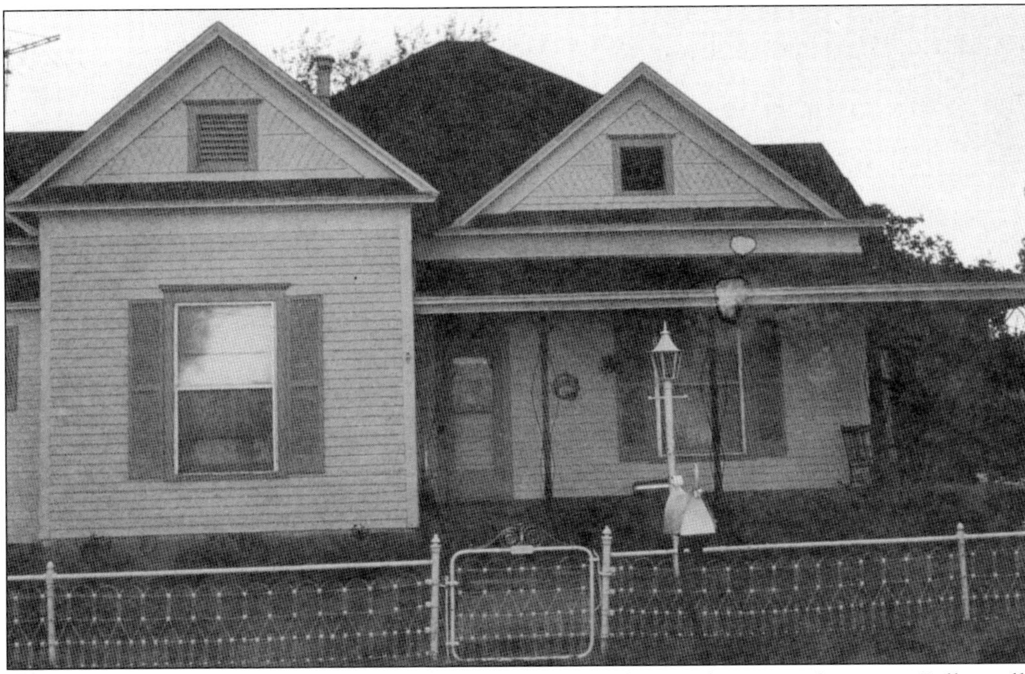

This beautiful house belonged to Elsie Bruce in the 1940s. She ran the movie theater in Collinsville and was a member of the Order of the Eastern Star. When she owned this house, it was always pink with white trim. She was a neat lady. (Authors' collection.)

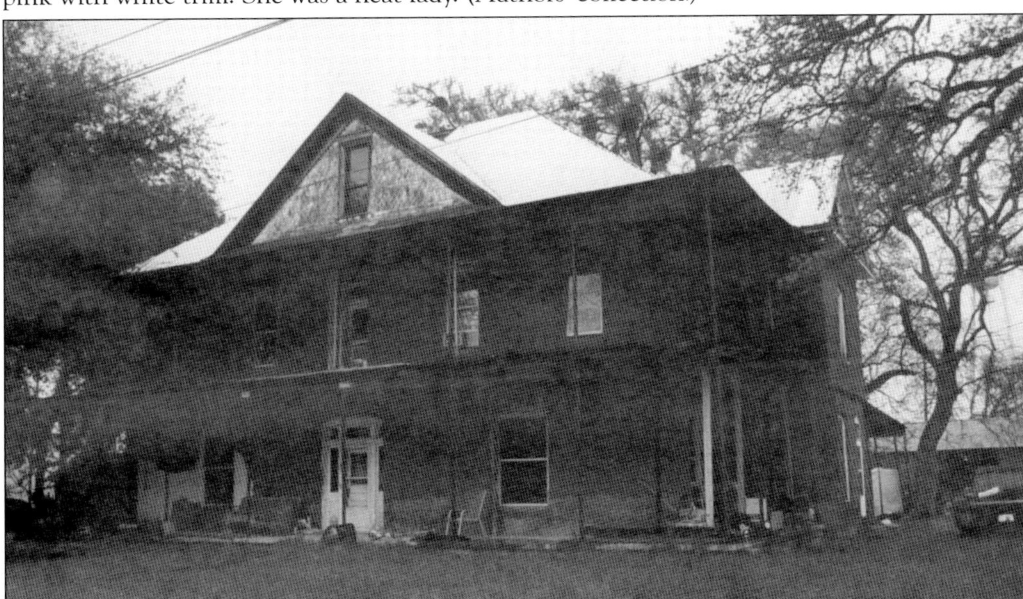

Here is what was the home of James Lee and Hattie Belle Harbison. James came to Texas from Arkansas to teach. In 1886, he settled in Collinsville and helped create the town by constructing several brick buildings to be used for commercial purposes. He married Hattie Lamb in Collinsville Methodist Church in 1888, and they raised their family in this house. For more about the interesting Harbison, see chapter eight. Another colorful resident, Noel Lewter, purchased the home in 1967. (Authors' collection.)

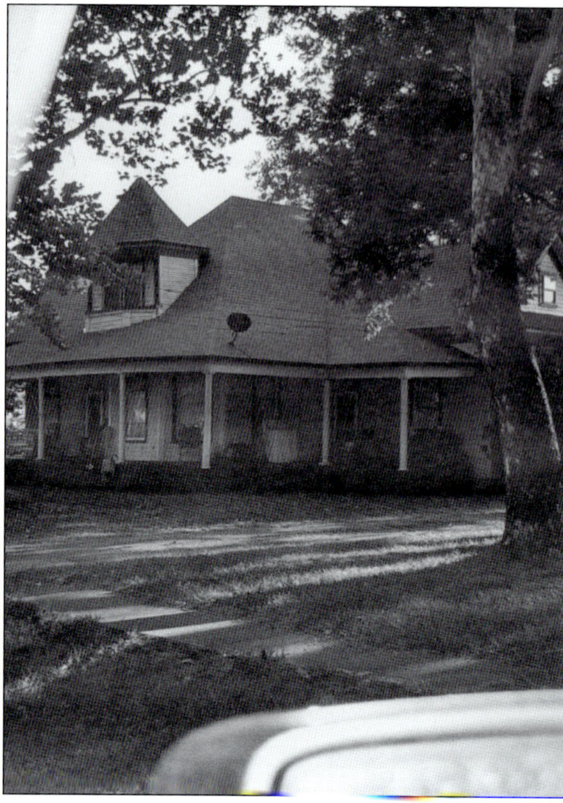

The deCordova house was completed in 1904 by William F. deCordova. Electricity was furnished to the home in the 1920s. Prior to that, gaslights had been used. The lot had two barns, a windmill, a cellar, and a log smokehouse. The deCordova era spanned nearly 70 years. During that time, celebrities such as Gene Autry and Oklahoma governor "Wild" Bill Murray were entertained in the deCordova's dining room. (Authors' collection.)

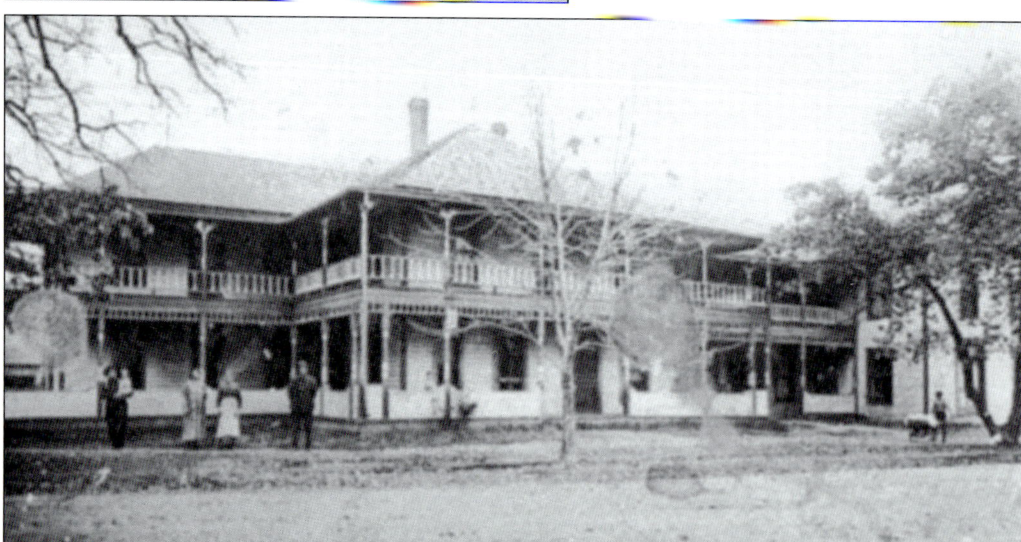

The St. George Hotel was built early 1900s; this photograph was taken in 1917. It served the area with hot baths, good food, and comfortable quarters. Early operators of the hotel were George Campbell and his wife and Grover Walker Sr. and his wife. The people pictured are, from left to right, James Madison Snow, holding Maggie Walker; Maggie's mother, Etta Snow Walker; unidentified; and George Moser Snow. The boy on porch is Grover Walker Jr. The photograph was originally the property of John Davis. (Ken Kemp.)

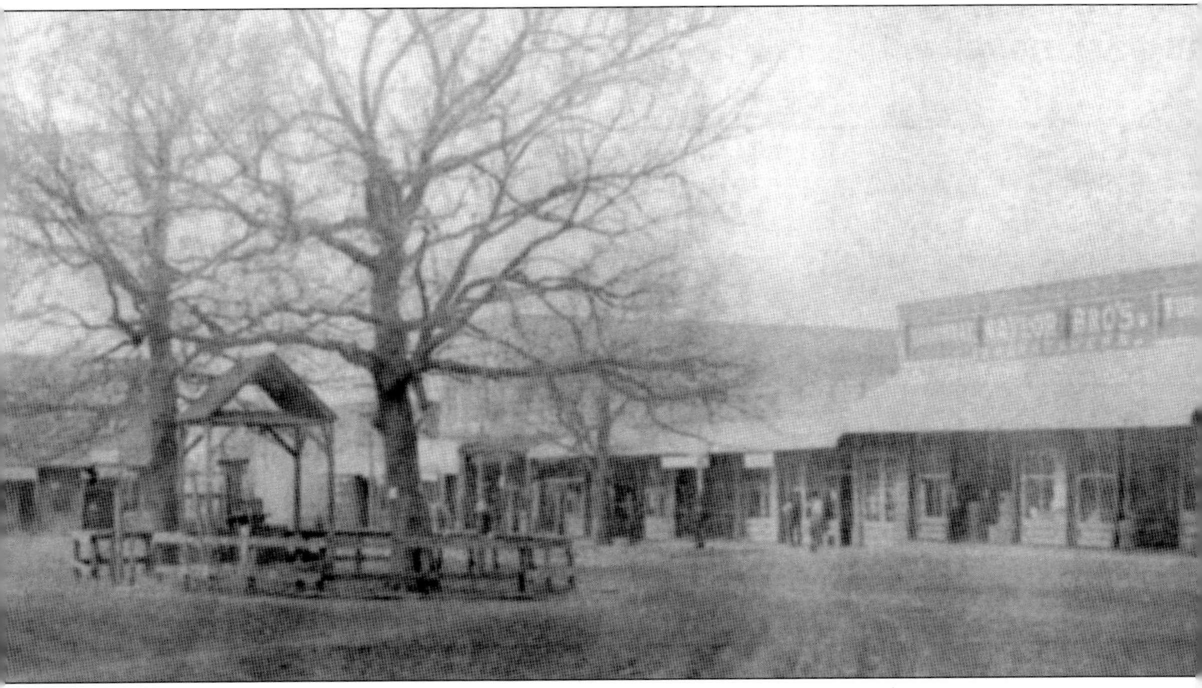

Here is downtown Collinsville in the late 1800s or early 1900s. (Ken Kemp.)

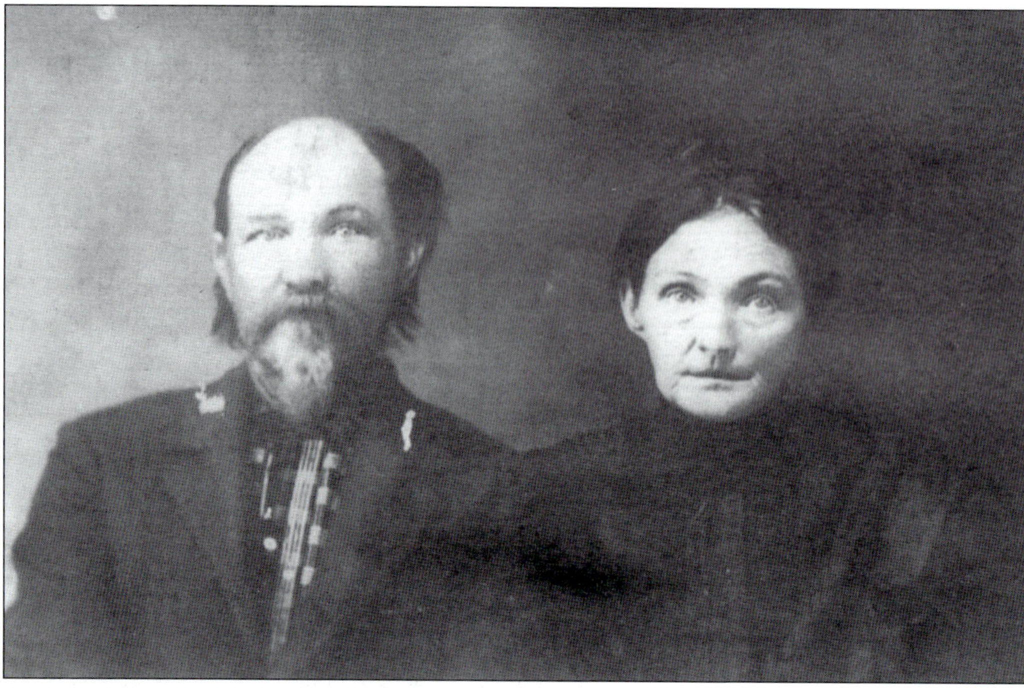

This is George Washington (G.W.) Cox and his wife. They are the great-grandparents of Don Cox, the owner of Cox Land Survey Company. This image was taken in the 1800s. (Cox Land Survey.)

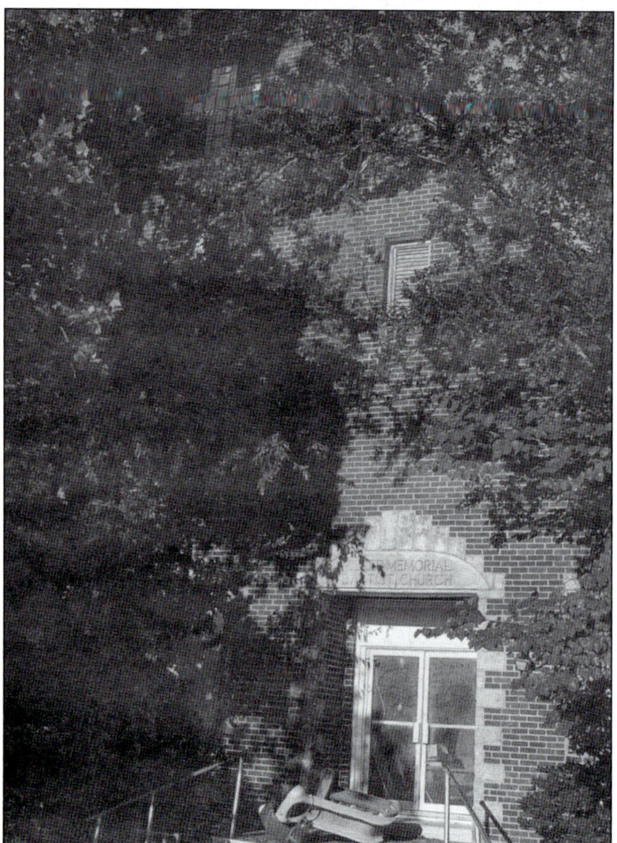

Pictured is the old Miller Memorial Baptist Church of Collinsville, which is now a child-care center. Note the glass cross at the top left of the image peeking through the trees. The church was built in the 1920s. (Authors' collection.)

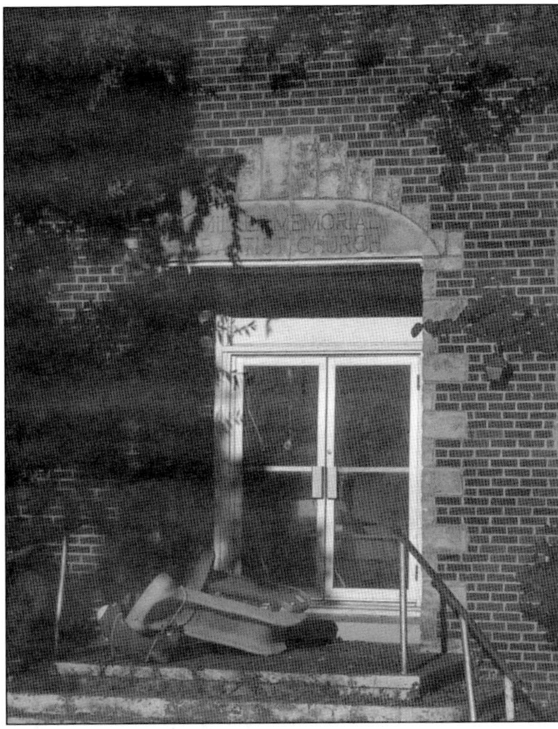

The inscription "Miller Memorial Baptist Church" over the doorway is more visible in this photograph. It was also the previous home of First Baptist Church of Collinsville. (Authors' collection.)

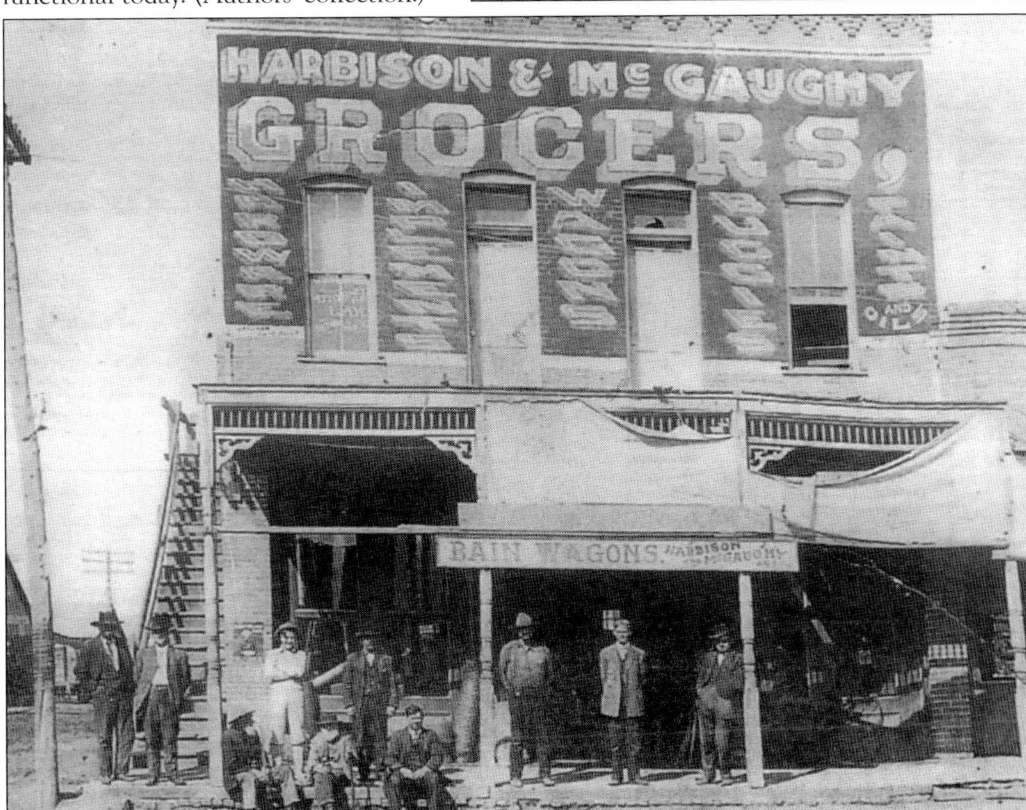

Pictured in the early 1900s is the corner of what is now Main and Hughes Streets. The Harbisons owned this business; it could have been one of the buildings J.L. Harbison constructed when he came to Collinsville to help the city grow. The building is still functional today. (Authors' collection.)

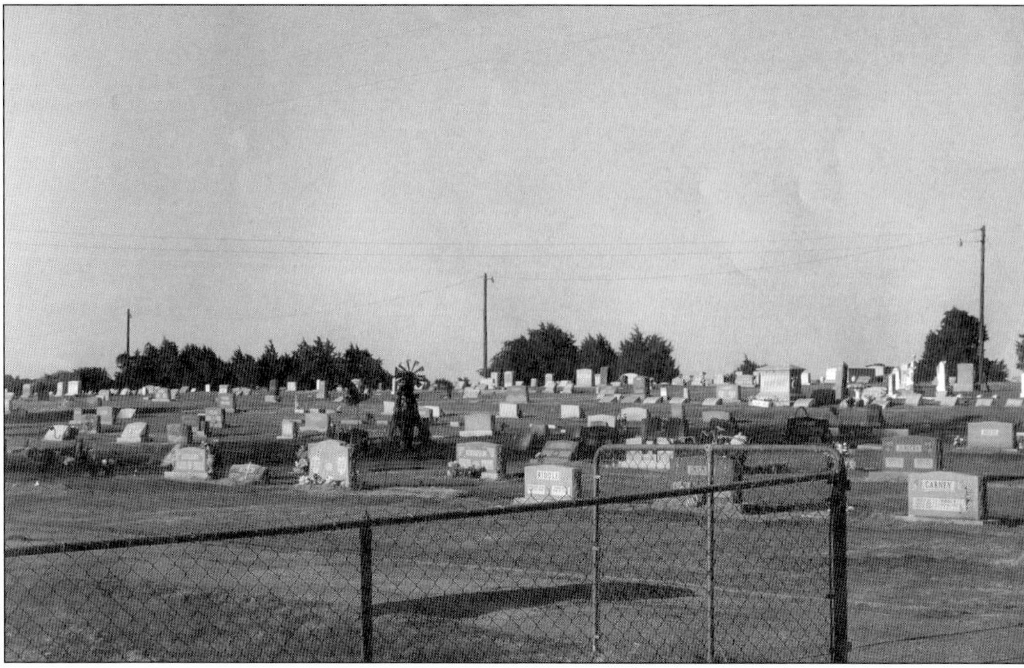

This is the north side of Collinsville Cemetery, a huge cemetery that is very much in use today. It is a beautiful place, with tall oak trees that have probably been standing since the cemetery's inception. It is also a peaceful final resting place. (Authors' collection.)

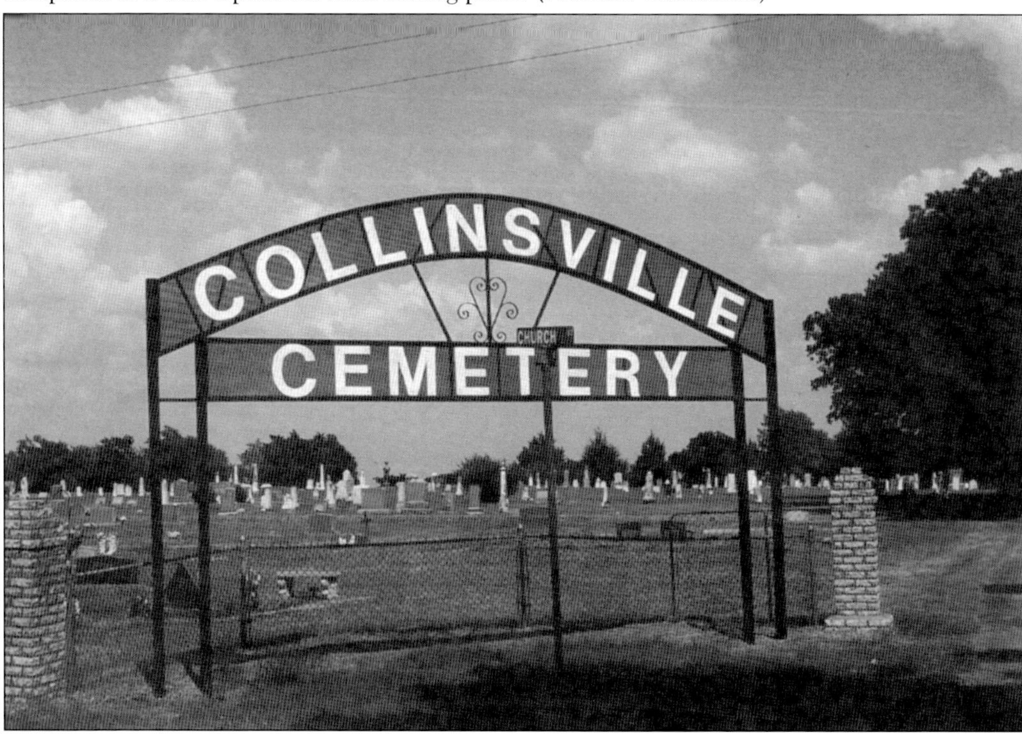

The main gate of Collinsville Cemetery is seen here. Its grounds are kept up and are very well maintained. (Authors' collection.)

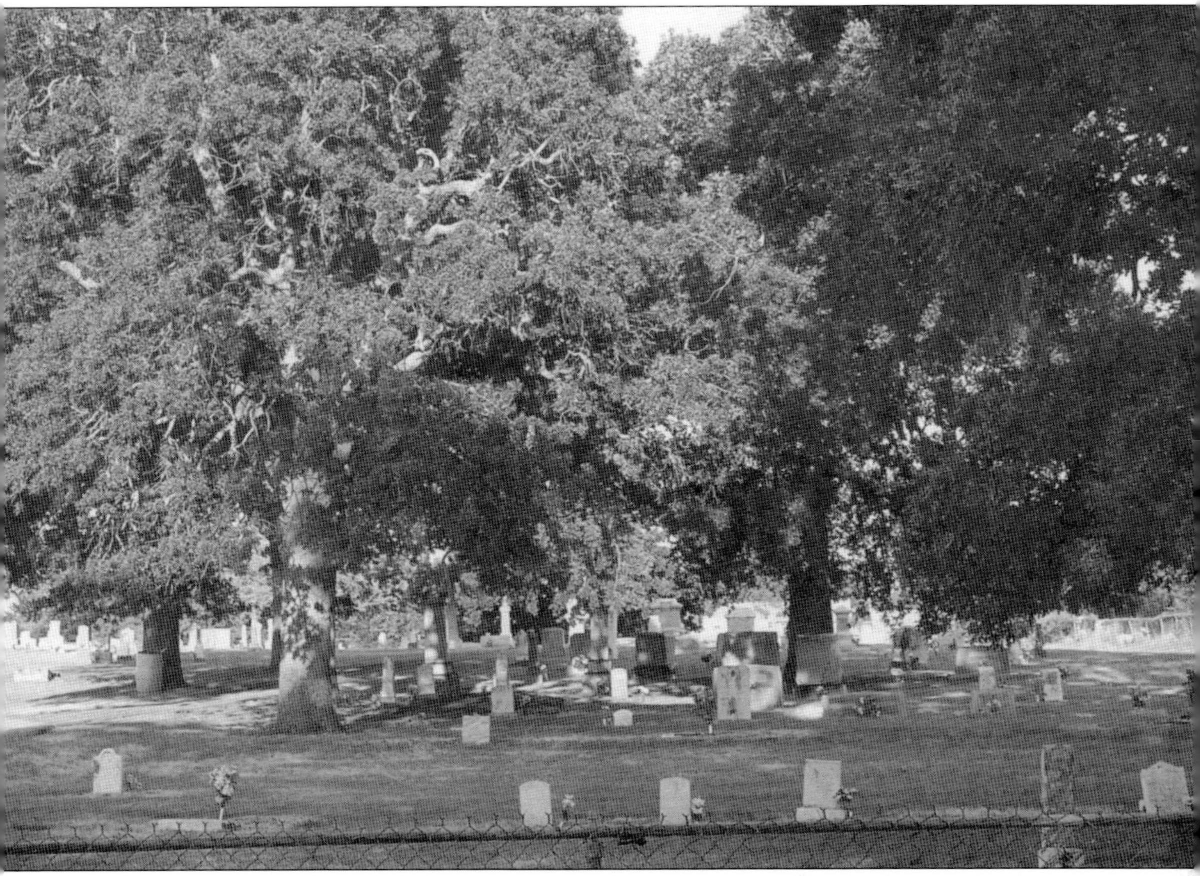

This is the south side of the cemetery, the oldest section. Huge oak trees shade the many headstones. Some of the markers are "moss green" with age and date back to the 1870s. It is evident that Collinsville residents are proud of their cemetery. (Authors' collection.)

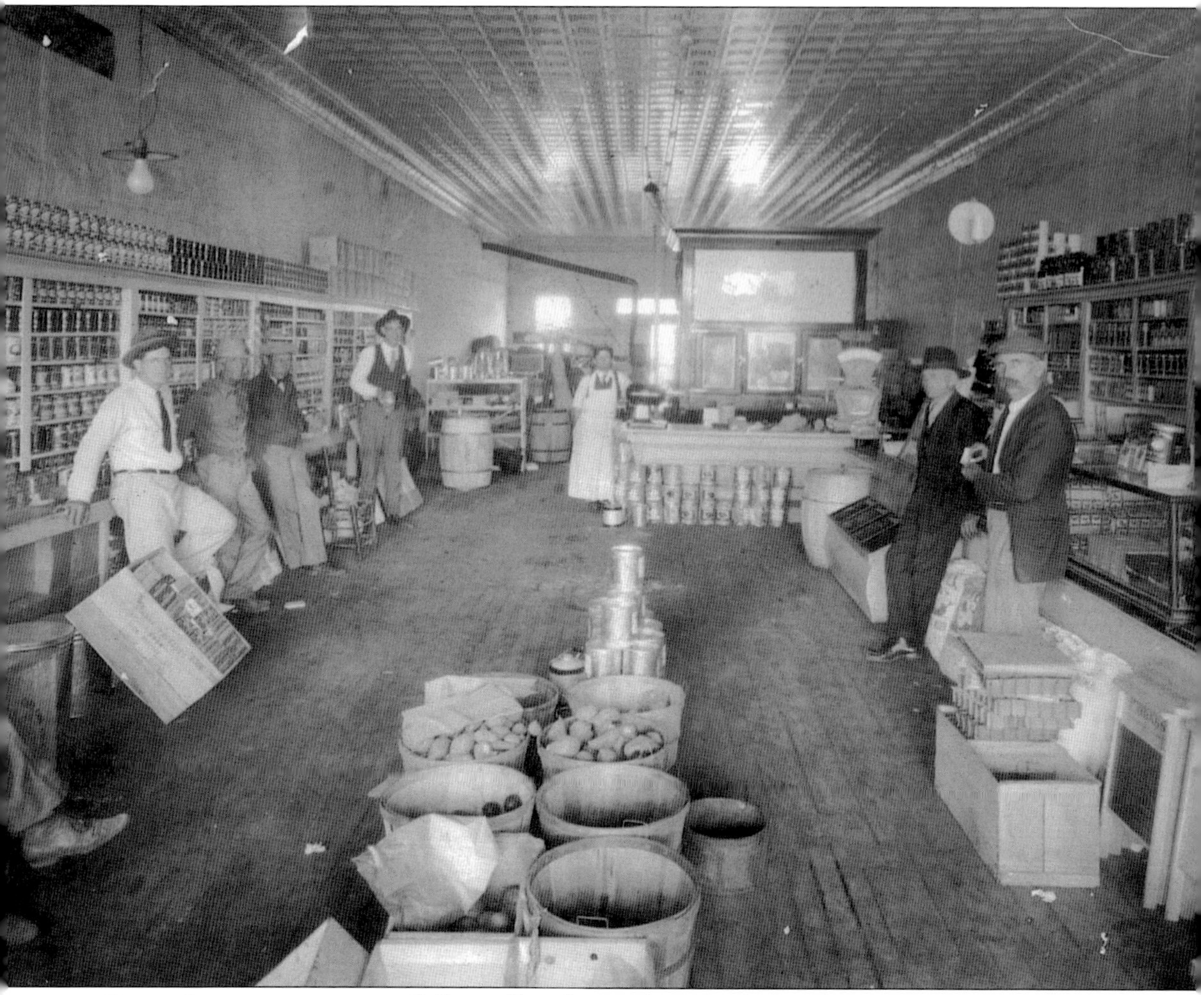

Pictured is a grocery store in Collinsville either in the 1920s before the Great Depression or when things were getting better and folks were pulling out of the Depression. (Cox Land Survey.)

Seven

COLLINSVILLE
SCHOOL DAYS

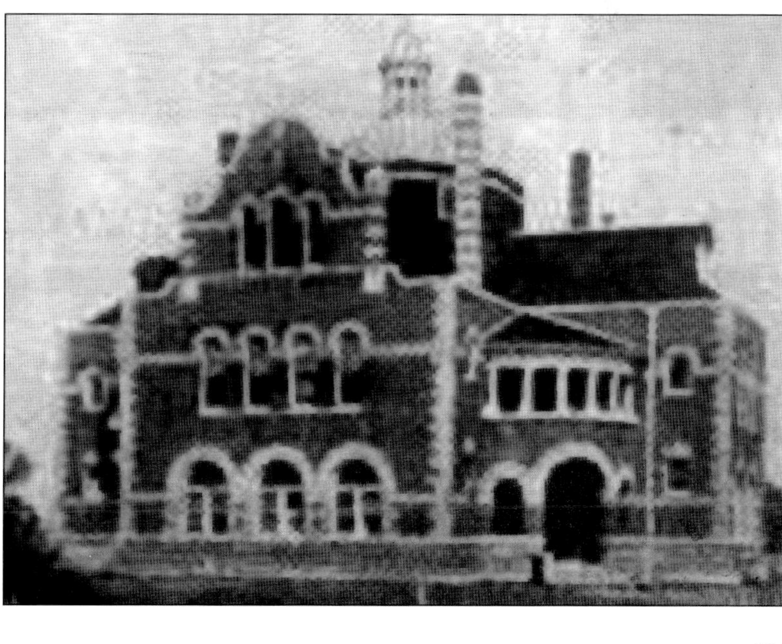

Here is Collinsville Academy that Lodi Collins was instrumental in obtaining. She is the reason Collinsville got its name. Thanks in part to her efforts, Collinsville had the first free school in the state of Texas. (Ken Kemp.)

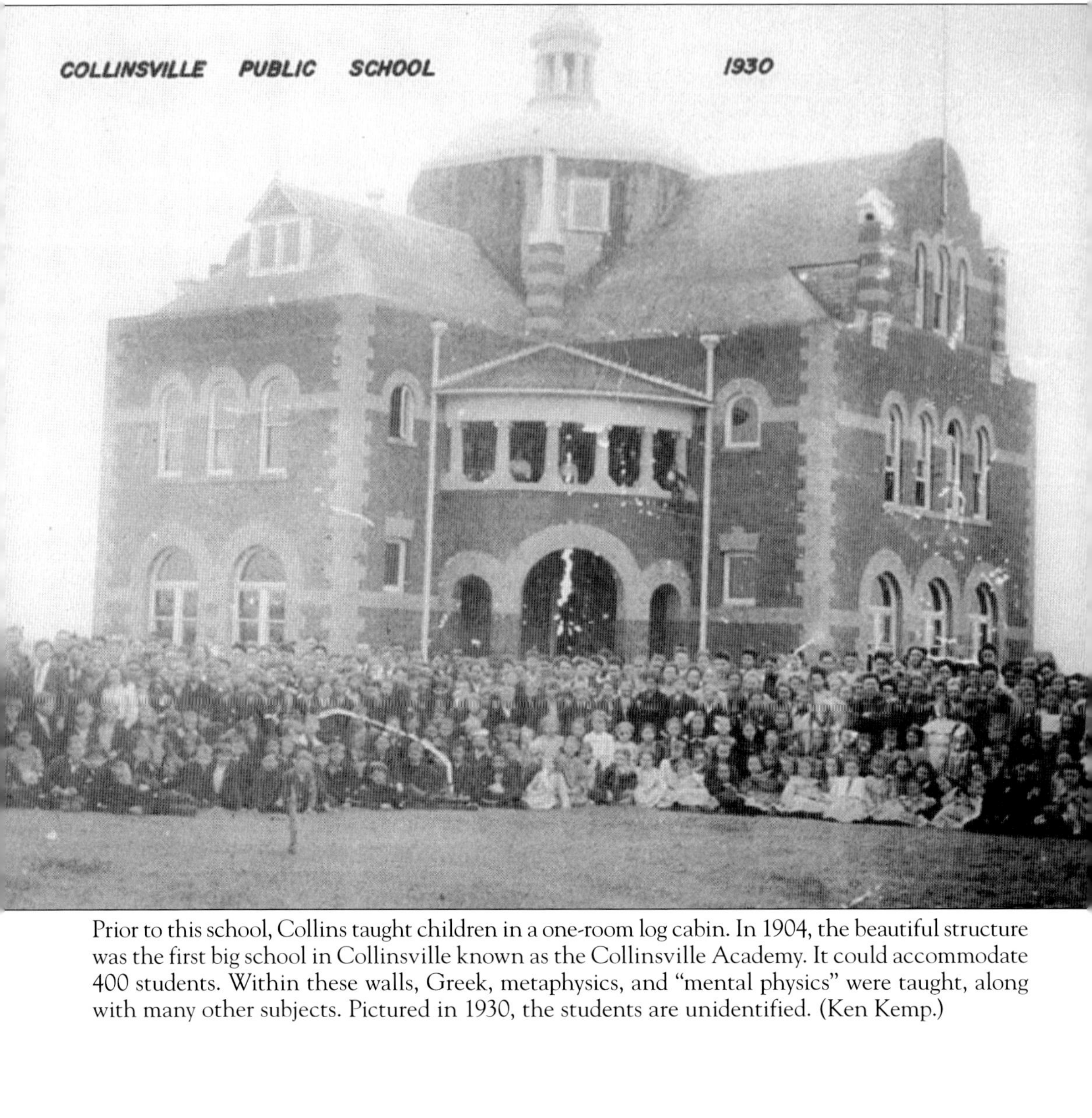

Prior to this school, Collins taught children in a one-room log cabin. In 1904, the beautiful structure was the first big school in Collinsville known as the Collinsville Academy. It could accommodate 400 students. Within these walls, Greek, metaphysics, and "mental physics" were taught, along with many other subjects. Pictured in 1930, the students are unidentified. (Ken Kemp.)

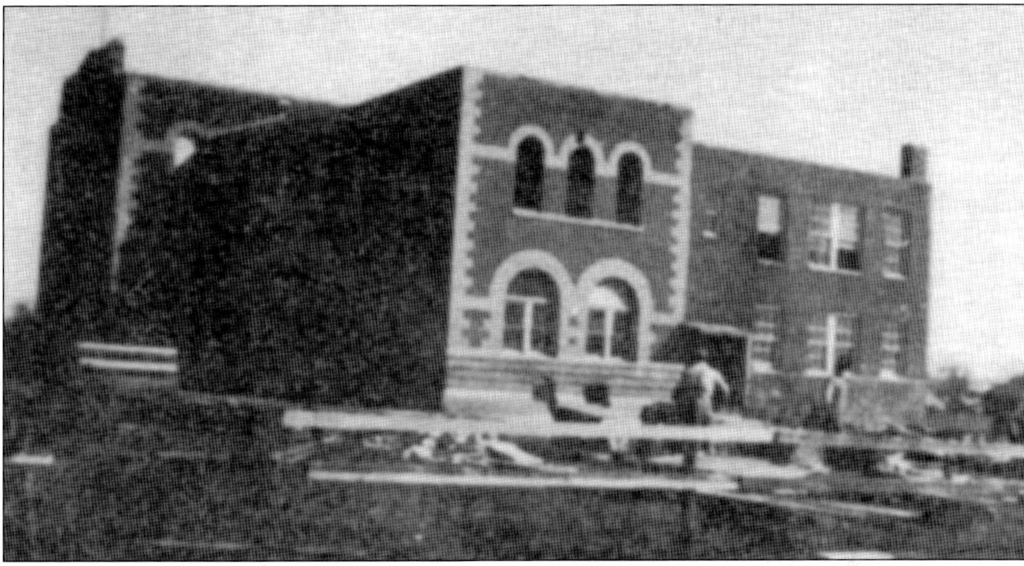

This 1930s image shows remodeling being done after the school caught fire and the whole upper structure fell into the bottom part of the school—Collinsville was devastated. Lodi Collins's son had given land to settlers to help Collinsville grow, and Horatio Waldo had done the same. Collinsville looked as if it were set on a path to become a big city, but the Great Depression almost broke its back. When it burned, it looked like the end of school and maybe Collinsville as well. (Ken Kemp.)

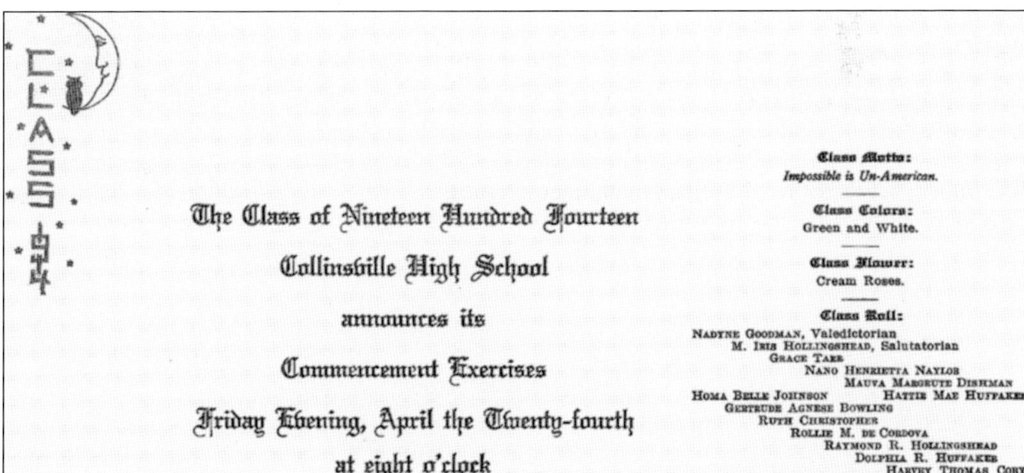

CLASS 1914

The Class of Nineteen Hundred Fourteen
Collinsville High School
announces its
Commencement Exercises
Friday Evening, April the Twenty-fourth
at eight o'clock
Opera House

Class Motto:
Impossible is Un-American.

Class Colors:
Green and White.

Class Flower:
Cream Roses.

Class Roll:
Nadyne Goodman, Valedictorian
M. Iris Hollingshead, Salutatorian
Grace Tarr
Nano Henrietta Naylor
Mauva Margrute Dishman
Homa Belle Johnson
Hattie Mae Huffaker
Gertrude Agnese Bowling
Ruth Christopher
Rollie M. de Cordova
Raymond R. Hollingshead
Dolphia R. Huffaker
Harvey Thomas Coby

Principal, Miss Stella Shelton.
Superintendent, E. R. Benedict.

At the time of this 1914 invitation, things were looking good for Collinsville. Little did residents know that graduation in June would be followed by World War I in July. The world, as well as the town, struggled with this war. Yet, note the motto on the invitation that reads, "Impossible is Un-American." Apparently, rumors of war were already circulating. (Ken Kemp.)

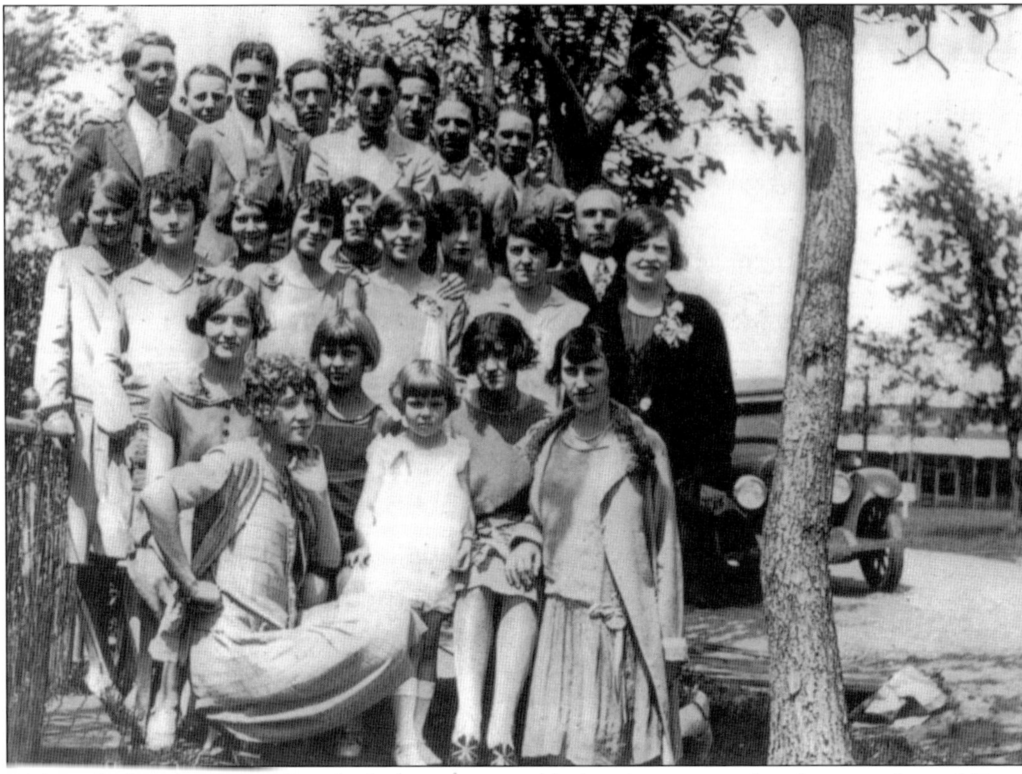

Although this class is unidentified, their dress and hairstyles suggest the photograph could have been taken in the 1920s. Small towns across America were trying to get back on their feet after World War I, and everyone was glad the war was over. This class looks very dapper and ready for the world. (Ken Kemp.)

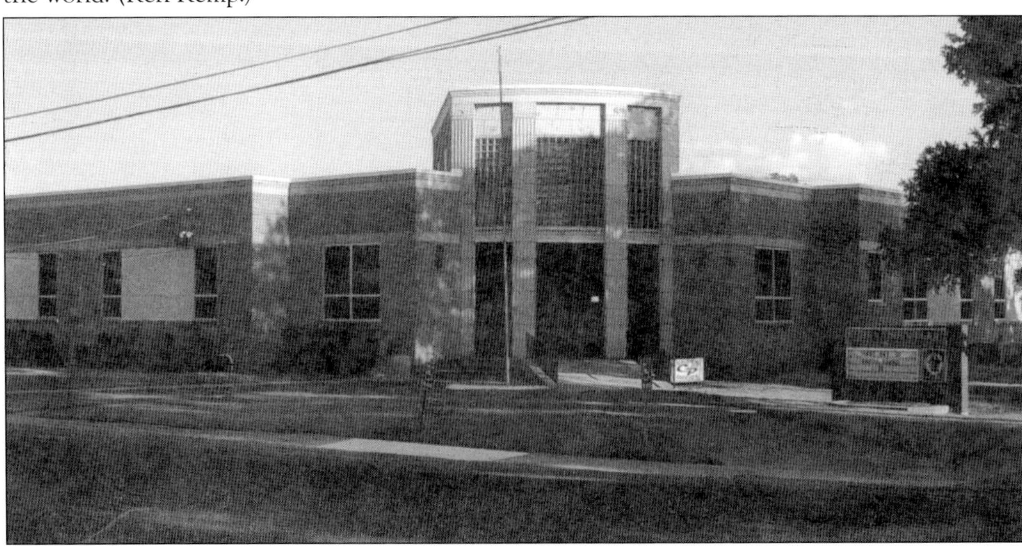

In 1941, work began on Collinsville's new school. Excitement ran through every home in the small town. The Works Progress Administration was responsible for its construction. It was a relief, as the Great Depression, the school fire, and World War II had almost finished Collinsville. (Ken Kemp.)

The 1938 freshman class motto of "green but growing" seems to bolster a positive attitude toward the school days ahead. Students would see the construction of a new school for Collinsville and be the right age when they graduated to be involved in the draft call for World War II. (Ken Kemp and Collinsville ISD.)

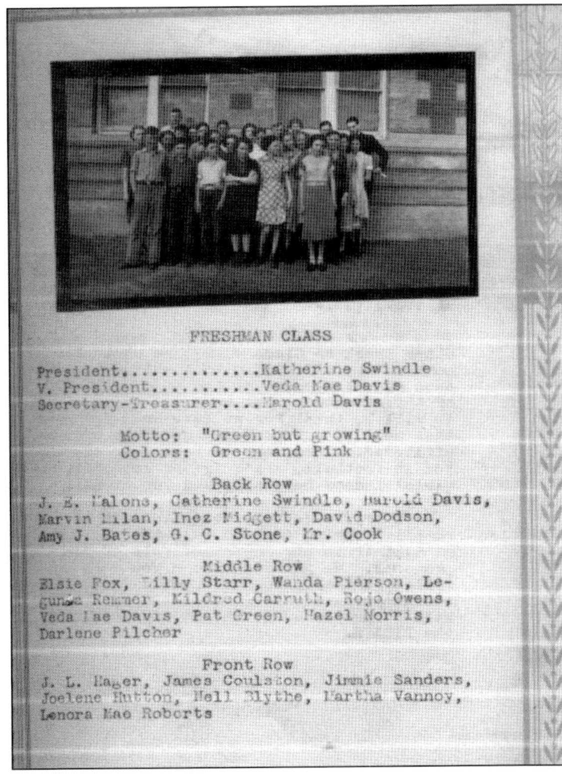

FRESHMAN CLASS

President.............Katherine Swindle
V. President..........Veda Mae Davis
Secretary-Treasurer....Harold Davis

Motto: "Green but growing"
Colors: Green and Pink

Back Row
J. E. Malone, Catherine Swindle, Harold Davis, Marvin Lilan, Inez Midgett, David Dodson, Amy J. Bates, G. C. Stone, Mr. Cook

Middle Row
Elsie Fox, Lilly Starr, Wanda Pierson, Legunde Remmer, Mildred Carruth, Rojo Owens, Veda Mae Davis, Pat Green, Hazel Norris, Darlene Pilcher

Front Row
J. L. Hager, James Coulston, Jimmie Sanders, Joelene Hutton, Nell Blythe, Martha Vannoy, Lenora Mae Roberts

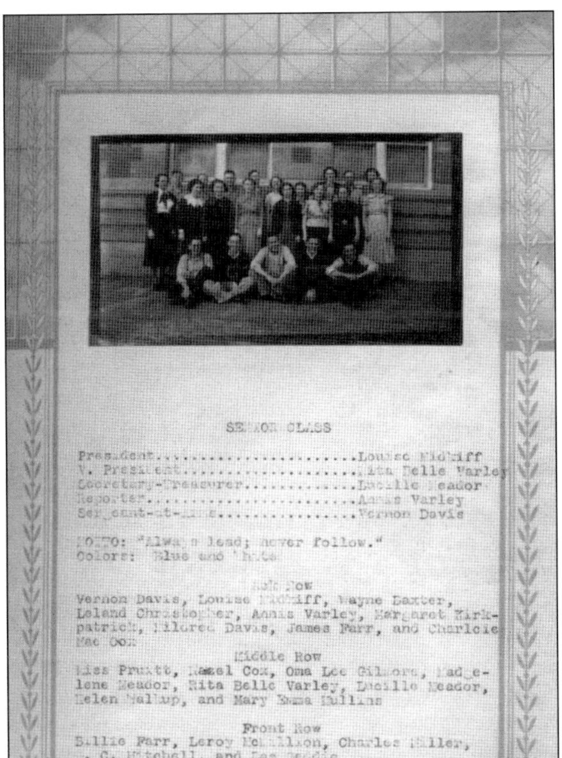

SENIOR CLASS

President......................Louise Midkiff
V. President...................Rita Belle Varley
Secretary-Treasurer............Lucille Meador
Reporter.......................Annis Varley
Sergeant-at-Arms...............Vernon Davis

MOTTO: "Always lead; never follow."
Colors: Blue and White

Back Row
Vernon Davis, Louise Midkiff, Wayne Baxter, Leland Christopher, Annis Varley, Margaret Kirkpatrick, Mildred Davis, James Farr, and Charlcie Mae Cox

Middle Row
Liss Pruitt, Hazel Cox, Oma Lee Gilmore, Madelene Meador, Rita Belle Varley, Lucille Meador, Helen Mallup, and Mary Emma Mullins

Front Row
Billie Farr, Leroy McMillon, Charles Miller, [illegible] C. Mitchell, and [illegible]

This 1938 senior class was still in the old school Lodi Collins had helped build. Students had survived the worst of the Great Depression and were optimistic about their future. (Ken Kemp and Collinsville ISD.)

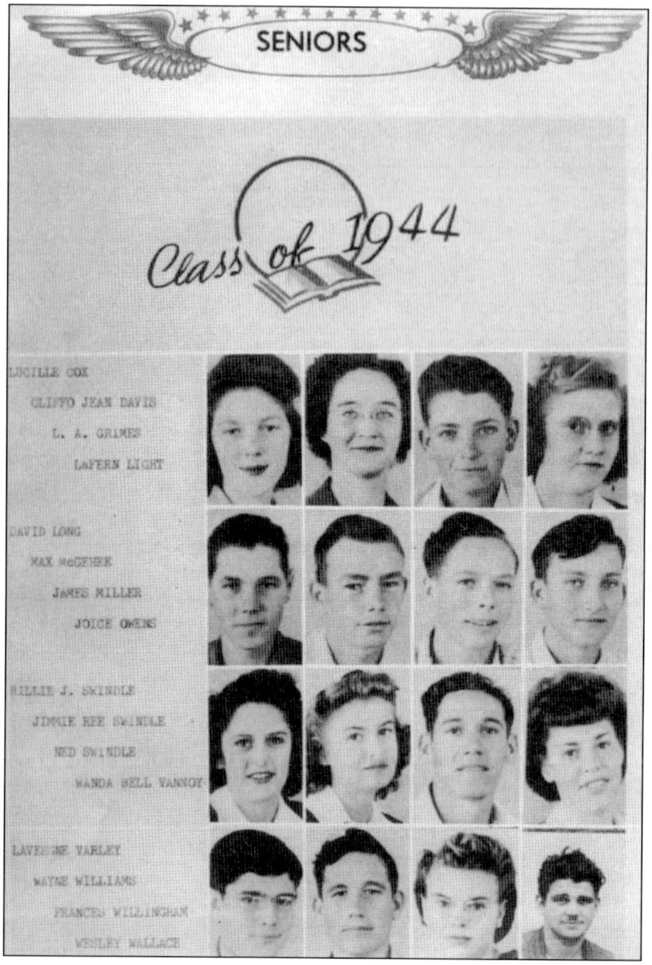

The 1944 graduating class of Collinsville High School was still in the throes of World War II. Male students were at the right age at their graduation to be drafted. This had to be on their minds as they looked toward the future. (Ken Kemp and Collinsville ISD.)

The 1938 girls' basketball team poses on the steps of the original school. Collinsville has always supported the athletic department of its school. The town has always joined in and still plays a big part in the athletics today. (Ken Kemp and Collinsville ISD.)

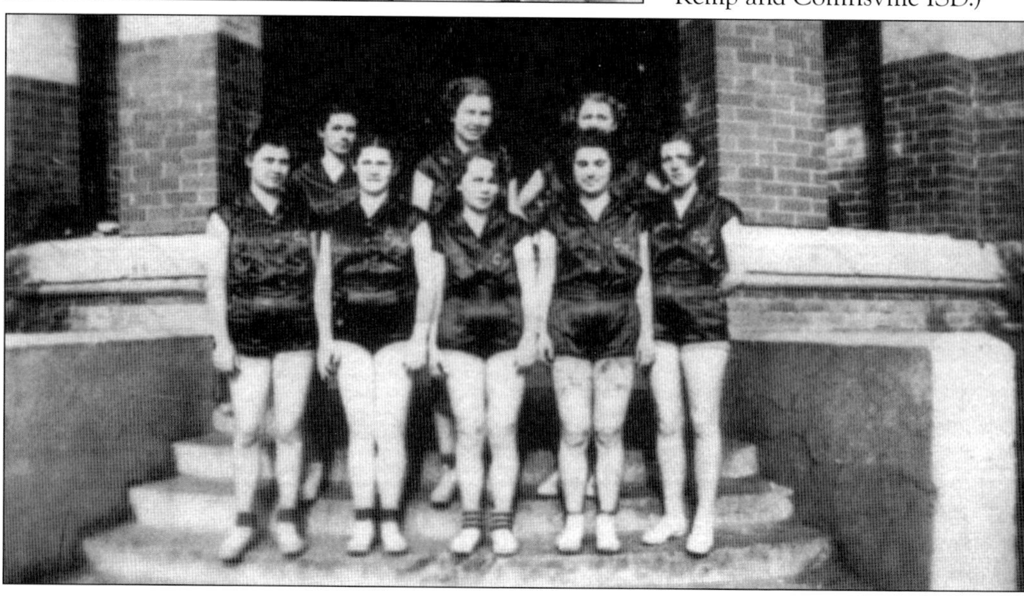

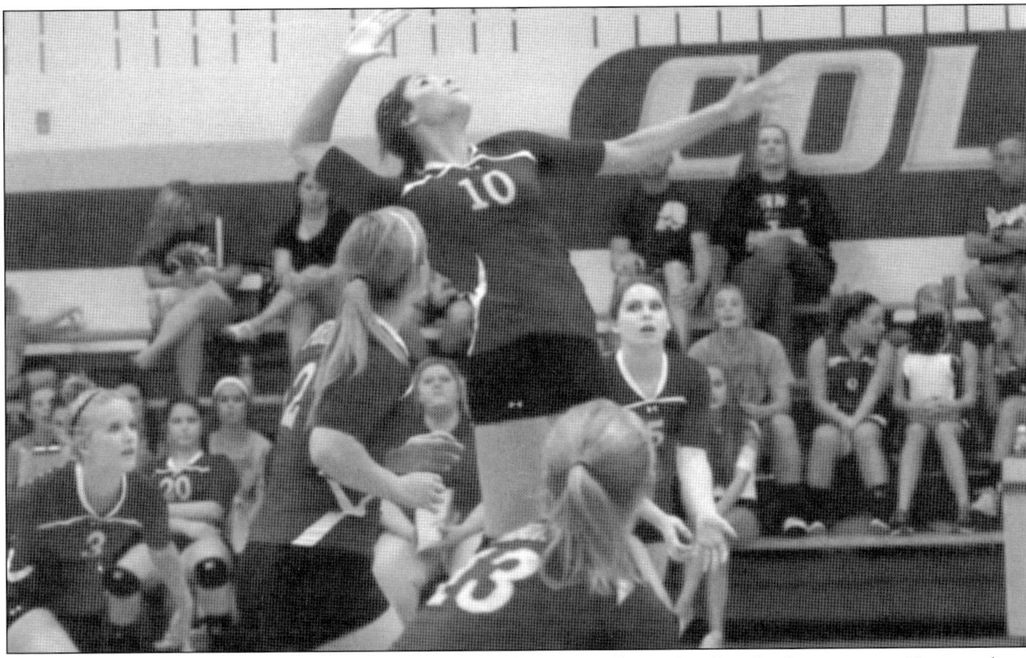

Here, the 2013 girls' volleyball team is engaged in a modern-day battle for victory. Pictured are Brooke Johnson (No. 10) jumping high, Callie Woosley (No. 5) going low, and Holly Theall (No. 13) looking on. Morgan "Mo" Irelan (No. 2) and behind her Emily Dishman (No. 3) are ready for action. The rest of the players are unidentified. (Ken Kemp and Collinsville ISD.)

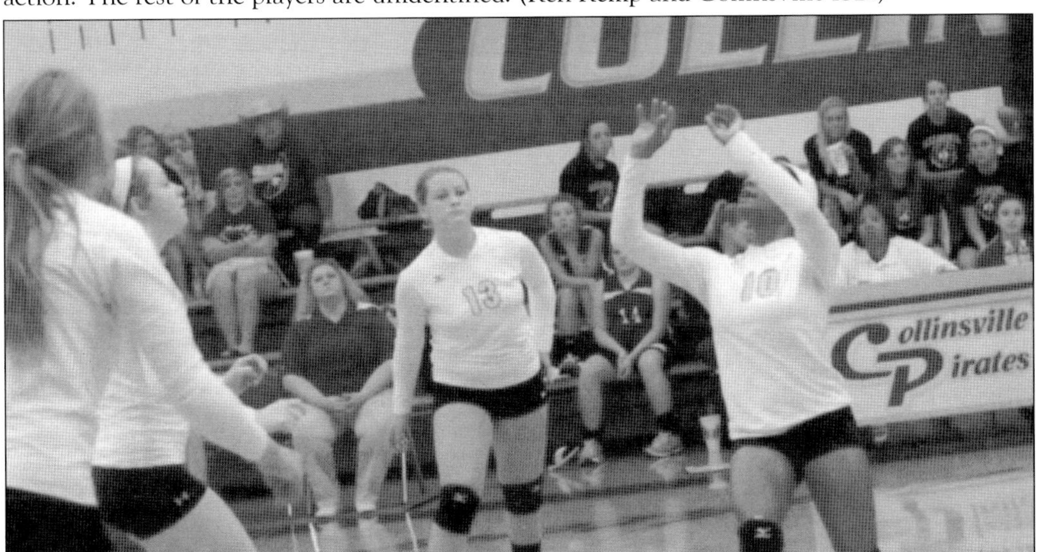

Junior varsity volleyball players Jorey Polly (No. 13) and Michelle Moore (No. 10) are playing hard for victory. (Ken Kemp and Collinsville ISD.)

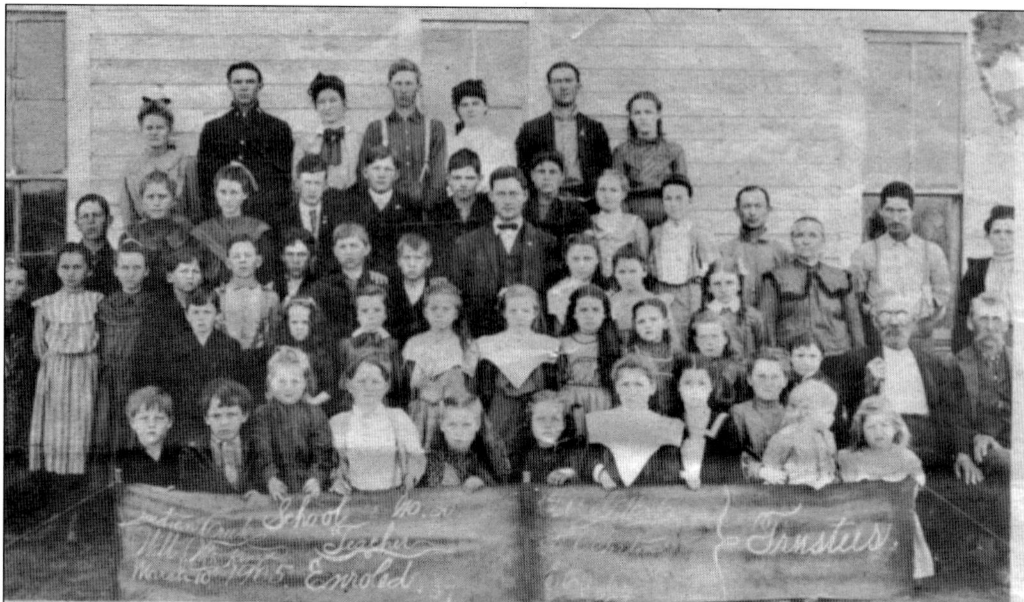

NDIAN CREEK SCHOOL 1905

Top row, left to right:- Daisy Mitchell, Charlie Gilbert, Annie McBride, Marian Allen, Myrtle Gilbert, Jim McBride, Myrtle Dillon. Second row-Bob Fulmer, Ruby Allen, Mollie Moore, Avner Steel, Claude Kaylor, Lee Gilbert, Everett Baxter, Laudie Kaylor, Leta Gordon, Bud Rawlins. Third row-Alma Baxter, Eva Moore, Gertie McBride, Harold Kaylor, Pink Fulmer, Dillon Boy, Scott Baxter, Joe Hardy, Will McKinzie (teacher), Ruth Hall, Lillie Moore, Luella Bryant, Mrs. T. A. Gilbert. Iris Allen. Mrs. Fulmer. Fourth row-Tony Moore, May Hooks, Bryant girl, Thelma Allen, Avis Autry, Edna Gordon, Ollie Autry, Fulmer girl, Cecil Rawlins, T. A. Gilbert, H. O. Gordon. Fifth row-Gordon Autry, unknown, Fulmer girl, Jack Fulmer, Iva Gilbert, Mattie Fulmer, Mable Autry, Bertha Rawlins, Viola Allen, Bernice Allen, Grace Allen. (Picture submitted by Scott Baxter.)

Indian Creek School, which was west of town, joined Collinsville to become a part of Collinsville School. This image was taken in 1905. (James Hilliard.)

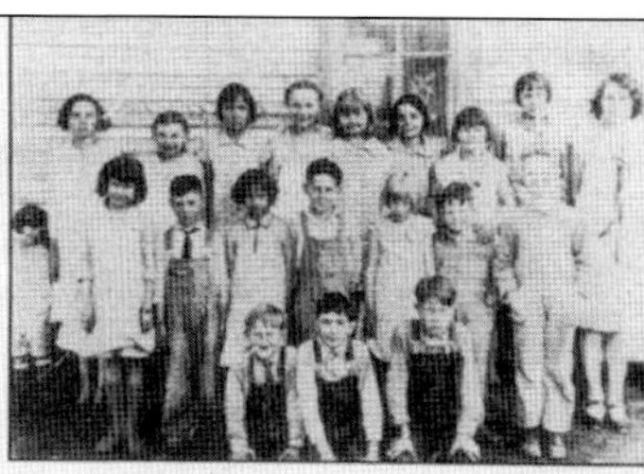

MT. ZION SCHOOL Circa 1928

Front Row L-R: Clarence Walker, James Cox & Clifford Cox

2nd Row L-R: Hazel Cox, Alden Dove, Gladys Dinkens, Joe Conner, Bernice Cox and two sons of Leonard Cox

3rd Row L-R: Merle Dove, Stella Dove, Charlsey Mae Cox, Cleta Fae Conner, Lucy Cox, Blutie Cox, Maudine Conner, Thelma Walker, Jessie Cox and Teacher Evelyn Martin.

****

KNOWN MT. ZION SCHOOL TEACHERS

1898–99	Sam Briggs
1902–03	J. B. King
1907–08	Ethel Osborn
1912–13	Minnie Enderby
1917–18	Mrs. Belle Brown
1922–23	Ruby South
1927–28	Luella Brown
1932–33	Nina Dennis
1934–35	Mr. Harrison (1st Grade)

Mount Zion School had to join Collinsville School in the 1930s. Pictured is the class of 1928. (Ken Kemp.)

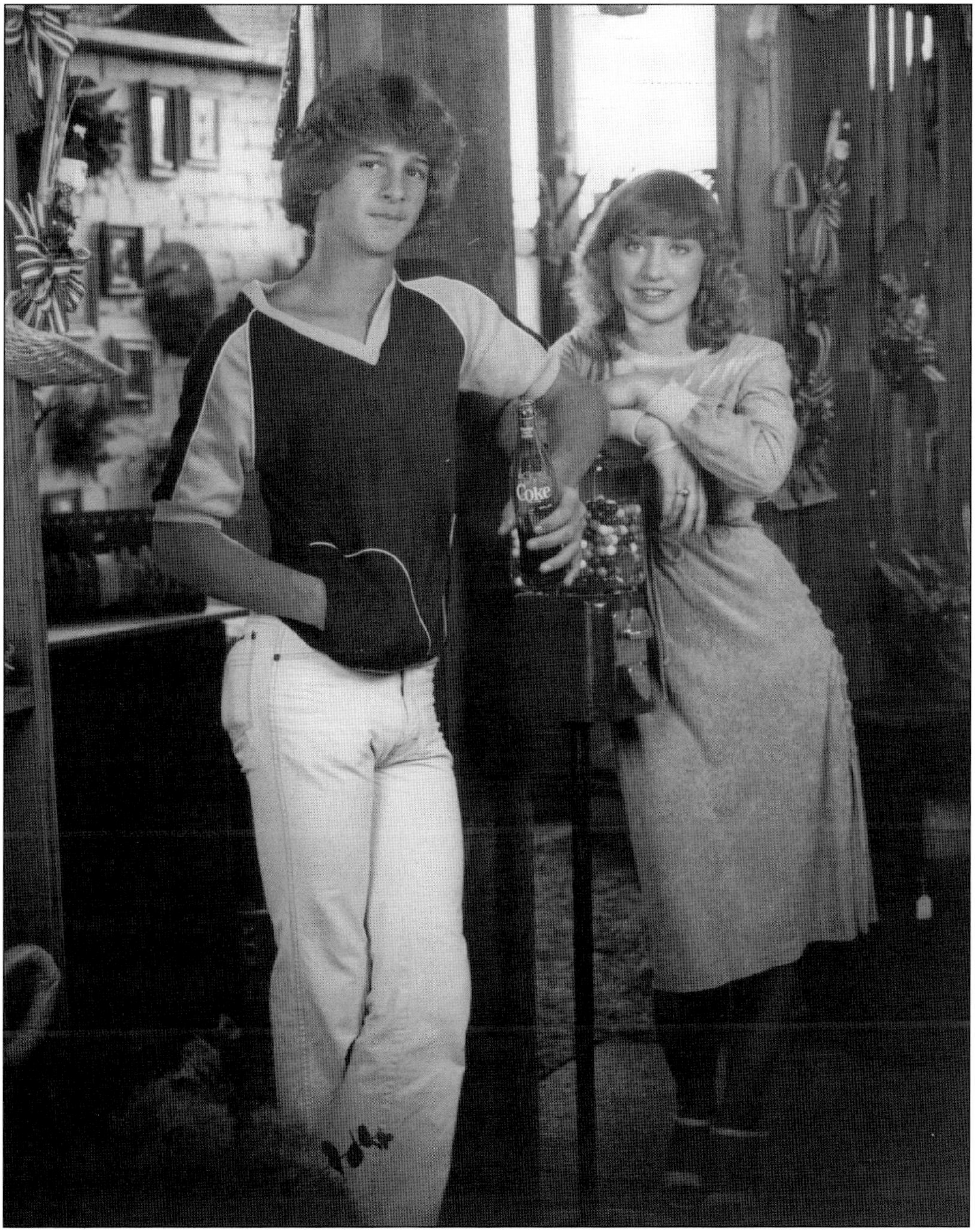

Collinsville High School's most popular male and female students in 1975, Kenny McKnight and Carol Mitchell, are seen here. Carol married Jerry McKnight, and they raised their children—Ben, Hannah, Lydia, and Spencer—in Collinsville. In later years, Carol became mayor of Collinsville. Her grandchildren now attend the schools Carol attended. Roots go deep in this small town. (Ken Kemp.)

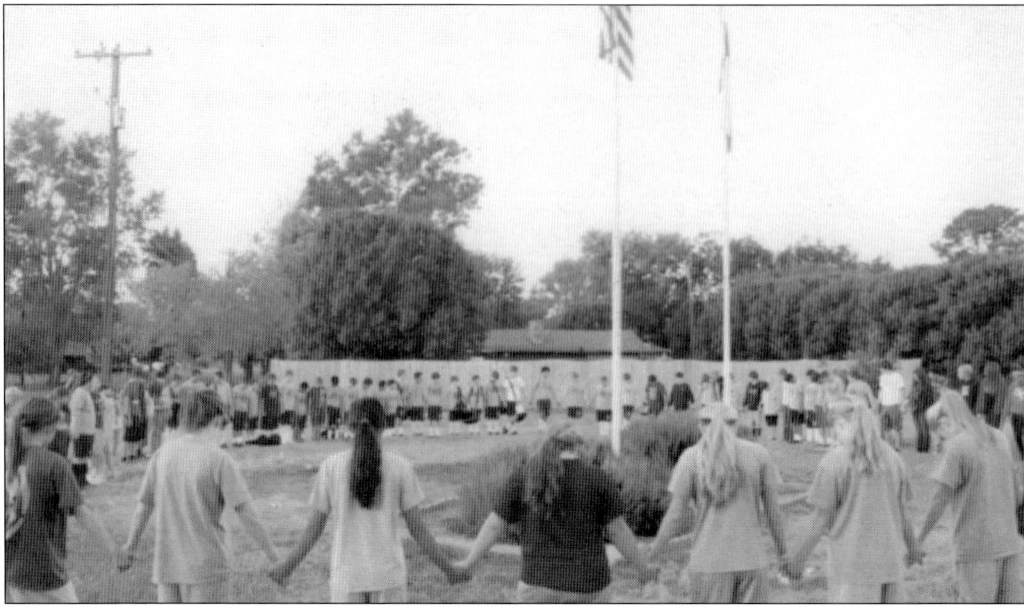

Students of Collinsville Independent School District invoke their first amendment right as they gather around the flagpole in 2013. The community has always held the love for one's God, country, and family in high esteem. (Ken Kemp and Collinsville ISD.)

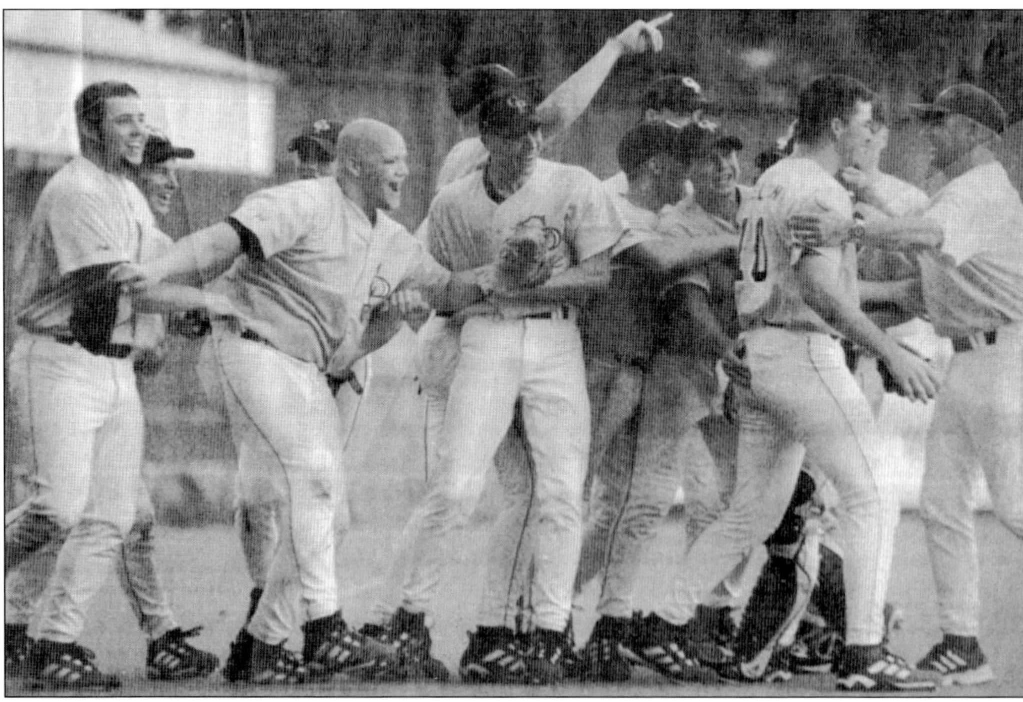

Here the Collinsville High School Pirates baseball team is seen at its finest in the 1990s. The team brought home the state title for their division. Ben McKnight was on this team, who is Carol and Jerry McKnight's son. The school added another trophy to its hall of fame with this championship. (Arvella McKnight.)

Eight

Collinsville Colorful Residents

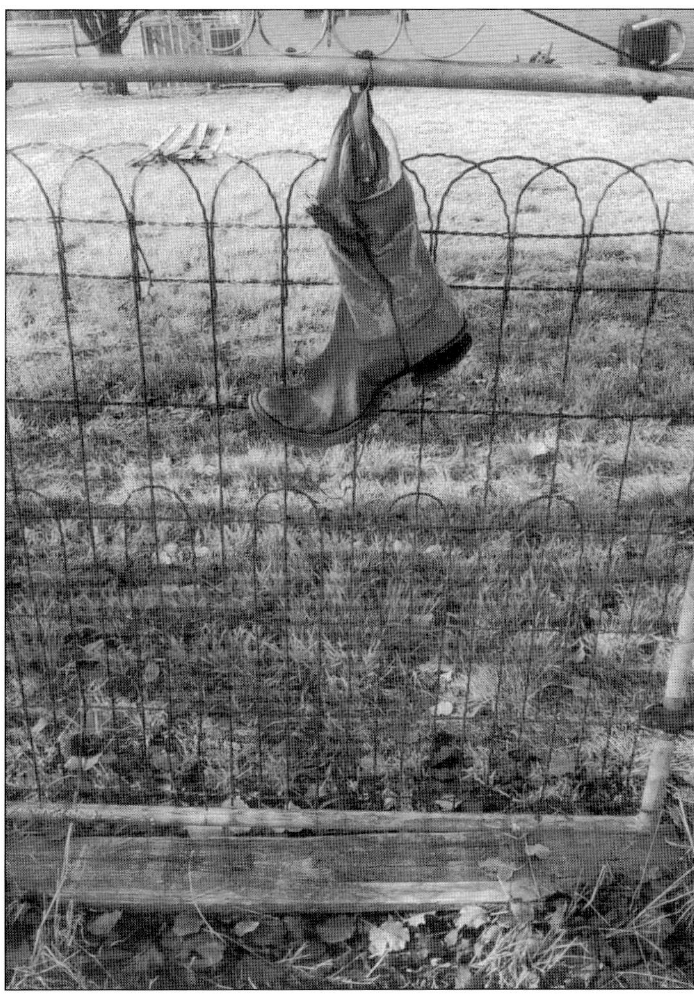

The old gate with a weathered boot is symbolic of the colorful residents who have and do call Collinsville home. They have brought honor, glory, and respect to their hometown. The following pages portray a few of them. (Authors' collection.)

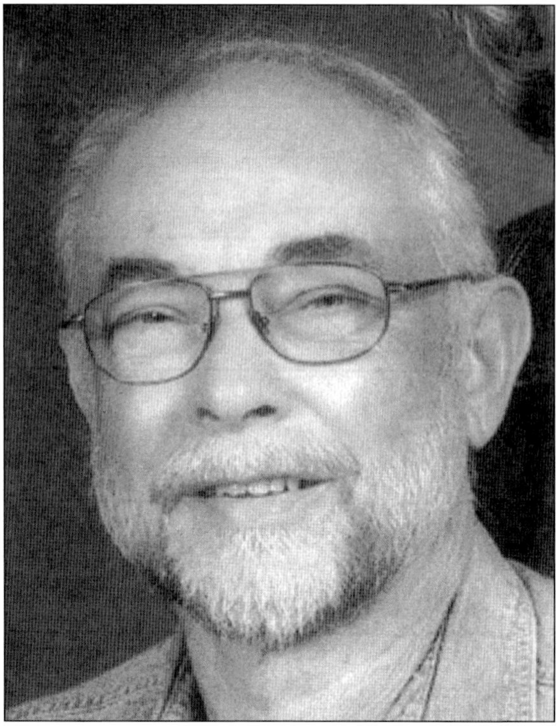

Noel Lewter was a carpenter by trade and a philanthropist by nature. He loved people, places, and things. If Noel did not know a person, he made a point to make him or her his friend. He came to Collinsville at a very young age and lived in the old Bates house, pictured on page 92. He later married Jacquita Hughes, and in 1967 they bought the Harbison house, pictured on page 93. They had three children, Layne, Gina, and Dorsey. (Lewter family.)

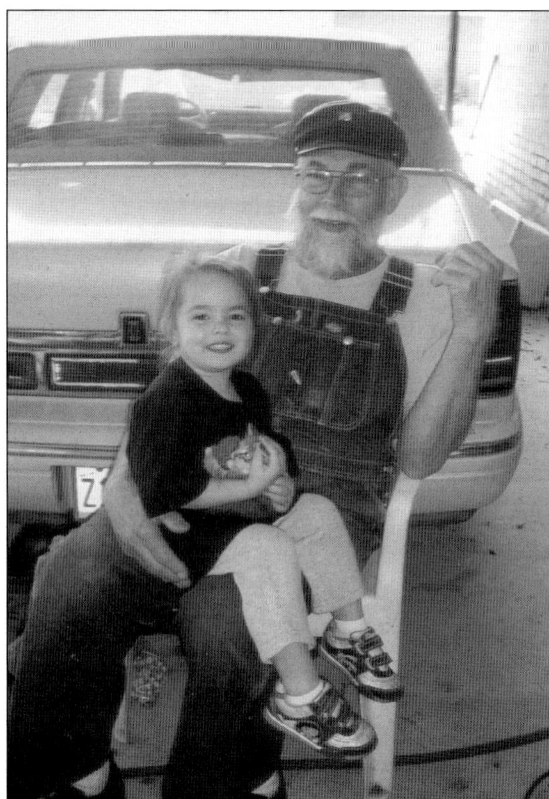

This is the way most people remember Noel Lewter: a big smile, overalls, French farmer cap, and sometimes red suspenders. He spent time in Lewter's Cabinet Shop in Collinsville. He is pictured here with his only granddaughter, Jasmine. In later years, his son Dorsey did most of the cabinetmaking with Noel supervising. Dorsey still conducts business there and is as good a carpenter as his father. Noel's oldest son, Layne, and his wife, Carrie, run the Pirate Island across the street, where good meals feed many Collinsville people. Noel passed away in 2013. Collinsville lost an ambassador, and he is greatly missed. (Lewter family.)

Neil Jones resides just outside Collinsville city limits on his La Cima ranch. He came to Collinsville in 1984 because of the sandy soil; he was sick of the black dirt and mud. La Cima translates to "top," and Neil certainly has accomplished that. His weathered countenance tells of days past when his journey was on the back of a cutting horse. He rode and sold cutting horses of fame. The walls and shelves of his home are loaded with trophies that he and his wife, Lee, have won. Racehorses and jumping horses have also called La Cima home and have credentials to prove their value. Lee passed away in 2012 and is interred just south of the main house in the family plot on top of a hill. (Neil Jones.)

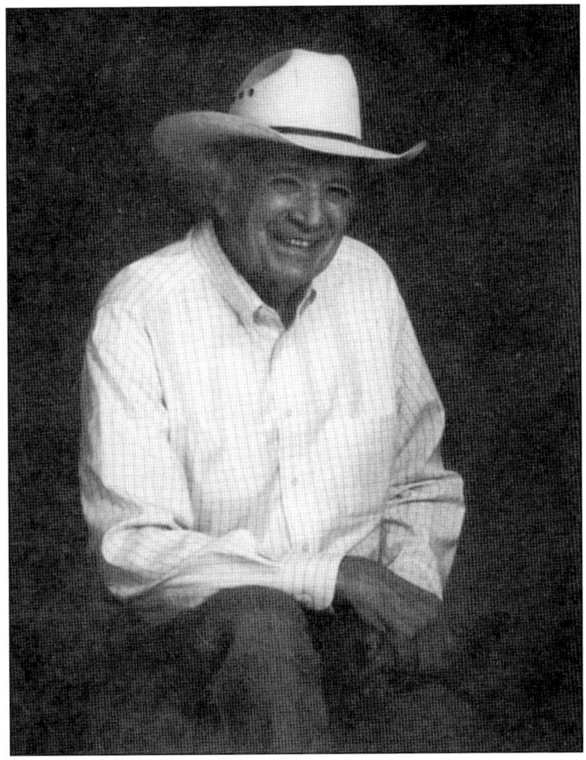

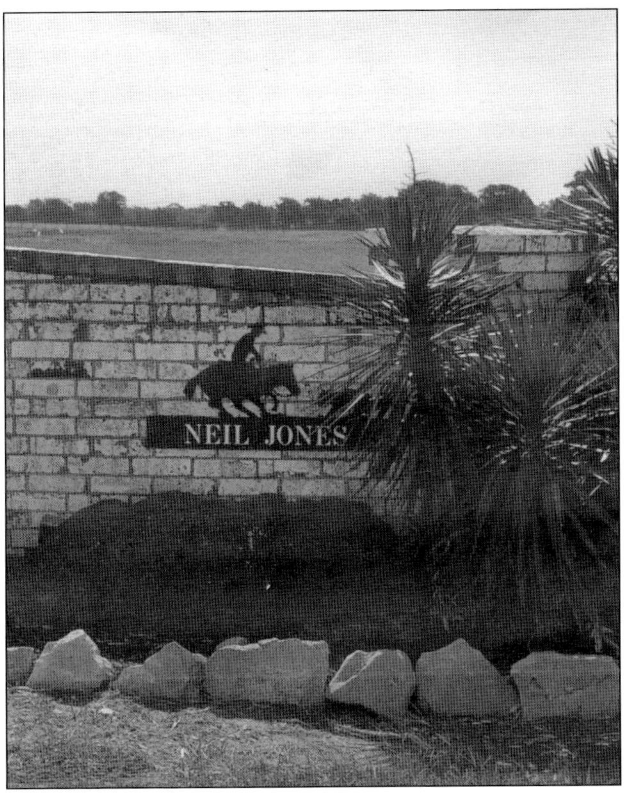

This is the entrance is to La Cima ranch where Long Horn cattle graze peacefully in the front pasture. Guests travel a curving drive to the ranch house on top of the hill, where pets and a tall, slow-talking cowboy greet visitors. Horses graze in several pastures that surround the ranch house, and trees offer shade on a hot summer day. People are invited to have a tall glass of sweet ice tea and enjoy the view from the top with Collinsville's Neil Jones, a real Texas Cowboy. (Authors' collection.)

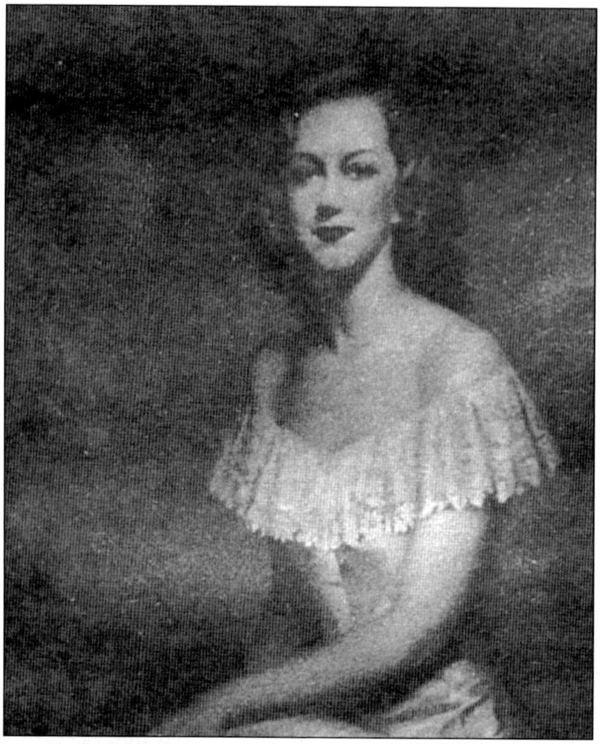

Lee Richardson Jones was a true Southern belle raised in Richmond, Virginia. Her love of jumping horses began at a very young age, and it love remained throughout her life. In younger years, Lee was somewhat of a socialite. Greta Kempton, an artist who painted presidents, did this painting. The one she painted of Harry Truman still hangs in the White House. In 1987, Kempton's paintings, called "Greta Kempton, 40 Years on Canvas," were on exhibit at the Harry Truman Library in Independence, Missouri. This 36-inch-by-46-inch painting of Lee was in that impressive collection. To be painted by Kempton was almost by invitation only. Lee, though, was a friend of Drucie Snyder, who was the daughter of Secretary of Treasury John Wesley Snyder, and Drucie was a personal friend of Margaret Truman, daughter of the president. (Neil Jones.)

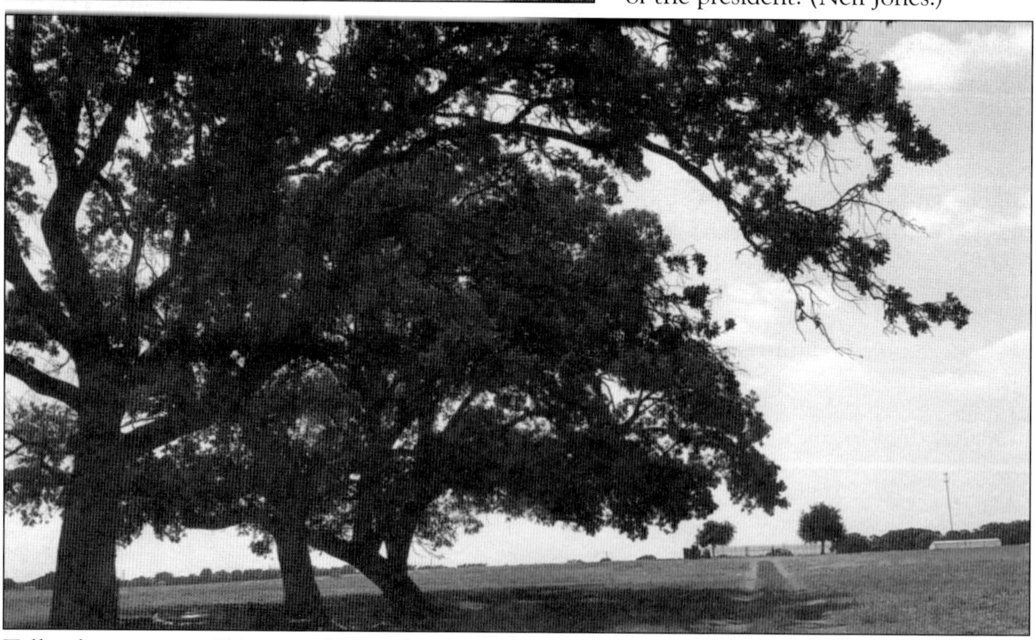

Tall oak trees over 100 years old stand as sentinels to the gate that leads to La Cima's cemetery. The road ends at a beautiful iron fence that surrounds the gravesite of Lee Jones. From Highway 377, travelers might wonder what is up on the hill where three trees and a beautiful cross stand regally watching over the countryside. Horses appropriately reinforce the sentinels on duty as they peacefully graze around the family plot. Lee picked the spot while she was alive. Now, she rests peacefully at the "top" of the hill. (Authors' collection.)

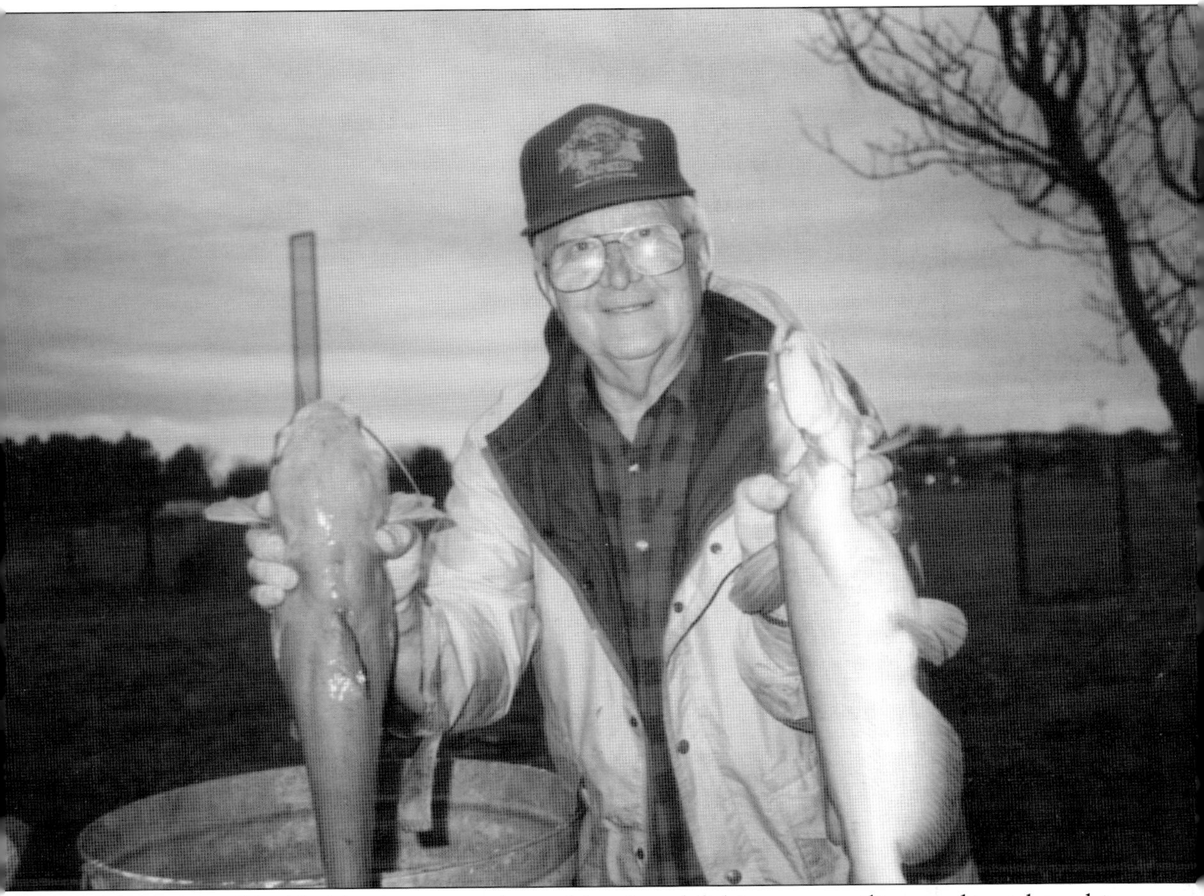

Tom Byrom, "Daddy Tom" as many knew him, loved fishing, parasailing, and watching his grandchildren play sports. He was not embarrassed to loudly disagree with a referee if they made a call against one of his grandchildren that he did not agree with. He supported the Collinsville high School Pirates at every game he could attend. He smiled often and loved with all his being. He arrived in Collinsville in the early 1990s, but he was born and raised in the surrounding area of Aubrey. Tom served 20 years in the US Air Force and then served 20 years as a field representative for the Veterans Administration. His love of gospel music and the Texas Rangers was only outdone by the love for his Lord, wife, children, grandchildren, and his church. He served the community by helping any and all who needed a hand up. He passed away in 2013. All who knew him miss him, and the Collinsville community appreciated him. (Byrom family.)

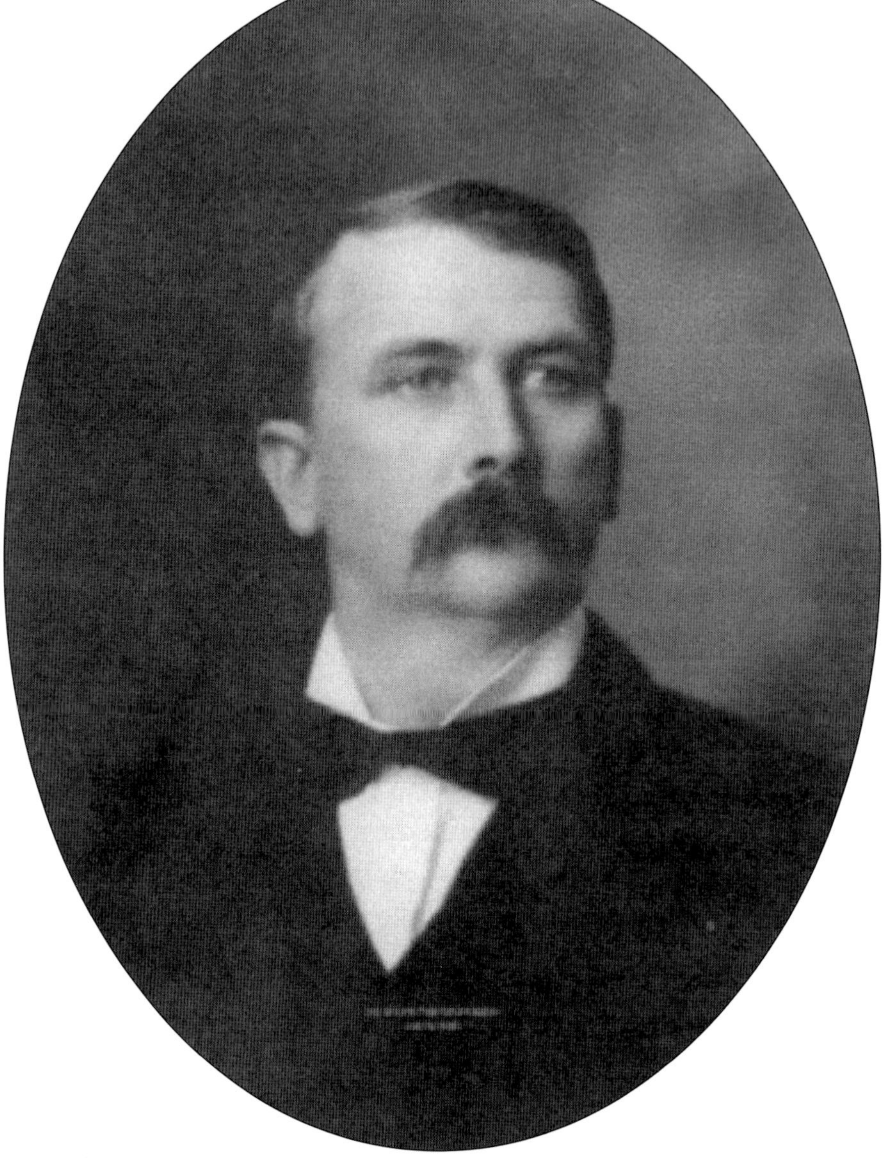

James Lee Harbison was born in 1860 in Arkansas, five years before the end of the Civil War. He left Arkansas at an early age and came to Texas to teach school. He settled in Collinsville in 1886. He helped create the town by constructing several brick buildings to be used for commercial purposes. He married Hattie Belle Lamb at the Collinsville church in 1888. They had one son and seven daughters. It is probable that he built the Harbison house, found on page 22. The Harbisons lived in that house for over 40 years. In 1903, he drew a two-year term in the Texas Legislature. In 1905, he became a senator for the 29th Legislature, and then in the 30th Legislature he remained as senator. He served as a senator from Grayson County for over eight years. During his life, he was an editor of the *Collinsville Times*, a merchant, and a senator of Texas. Nowhere does legend state that he helped Collinsville get the first free school, but his background was conducive to this, and he did go to the legislature in 1903. Apparently, he was a well-educated, resourceful man.

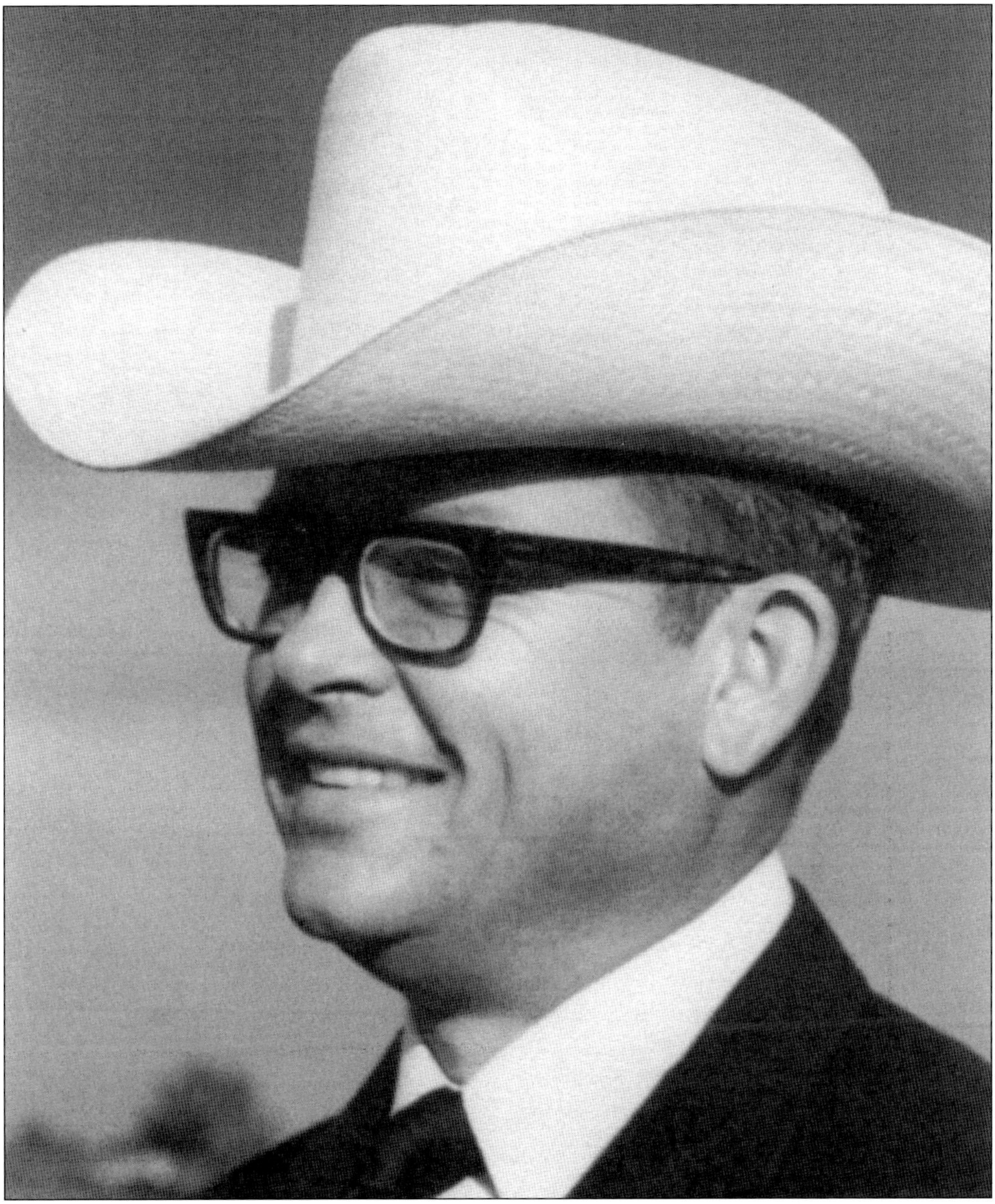

Joe Turner Jr. was a busy man. He bought a farm in Collinsville, located on Southmayd Road, in 1972 from Mamie Bryan; however, he did not get to move to his farm until 1983. During that time, he continued to work for the Corrigan-Jordan family in Dallas. His tenure there would span 40 years, and he became president of InterCity Investments. He was married to Norma Turner for 53 years, and they had three daughters: Cindy, Cathy, and Sally. Cathy still resides in Collinsville area with her husband, Ronnie Weems. Joe had a business degree from Southern Methodist University and served in the US Army. He was a lifetime member First United Methodist Church and was on its building and finance committees. He joined up with Bob Rheudasil and Bob Light in starting a tree farm in Collinsville. He was cofounder and president of the Texas Quarter Horse Association Heritage Center. (Cathy Weems.)

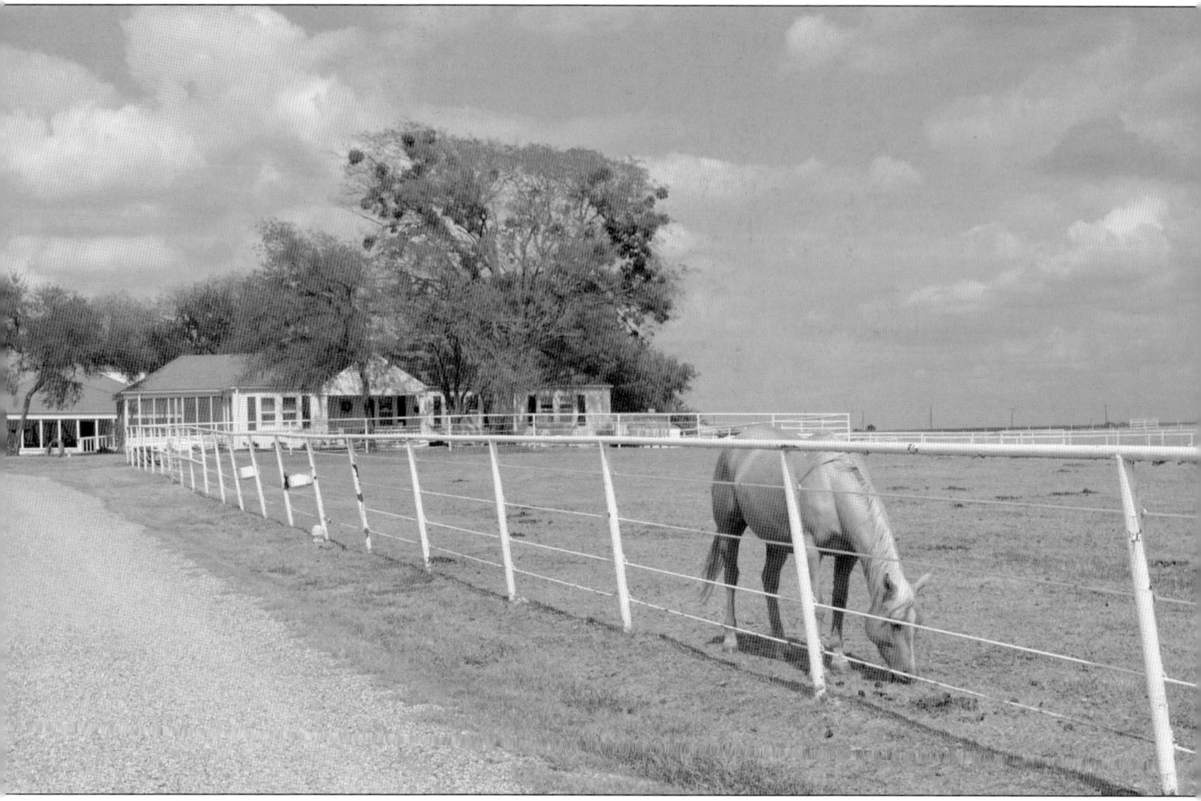

Joe and Norma named their ranch in Collinsville Turner Farms. Many fine Quarter horses came from this ranch and were raced all over the United States. Trophies lined the walls and shelves of the stables, and Joe continued his work in helping others. He was president of Big Brothers in Dallas, was cofounder and served on the board of the Retina Foundation of the Southwest, and was a Texoma Medical Center Foundation board member. In 1998, working with Chico Light, Ricky Patterson, Kevin Hale, Tom Anderson, and Mark Henry (superintendent of CISD at the time), they created the Collinsville Education Foundation. In his spare time, Joe enjoyed his family, the ranch, and his horses. The Turner family and their many friends enjoyed countless happy days on this farm. Part of the house is an old farmhouse that the present home is built around. Maime Bryan's husband, it is believed, built the original house for her. The present owners have named the ranch the Rockin M. Their children's laughter now reverberates throughout the ranch. Registered Charolais cattle graze the pastures where Quarter horses once called home. (Authors' collection.)

Nine

Collinsville
Collinsville Today

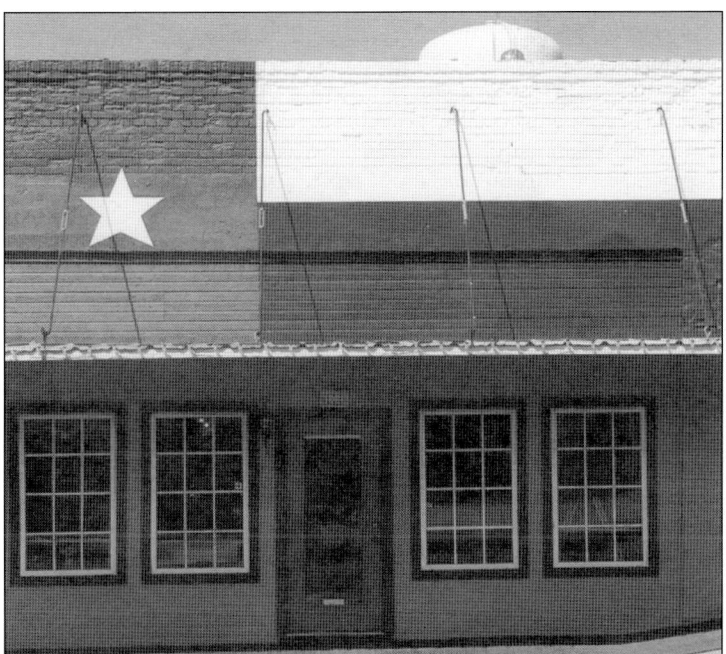

The Texas flag decorates the exterior of Cox Land and Survey Company. Cox is located on Main Street in Collinsville and has probably been a part of the metes and bounds of most places located anywhere near the town. Don Cox and his ancestors have been in and around Collinsville a long time. Many of their images were loaned to the author to use in this book. Inside the office are many old photographs of the area. The folks in the office are always nice and friendly, welcoming visitors with smiles. (Authors' collection.)

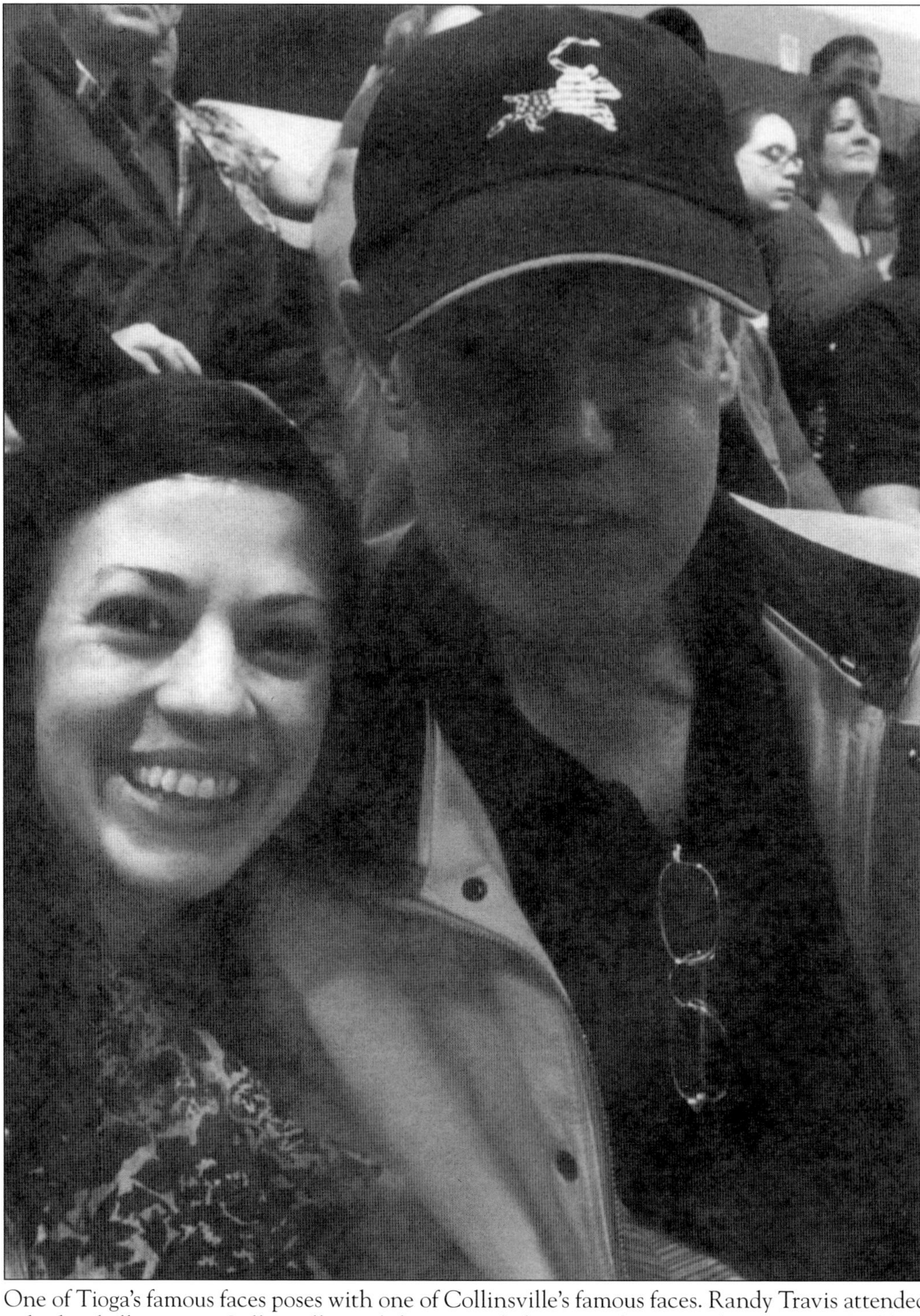

One of Tioga's famous faces poses with one of Collinsville's famous faces. Randy Travis attended a donkey ball game in Collinsville, and this young lady, Hannah McKnight Martin, asked him to pose with her, which he graciously did in 2012. She may not be as famous as Travis, but she is well known in Collinsville where she grew up. (Authors' collection.)

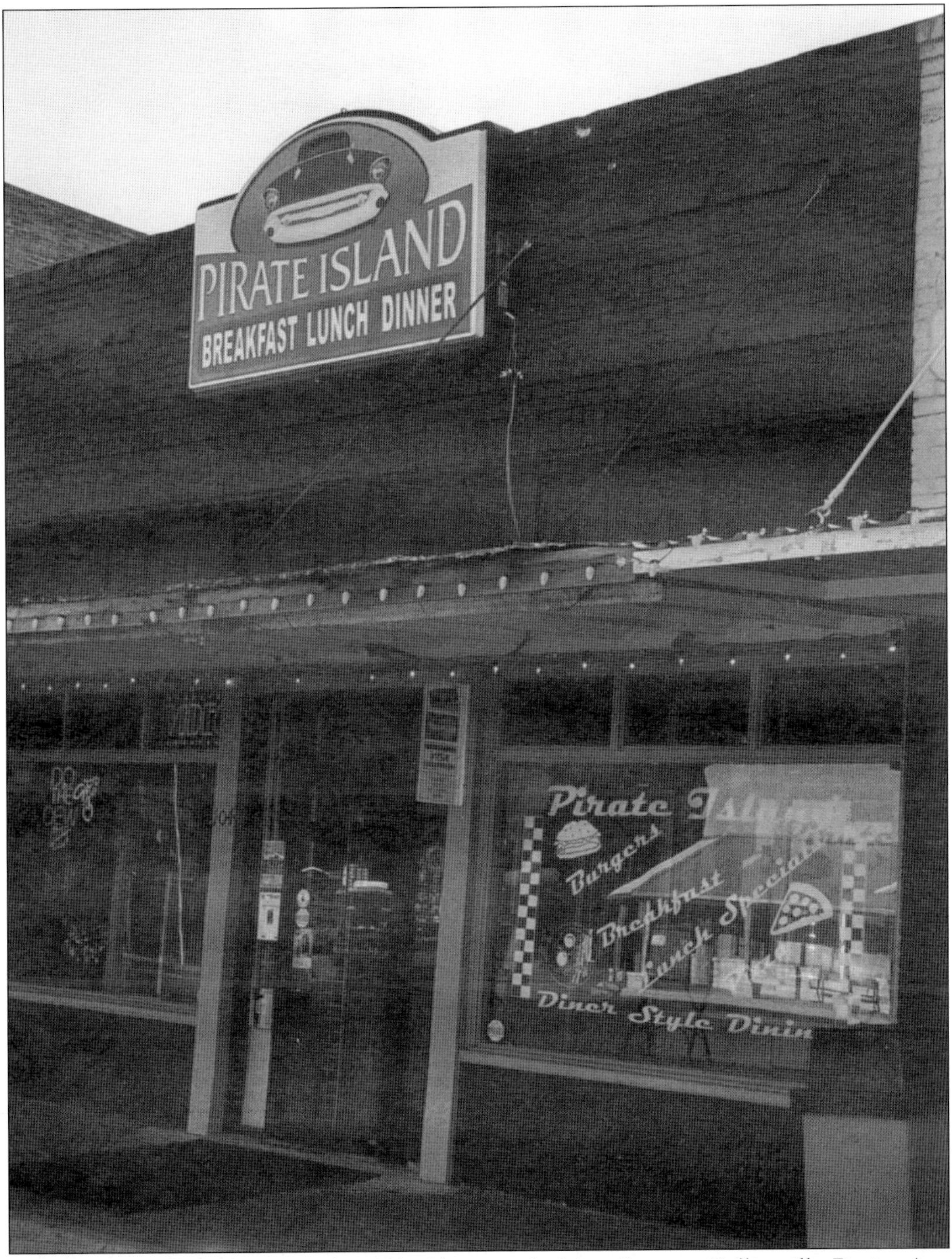

Pirate Island is located in one of the old buildings on the Main Street in Collinsville. During Any hometown ball game, Pirate Island will be open. Layne and Carrie Lewter own and operate this establishment. It is not just an eatery, but it is also a place to rent videos or purchase a memento for a special occasion. Layne is the son of Jacquita and Noel Lewter, and so he knows everyone in town because he grew up here. Pirate Island's walls are covered in old images of the town's past and cars of all kinds. Here, one can get an old-fashioned ice cream float. (Authors' collection.)

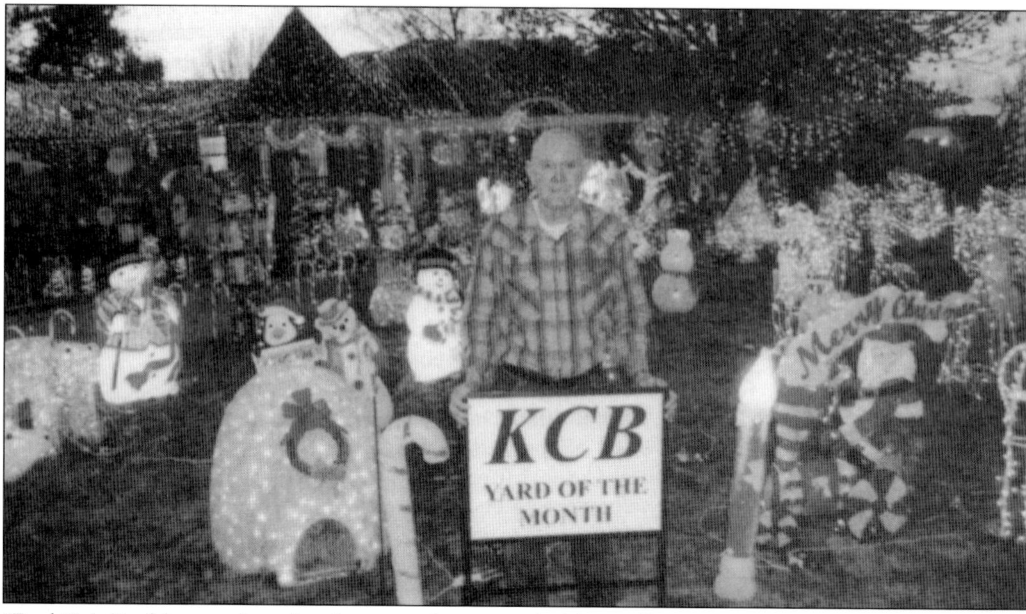

"Red "McCorkle stands in his front yard surrounded by millions of Christmas lights he puts up every Christmas season. Note the sign stating he was awarded Collinsville Yard of the Month. Often, the only time when there is traffic in Collinsville is when Red turns on the Christmas lights. He starts every year right after Thanksgiving and works until all the lights are up. His children have long since left, and Red lives alone. He enjoys knowing that others appreciate the Christmastime lights. He attends almost every ball game of any kind that the Collinsville High School Pirates play. He supports the youth and the school in his hometown. (Red McCorkle.)

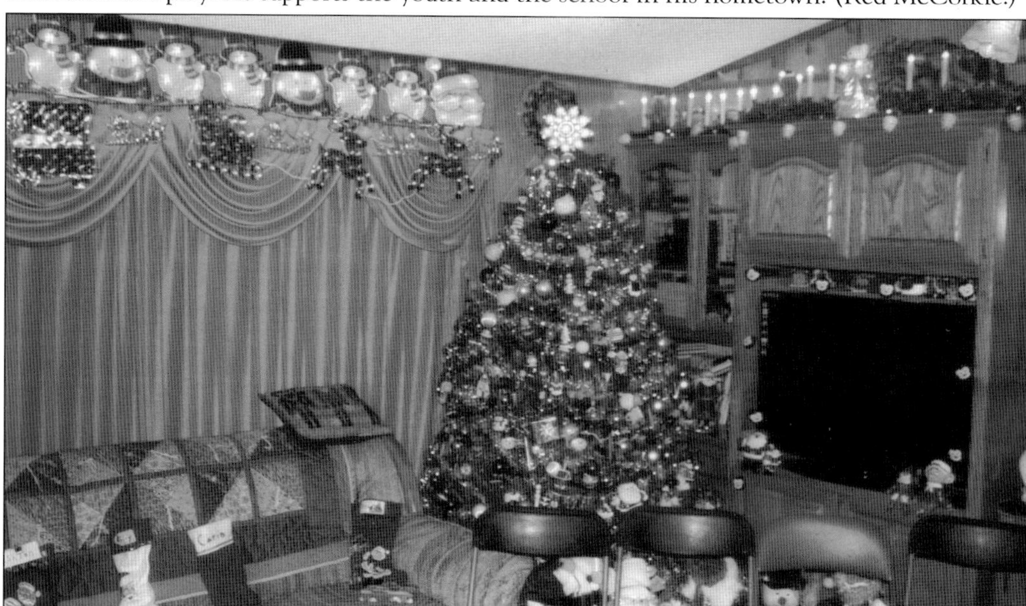

Red not only decorates the outside of his home, but the inside also gets a dose of Christmas spirit. His living room is full of lights, and a majestic Christmas tree is decorated to the hilt. Light floods the room; merriment is felt throughout the home and spreads through the entire neighborhood. This is December in Collinsville, Texas. (Red McCorkle.)

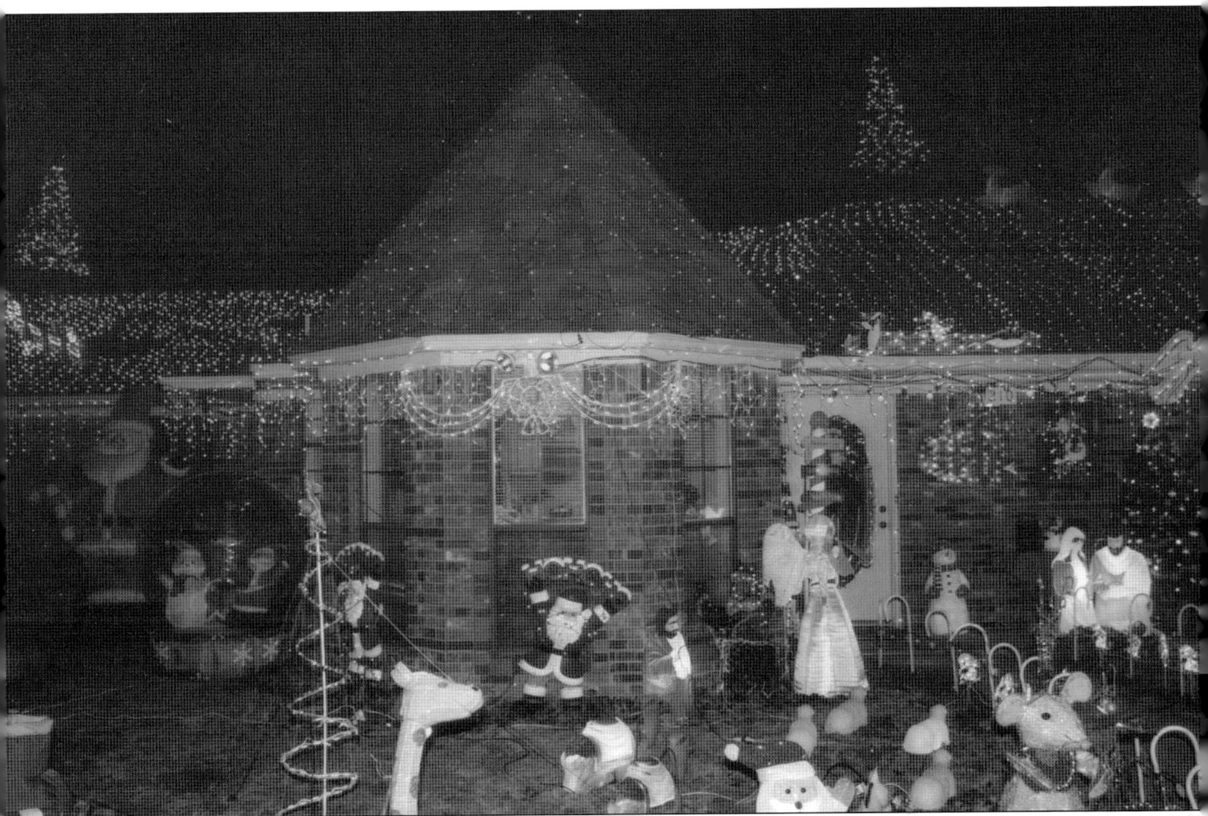

The night is filled with starry wonderment. When asked if his light bill increases in December, Red just chuckles. Of note is that Red does not leave up any lights after Christmas. He removes them and packs them away for another 11 months. If residents of Collinsville were asked if they would object to Red McCorkle leaving his lights up all year, the majority would most likely reply, "No, I would love it." (Red McCorkle.)

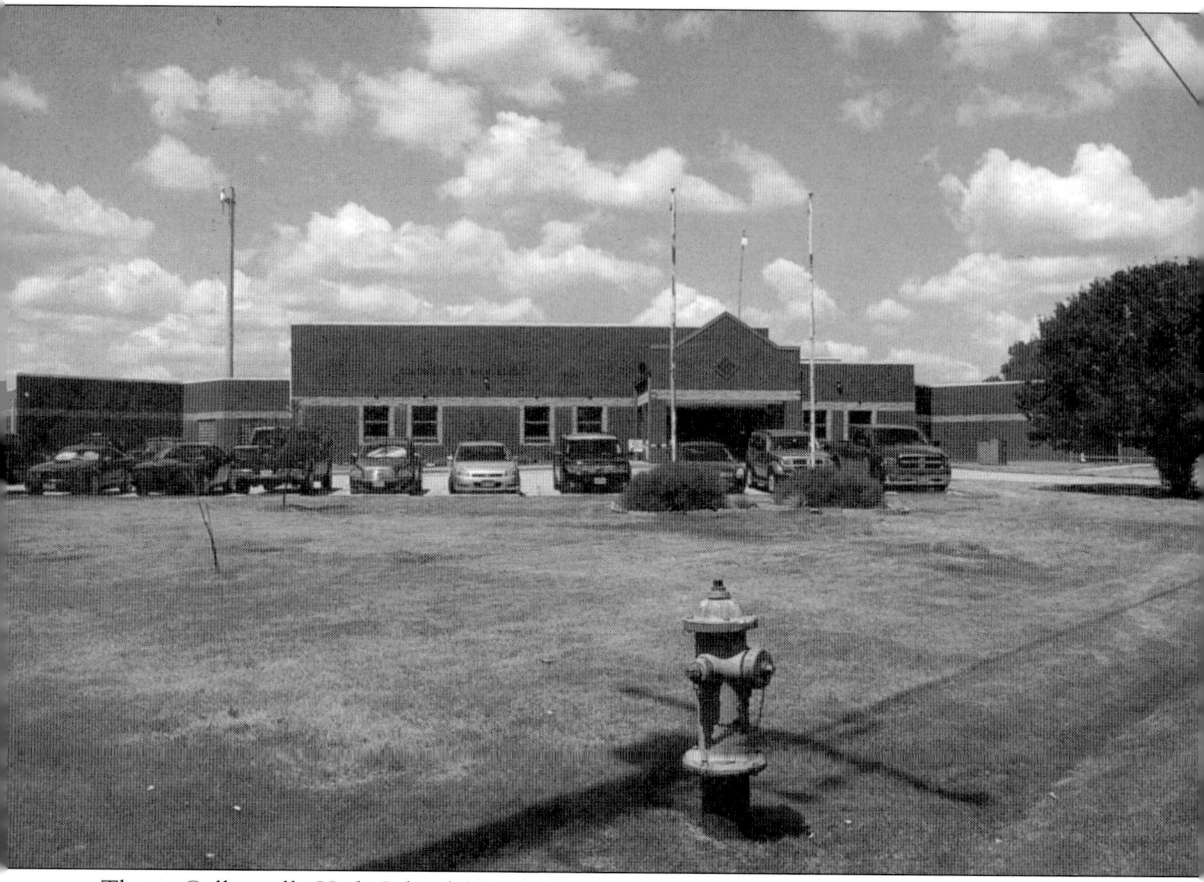

This is Collinsville High School (CHS), home of the Pirates. The school was built in 1995 for high school students and the eighth grade. Students moved from the school built for all students in 1941 into this brand-new facility. It is filled with glass trophy cases that line the walls. Images of students long gone from the school corridors line the wall as well. The school honors its past and present students and respects them while offering the best education that is available. When it comes to the school, it is the heart of the city. Everyone supports it and encourages all who enter the hollowed walls of CHS. "Once a Pirate, always a Pirate," is yelled, screamed, and honored throughout the town. Lodi Collins caught that spirit many years ago and passed it on to the entire town of Collinsville. (Authors' collection.)

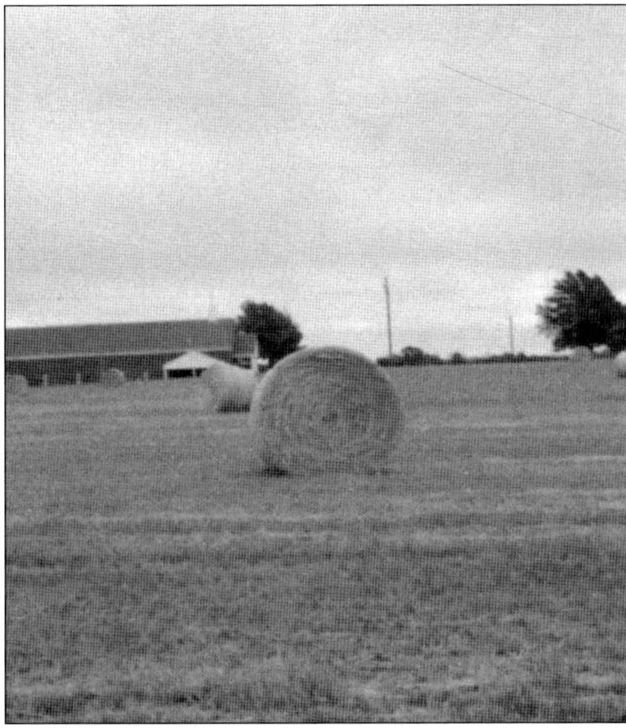

People know they are in the country when they see bales of hay surrounding a church. The city does not come out and have the bales removed, and the church does not get bent out of shape about it; no one thinks it is one bit out of the ordinary. In fact, residents may comment, "Old so and so had a good hay crop this year, bless his heart." Maybe that is not quite the way to word it. Leave out "bless his heart." In Texas, that phrase has a whole different connotation. Anyway, they are happy it has been a bountiful year for their neighbor. (Hannah Martin.)

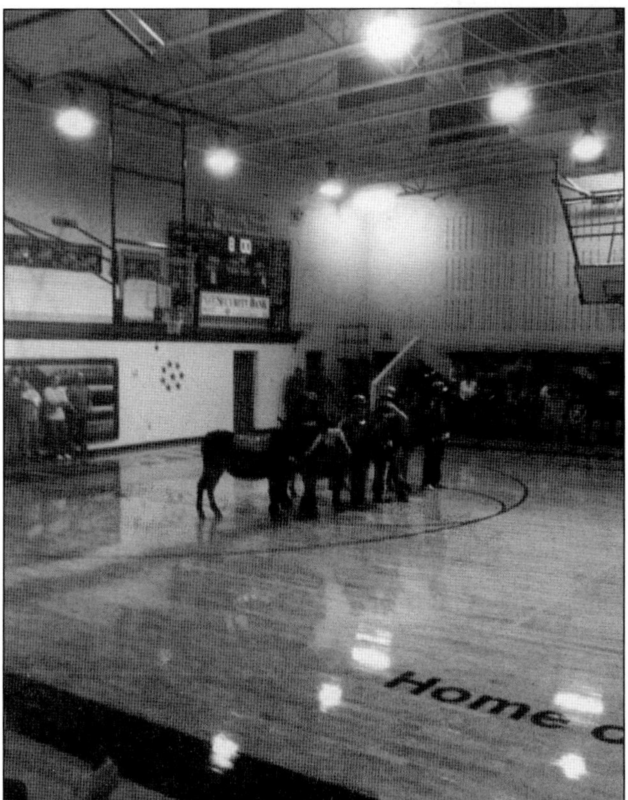

Here, the gym hosts a different kind of ball game: a donkey basketball game. The stands are full of cheering fans as the senior girls take the floor. They have put on helmets and are advancing toward their rides for the night. It is a sight to behold. The senior girls of the class of 2012 will never forget their night of donkey basketball. (Authors' collection.)

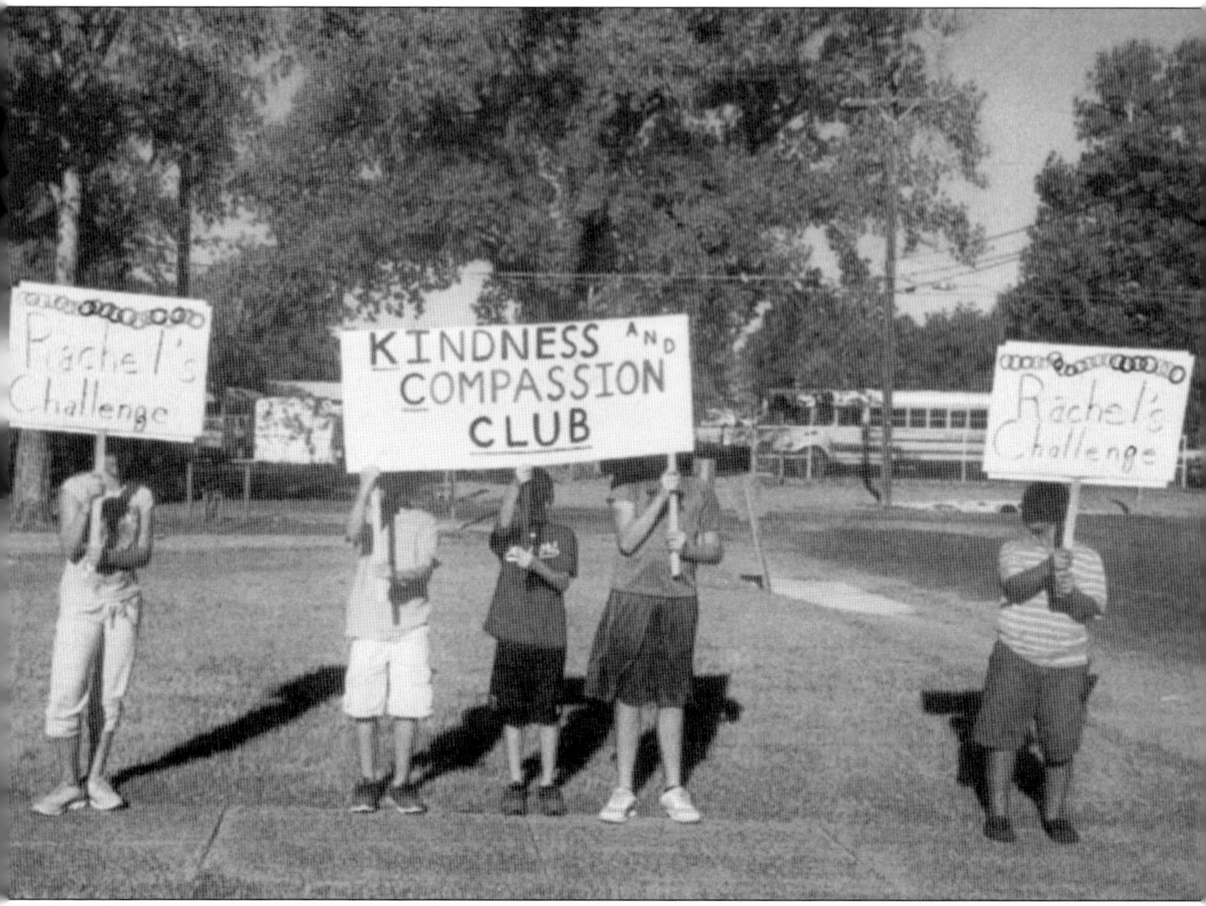

Every year, Collinsville has a Pioneer Days Celebration. Folks get dressed up in 1800s attire and act as though the town has just changed its name from Toad Suck to Collinsville. At this annual event, the town is full of excitement. The mayor of the town rides either in a personal float or shares one with fellow pioneers. People set up booths on the sidewalk, and food, beverages, and trinkets of all kinds are sold. The town has bands that play country music, and there is dancing in the street. Pictured at the 2013 Pioneer Days Celebration is the fifth- and sixth-grade Kindness and Compassion Club. (Ken Kemp and Collinsville ISD.)

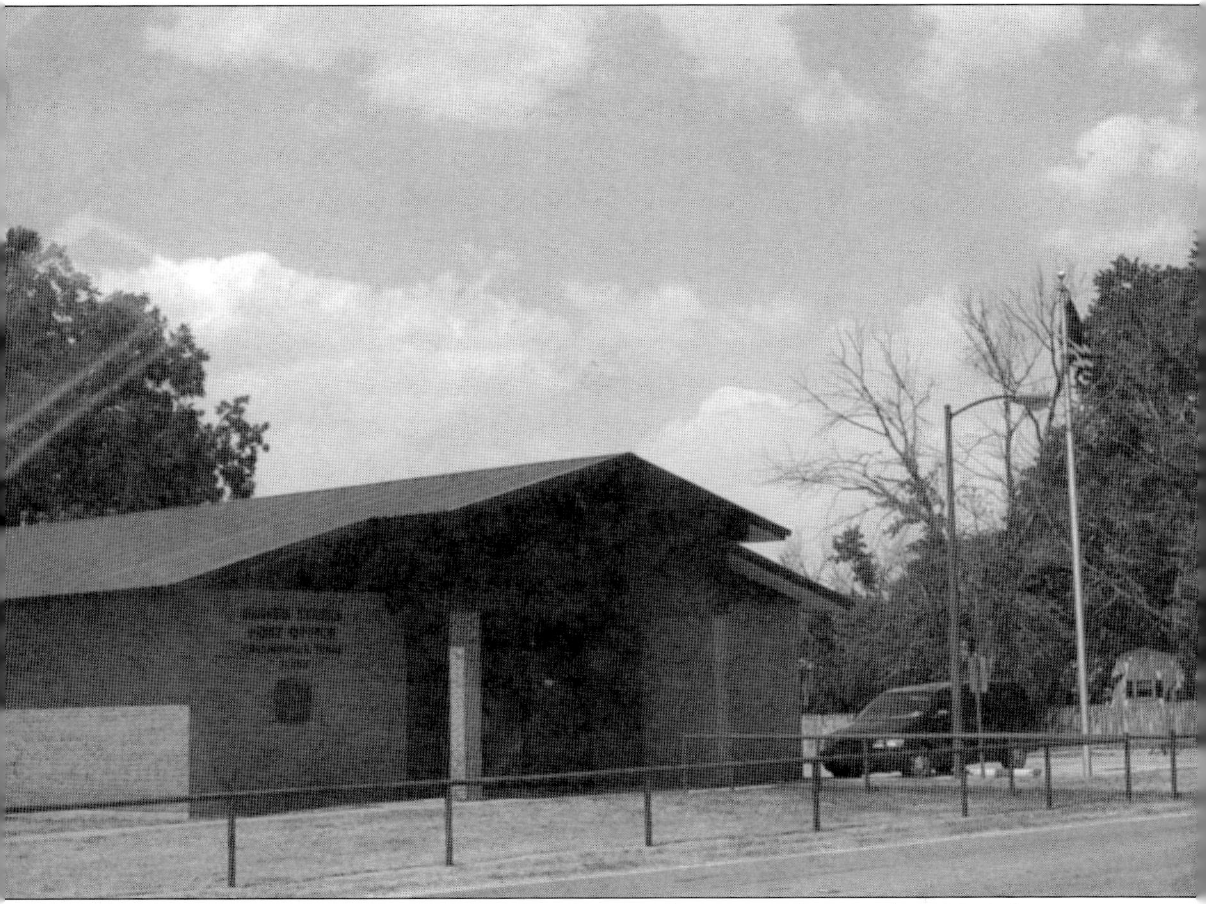

This modern-day post office gives credence to days long past when Nadine McGehee was postmistress. She held that position for over 40 years and served the town well with her loyalty and dedication to the job. Collinsville salutes the postmasters and postmistresses of the past and present and says thank you. This is the perfect time to acknowledge a few of the names that may not have been mentioned before. This town has had so many wonderful families support and invest time and money into Collinsville, including the Hughes, Vannoy, Hite, Graham, Light, deCordova, Phelphrey, Landers, Rodgers, Cobler, Collins, Neathery, Huffaker, Adamson, Roberts, Harbison, Cox, Midkeff, Goodman, McCorkle, Swindell, and Lewter families, among many others. As long as there is a town called Collinsville, Texas, and a historian to record its history, these names will live on. (Authors' collection.)